Creating Cyber Libraries

Recent Titles in the Series*

Collection Assessment and Management for School Libraries: Preparing for Cooperative Collection Development. By Debra E. Kachel.

Collection Development for a New Century in the School Library Media Center. By W. Bernard Lukenbill.

Creating Cyber Libraries: An Instructional Guide for School Library Media Specialists. By Kathleen W. Craver.

Curriculum Partner: Redefining the Role of the Library Media Specialist. By Carol A. Kearney.

Leadership for Today's School Library: A Handbook for the Library Media Specialist and the School Principal. By Patricia Potter Wilson and Josette Anne Lyders.

100 More Research Topic Guides for Students. By Dana McDougald.

Teaching Electronic Literacy: A Concepts-Based Approach for School Library Media Specialists. By Kathleen W. Craver.

Using Educational Technology with At-Risk Students: A Guide for Library Media Specialists and Teachers. By Roxanne Baxter Mendrinos.

Using Internet Primary Sources to Teach Critical Thinking Skills in Geography. By Martha B. Sharma and Gary S. Elbow.

Using Internet Primary Sources to Teach Critical Thinking Skills in Government, Economics, and Contemporary World Issues. By James M. Shiveley and Phillip J. VanFossen.

Using Internet Primary Sources to Teach Critical Thinking Skills in History. By Kathleen W. Craver.

Using Internet Primary Sources to Teach Critical Thinking Skills in Mathematics. By Evan Glazer.

Using Internet Primary Sources to Teach Critical Thinking Skills in the Sciences. By Carolyn Johnson.

Using Internet Primary Sources to Teach Critical Thinking Skills in World Languages. Edited by Grete Pasch and Kent Norsworthy.

Creating Cyber Libraries is the first title to be published by Libraries Unlimited; previous titles were published by Greenwood Press.

Creating
Cyber Libraries

AN INSTRUCTIONAL GUIDE FOR
SCHOOL LIBRARY MEDIA SPECIALISTS

Kathleen W. Craver

**Libraries Unlimited Professional Guides in
School Librarianship Series**

HARRIET SELVERSTONE
Series Advisor

2002
Libraries Unlimited
A Division of Greenwood Publishing Group, Inc.
Greenwood Village, Colorado

LIBRARIES UNLIMITED
A Division of Greenwood Publishing Group, Inc.
7730 East Belleview Avenue, Suite A200
Greenwood Village, CO 80111
1-800-225-5800
www.lu.com

Library of Congress Cataloging-in-Publication Data

Craver, Kathleen W.
    Creating cyber libraries : an instructional guide for school library media specialists / Kathleen W. Craver.
        p. cm. -- (Libraries Unlimited professional guides in school librarianship series)
Includes bibliographical references and index.
    ISBN 0-313-32080-2 (alk. paper)
    1. Internet in school libraries. 2. Digital libraries. 3. Libraries--Special collections--Computer network resources. I. Title. II. Series.
    Z675.S3 C758 2002
    027.8--dc21
                                                        2001055619

Contents

Acknowledgments

I wish to thank my husband Charlie for his unremitting enthusiasm and encouragement while I worked on this book. I gratefully acknowledge the advice, interest, and support that my Greenwood Press editors, Debra Adams and Harriet Selverstone, gave me throughout this challenging project. I would also like to express my appreciation to copyeditor Steven Long whose attention to detail greatly improved the book and Emma Bailey, production editor, for her highly professional assistance. Finally, I would like to thank all the creators of Internet sites who gave me the inspiration and perseverance to finish this book.

Introduction

Before 1994 and the availability of the Internet, school library media centers (SLMCs) were totally bound by place, collection size, and time. New SLMCs or additions to existing ones are almost never built to accommodate growing collections. By necessity, school library media specialists (SLMSs) dutifully weed collections to fit within their original architectural footprints. Access to the collection is equally constrained. Without exception, most SLMCs remain open until late afternoon and are rarely open on the weekends.

Almost overnight, access to the Internet provided SLMSs with the ability to design and build SLMCs that previously existed only in biblio-dreams. These libraries possess benefits that not even newly constructed conventional SLMCs exhibit. The size of their collections is limitless. Weeding can be accomplished at the click of a mouse, and acquisitions, in most cases, are free. Students, faculty, and parents can use the materials from any Internet-accessible location on any day and at any time they desire. Libraries that require only an Internet connection to retrieve information are called cyber libraries, and cyber libraries offer SLMSs unprecedented opportunities to provide their users with a learning and research-rich environment that is unsurpassed in the history of education.

What Is a Cyber Library?

An exact definition of a "cyber library" is difficult to agree on. Even the Association of Research Libraries is unable to succinctly define the term. It has succeeded, however, in identifying characteristics common to all cyber libraries: (1) cyber libraries constitute more than one entity; (2) they employ technology to link many resources; (3) the links between various cyber libraries and information services are transparent to users; and (4) collections are not restricted to printed materials and also include material formats never distributed in printed formats (Ensor 2000, 147–148). Garlock and Pointek in *Building the Service-Based Library Web Site* further define "cyber library" as a library unconstrained by "space, geographic location, or specific type of computer system" (1996, 9).

Both definitions leave ample room for SLMSs to easily design cyber libraries that uniquely meet the information, research, and recreational reading needs of their faculty and students. For SLMSs, a cyber library can be as simple as a "home page linked to a collection of electronic texts, databases, and other existing Internet resources" (Garlock and Pointek 1996, 9). It is the applied, professional expertise in selecting, classifying, and evaluating materials for inclusion in a cyber library, however, that distinguishes it from a compendium of "best sites" or bookmark files. SLMSs need to possess an intimate knowledge of the curriculum and the contents of their SLMCs to create a well-organized and maintained set of Internet-accessible databases, texts, and Internet sites. These elements constitute the building blocks for what can correctly be termed a cyber library.

A Rationale for Cyber Library Construction

The main reason for creating cyber libraries is that it is the most efficacious means to deliver information, much more so than was ever possible in the past. Specific reasons, however, involve several forces and incentives that are impacting SLMCs now and that necessitate their construction. The forces and incentives for change are technological, economic, educational, and professional.

Technological Forces and Incentives

Cyber libraries are not new to the library profession. Academic, public, and special libraries have already paved the way by creating excellent ones that are rich in content, feature full-text databases, provide online tutorials, and much more. All of these libraries, however, had the financial capital, technological expertise, and personnel to initiate construction before school library media specialists could even contemplate the creation of such electronic facilities. With the progress that schools are making in connecting to the Internet, the types of Internet connections used, and the improved ratio of students to computers with Internet access, the time is propitious for SLMSs to create individual cyber libraries or join with other SLMSs to design consortium-based cyber libraries.

According to the National Center for Educational Statistics, more than 98 percent of public schools were connected to the Internet by the fall of 2000. In comparison, only 35 percent of schools were connected in 1994. The types of connections also improved. In 1996, dial-up connections that are much slower than dedicated-line Internet connections were used by 74 percent of public schools. By 2000, 77 percent of public schools were using connections ranging from 56 KB to T1 and T3 lines.

The ratio of students to instructional computers with Internet access also improved from nine to one in 1999 to seven to one in 2000. Even in schools with the highest concentration of poverty, the ratio of students with Internet access improved from seventeen to one in 1999 to nine to one in 2000 ("Internet Access in U.S. Public Schools and Classrooms" 2000, 3–5).

While Internet connections at school are a necessity for on-campus cyber library use, Internet access at home is the other half of the equation for maximum use of a cyber library. Students need to be able to access cyber libraries from home to do research and complete assignments. In this area, there are significant increases to report as well. In 1997, just over 50 percent of all households with computers had Internet access. By 2000, the figure had surged to four out of five households. During this time, computer penetration rose by almost 40 percent while Internet access soared by 123 percent. Growth in rural household access also increased at all levels, with the lowest income levels showing some of the highest growth rates ("Falling through the Net" 2000, 2–3).

The need for speedier Internet connections and Internet access from home were not the only impediments that previously stopped SLMSs from creating cyber libraries. There also remained the investment in expensive equipment and technical support for an on-site Web server connected to the Internet with a dedicated line. Even when a school chooses a less expensive route by leasing or renting space on an Internet server from a Web hosting company, monthly charges can be prohibitively costly for many school districts.

Now, a third choice exists that enhances the capacity of SLMSs to provide increased access to more materials and services without regard for location, time, or day. Many companies and nonprofit organizations offer free Web site hosting and creation services as an incentive for paying for future services or placing a small fixed banner ad at the top of each page (Burnett 2001, 7). Netscape Netcenter (www.netscape.com/Websites), for example, provides a fast, visual online editor, 10 MB of free space, a guest book, and a hit counter. Another site, Red Rival (www.redrival.com) furnishes users with 20 MB of free space and a text editor.

Economic Forces and Incentives

The disappearance of technical and economic impediments to creating cyber libraries frees SLMSs to examine the economic forces and incentives that compel their construction. The first economic inducement is the cost-savings aspect of a cyber library. SLMSs can link to thousands of curriculum-related sites without having to purchase, classify, catalog, circulate, retrieve, bind, or weed a single one of them in the traditional sense. In many cases, there are entire Web libraries such as KidsClick! (www.sunsite.berkeley.edu/KidsClick!) and the American Library Association's site ALA 700+ Great Sites (www.ala.org/parentspage /greatsites) that have been professionally reviewed, attractively designed, and made available for the linking. At no time in the history of SLMCs has there been a greater economic and educational incentive to "acquire " materials for students and faculty. It can be accomplished in a few minutes with some hyper text markup language (HTML) programming software purchased or provided freely by a nonprofit organization and the click of a mouse.

A second economic incentive concerns the issue of access versus ownership. The cost of children's and general interest periodicals, for example, has increased steadily by about 2 percent per year since 1999 (Albee and Dingley 2001, 72). Hardcover (children's and young adult titles) books have increased by 5.7 percent since 2000 (Cummins 2001, 11). Without even factoring in the additional costs for ordering, cataloging, processing, labeling, and storing these stock items of a conventional library, it is readily apparent that providing electronic access to them would be cost efficient and beneficial. For major reference books and less frequently used periodicals, this choice makes a great deal of sense.

A third incentive centers on a SLMC's ability to acquire and maintain current materials. A recent survey of 3,097 users of public libraries and the Internet found that the Internet received higher ratings for currency of information (Roger et al. 2001, 58–59). Printed materials are much slower to update because of the printing and delivery process. It is far more economical, for example, to maintain versions of reference works such as *Encyclopaedia Britannica* through a cyber library so that it can be updated on a continuous basis by the vendor and accessed by more than one person on a 24/7 basis than it is to maintain a multivolume, usually noncirculating set in a conventional library.

Cyber libraries offer another economic motivation through their ability to share information. If a faculty member places a periodical article on reserve in a conventional library, students must access it on the library's premises. Its availability in a periodical's online database gives everyone the opportunity to read or print the article any time or day they desire. The constant availability of information in a cyber library is difficult to measure and evaluate. A study at a British university, however, found that almost half of the use of the library's digital collections occurred when the library was closed (Arms 2000, 6). The contents of cyber libraries share some additional features that make their availability so reliable. Because of their electronic format, cyber library materials cannot only circulate simultaneously to multiple users but also can never be misshelved or go missing from the collection. With the exception of a possible technical connection problem, they are more accessible than items in a conventional library.

Storage of materials is a constant concern for SLMSs. Conventional SLMCs, while absolutely essential to schools, are expensive to construct, maintain, and manage. They require a substantial budget and professionally trained personnel to acquire, catalog, process, and maintain items for the collection. In the future, this problem will become acute in many areas of the country as enrollments increase and more SLMSs retire from the profession.

The Projections of Education Statistics to 2009 Report found that between 1999 and 2000 public and private elementary school enrollment rose 4.2 million and secondary school enrollment rose by 2.4 million. These numbers reflect a 12 percent increase in elementary school enrollment and a 19 percent increase in secondary school enrollment. Between 2000 and 2010, some states will show a decrease in enrollment, but public school enrollment is expected to increase in the South and West. Idaho, New Mexico, Nevada, Alaska, Hawaii, Arizona, Wyoming, Utah, Georgia, Texas, Colorado, and California are projected to have large increases ("Growing Pains" 2001, 2).

Finding trained and state-certified SLMSs is also expected to be a challenge. In Maryland, Virginia, and the District of Columbia, more than half of all SLMSs are expected to retire in the next five to ten years. These numbers reflect a similar trend that is projected for other states as well (Schumacher 1999, DC5). Given the building costs associated with SLMCs and the anticipated dearth of professional SLMSs to staff them, the creation of cyber libraries that can provide 24/7 access to thousands of resources would seem not only economically feasible but also educationally essential to many school districts across the United States.

Educational Forces and Incentives

In addition to economic forces and incentives that rationalize cyber library design, there are significant educational considerations. Richard Reilly, the secretary of education, requests that "instead of building schools for 1950, let's build schools for 2050. Schools designed with the community and for the community. Schools that reflect a dedication to excellence and innovation" (quoted in "Growing Pains" 2001, 3). The state of Florida, for example, has taken this challenge seriously by constructing a cyber high school. Its doors are not the traditional schoolhouse red and no periodic bells sound. The "doors" are electronic and the principal has had to turn away as many students as she can accept to Daniel Jenkins Academy (Polk County, FL). All courses are taken online and all teaching is done online.

Unfortunately, the main reason for creating this cyber high school was not to achieve the ideal goal articulated by Secretary Reilly to build a school "dedicated to excellence and innovation." It was built because of space limitations. Construction on the crumbling Daniel Jenkins building could not be finished by the deadline necessary for a full high school schedule. So the cyber high school promised small classes, log-in time to coincide with students' most alert periods, and self-paced education. Although this school environment is not ideal to fulfill the social, behavioral, and cultural goals that educators might wish for students, it is a logical step as the Internet and computers become ubiquitous in educational institutions and homes (Thomas 2000, 1A–3A).

While most schools will not exist totally in cyberspace, as does Daniel Jenkins Academy, schools are beginning to offer more of a mix between cyber classes via distance education and traditional classes. Students in geographically isolated areas or who attend schools that do not have sufficient enrollments to support courses in various subjects are studying them through a variety of school-sponsored distance education programs (Cox 1997, R26).

Cyber libraries naturally complement online learning and are an absolute necessity when school construction is unfinished or the conventional curriculum is unable to meet students' needs for not only daily assignments but also longer projects such as laboratory reports or term papers.

A second educational force stimulating change in SLMCs is students' preference for online research in an information environment that lacks: (1) organization; (2) standards; (3) publication indicators or identifiers; (4) governance; (5) quality control; and (6) reliability. Students appear to view the Internet as either a one-stop shopping information and research center or the world's largest library. It is the first place they search for information and frequently the only place because it requires few skills and demands no special knowledge of organizational schemes. Lubans's study of seventh through tenth graders taking summer courses as part of Duke University's Gifted and Talented Program confirmed these findings in 1998. Lubans also found that students in the study rated the Internet highly for accuracy, timeliness, authoritativeness, and reliability of information (1998, 1–8).

While Lubans's study did not survey students concerning their searching skills, there is evidence that these are inadequate when students attempt to cope with 1 billion plus Web pages that currently comprise the Internet (Wiggins 2000, 27). A recent two-year study, for example, by Alexa Research, showed that a surprising number of Web users are inefficient at reaching their online destinations. Rather than entering a uniform resource locator (URL) into the search box of a chosen Web browser, millions of Internet users enter the name of the site they are searching in the search box of their home page or other search engine ("Alexa Research" 2001, 5).

These research studies confirm the Internet practices and beliefs by students that SLMSs have been anecdotally writing about during the past five years in various professional journals. The educational mandate and economic incentives for creating cyber libraries replete with relevant Web libraries and Internet tutorials are obvious if SLMSs do not wish to witness the birth of a new generation of students termed the "digital illiterati" (Majka 2001, 52).

Professional Forces and Incentives

As more SLMSs retire and schools rush to find replacements and additional SLMSs because of increasing enrollment, it will be a logical temptation to fill openings with people who are not certified SLMSs. I have personally observed the change in the qualification requirements for job postings in private schools. Just a few years ago the professional publication job listings stated that an M.L.S. was required. Now, more of the listings state that an M.L.S. is preferred.

This relaxation of qualifications for one of the more essential positions in a school, while understandable, could not come at a more dangerous, pedagogical time for schools. SLMSs are masters at incorporating new technologies into their collections, teaching curricula, and services. Books, periodicals, filmstrips, videocassettes, digital video, realia, posters, and art have been seamlessly classified and cataloged into SLMC online catalogs, thus making all of these materials formats imminently usable to students and faculty.

Internet-connected computers, however, are not as easy to integrate into SLMCs. Although computers are better than manual methods for finding information and have become the preferred searching tool within an electronic environment consisting of 1 billion plus unorganized Web pages, students and even faculty face a bewildering amount of information choices among materials that are not valid, objective, or reliable. Our new professional challenge is to accept this evolution and realize the incentives that exist for changing the way we place quality electronic content in our students' hands.

The opportunity for SLMSs to electronically expand collections by acquiring critically evaluated Internet sites, databases, texts, and tutorials is finally a reality for even the neediest SLMC. Offering our students and teachers electronic passage by constructing a cyber library that is reflective of the school's curriculum is imperative in light of today's electronic information maze.

Just as the conventional SLMC is a laboratory for teaching students how to locate materials, search the indices of reference books, and understand the difference between keyword and subject searching in the online catalog, so will a cyber library provide an electronic laboratory to teach students how to: (1) choose appropriate databases; (2) perform Boolean searching; (3) design an Internet search strategy; and (4) evaluate Web sites.

The expertise that SLMSs offer students and faculty in finding information, completing assignments, and performing research is essential to their future success in any endeavor. In the past, students could accept information as fairly accurate and reliable because SLMSs had preselected the periodicals, books, and videos from professional acquisition journals. Although SLMSs are aware that much of Internet information is not valid, objective, and authoritative, students and even faculty are ignorant of these information defects. They tend to accept most Web information as accurate and trustworthy (Majka 2001, 63).

The Internet provides SLMSs with the opportunity to demonstrate our essential value to our institutions. Our role as crossing guards on an information highway that is littered with trivial, superficial, and biased sites requires the highest organizational, searching, managerial, and evaluative skills. Only certified SLMSs are trained to distinguish Internet gold from the millions of pyrite sites that exist in cyberspace.

Purpose

I have had the privilege of practicing my profession in a variety of geographic locations, socioeconomic environments, grade levels, and secondary and university institutions. During my twenty-four years as a SLMS, I have always experienced disappointment when I have had to inform either students or faculty members that I could not supply them with the item they requested. Although I could obtain some items through interlibrary loan or refer them to a local public or academic library, I knew in most cases that the follow-up on their part would be too arduous or the desired item would arrive too late for their gratification.

The arrival of the Internet and a fast, dedicated line at my school has reduced the number of disappointments considerably by enabling me to provide my students and faculty with a wealth of content-rich sites in every area of the curriculum. The cyber library that I designed contains: (1) a Web library of 2,000 annotated sites that are keyword searchable; (2) several full-text online databases; (3) a cyber café reading room; and (4) a set of Internet and online database tutorials. It has become a second library that is open to everyone in my school community regardless of their location or the day or time. Its size is not dependent on the current school budget but on the willingness of many educational institutions, government organizations, and individual Web creators to share their information treasures without regard for profit or fame.

The purpose of this book is to provide SLMSs with practical guidelines and suggested Internet sites for designing cyber libraries that are reflective of their school's research, curriculum, and recreational reading needs. A secondary goal is to furnish ideas and hints that will enable SLMSs to build cyber libraries expeditiously, economically, and with presumably untrained staff.

Intended Audience

I have written this book primarily for SLMSs who work with students in grades 4–12. Recent research shows that the Internet is not particularly user-friendly to students below the fourth grade because it is rather slow and primarily text driven. The second reason is that studies are beginning to reveal that students younger than fourth grade are better served in environments that foster three-dimensional learning (Minkel 2001, 39).

The book is also written to awaken school library media coordinators and administrators to the economic, educational, and professional benefits to be derived from the creation of a cyber library that is maintained and managed at the district level. School library media coordinators and administrators faced with growing enrollments and a shortage of certified SLMSs may wish to design a cyber library as a supplement to conventional SLMCs or as a resource while a conventional SLMC can be completed and stocked.

Book Arrangement

The book opens with an introduction that provides SLMSs with a rationale for designing cyber libraries. Although creating cyber libraries is not dependent on extra funding, a sufficient number of studies and statistics are cited to enable SLMSs to use them to justify additional funding or staff to complete their projects.

Chapter 1, "Cyber Library Guidelines," addresses the need for planning cyber libraries that reflect the educational needs and interests of the entire school and the conventional SLMC. Consideration of the school's location, budget, population characteristics, and access to other libraries is stressed. The chapter also points out the need for economies of scale when constructing cyber libraries. According to Rifkin, organizations are in the "Age of Access" where ownership of hardware and software is no longer the goal so much as the ability to access the hardware and software (2000, 32). In keeping with this trend, cyber libraries may be designed to access SLMS-selected sites or link to other Web libraries that have received positive reviews in professional publications.

Criteria for selecting content, graphics, and design options are part of the chapter. An annotated list of cyber libraries that can serve as templates for future cyber library design is also provided.

Chapter 2, "Cyber Library Policies," discusses the need for a formal set of policies and operating procedures since a cyber library is open when a SLMC is closed and it is also open to millions of users beyond the traditional school population. Areas where policies and procedures are needed concern Web template development, Internet use by students and faculty, cyber library collection development, and privacy and copyright issues. A list of annotated sites containing other cyber libraries' policies and procedures is included to provide possible ideas and suggestions for adaptation by school cyber librarians.

Chapter 3, "Constructing Web Libraries," explores several options for the provision of the most essential component of a cyber library: a compilation of annotated, Internet sites that are grouped under a series of broad subject areas. It is a Web library that enables SLMSs to give students and faculty an additional free, full-text library of appropriate materials that are available on a 24/7 basis.

Constructing a Web library can be achieved by linking to other well-reviewed Web libraries or by selecting various curriculum-related sites and placing them within librarian-selected categories. The final part of the chapter includes a recommended set of Web libraries that SLMSs can either link to or use as templates for an original Web library design.

Chapter 4, "Using Portals," describes the use of commercial templates that allow SLMSs to create their own links and images in a matter of minutes. Knowledge of higher learning-curve programs such as HTML, Java, FrontPage, or basic Web design is unnecessary. This chapter introduces SLMSs to library-related education portals and discusses the advantages of portal hosting of a school's cyber library as opposed to SLMC hosting and how to estimate usage costs. A set of guidelines for evaluating education portals is provided, and an annotated list of leading educational portals is included.

Chapter 5, "Acquiring Fee-Based Cyber Libraries," addresses a growing trend toward accessing a database of academic and research-oriented books and periodicals within a prescribed period of time for a fee. The services and operating features of several fee-based libraries deemed suitable for high school students are discussed. The chapter explores their potential to expand the text offerings of a conventional SLMC. A set of guidelines is also included to assist SLMSs in deciding whether to subscribe to a fee-based library.

Chapter 6, "Establishing Remote Access to Subscription Resources," discusses the need that students and faculty have for remote access to commercial online databases from the SLMC's cyber library. Incorporating these databases and their remote log-in requirements into a cyber library is considered a major component of a fully operational cyber library. A set of option examples for structuring this type of access is provided.

Chapter 7, "Creating Cyber Reading Rooms," is devoted to encouraging SLMSs to think beyond the four walls of their SLMC and to experiment with new ideas such as hosting book discussions, starting an online book club, arranging for an author Internet chat with students, or sponsoring an online book review group. Ideas for providing reading guidance, giving booktalks, and posting vacation reading lists and bibliographies are just some of the activities described in this chapter. A list of annotated Web sites that SLMSs can either link to or use as possible templates for their own designs is also included.

Chapter 8, "Providing Cyber Library Instructional Services," furnishes guidelines for structuring cyber library instructional content. Cyber libraries should contain instructional aids and tutorials to enable students and faculty to become information literate. These skills consist of the ability to successfully search an online catalog, select appropriate electronic databases, employ Internet search strategies, and evaluate information resources.

Examples of Webquests (electronic course-integrated SLMC instructional units), pathfinders, interactive lessons, and other instructional components of a cyber library are supplied. An annotated list of recommended instructional

Internet sites and online tutorials is given so that SLMSs can either adapt or adopt them for their own cyber libraries.

Chapter 9, "Managing and Evaluating Cyber Libraries," reviews several management techniques and strategies for ensuring that a cyber library remains operative in cyberspace. Management criteria such as reliability, response time, downloading capabilities, and user-friendliness are stressed. Internet programs, such as Net Mechanic.com (http://netmechanic.com), that automatically check for broken links within a cyber library are introduced as timesaving devices. Since many SLMSs are sole practitioners and without sufficient support staff, a substantial part of the chapter addresses the employment of student library aides, parent volunteers, SLMC cyber library club members, and school district consortia of SLMSs to assist with the management of a cyber library. The chapter closes with an annotated list of software programs that perform some management functions within a cyber library.

Chapter 10, "Promoting Cyber Libraries," discusses the liberating use of the Internet for marketing and promoting library programs and services. SLMSs finally have access through the Internet to what every dot-com enterprise dreams of—free advertising. It is an opportunity that every SLMS should seize. This chapter provides SLMSs with a rationale for promoting cyber libraries. It stresses the inherent validity of SLMC programs and services and the reasons why they need to be constantly promoted in a school.

In addition to providing a rationale for promoting cyber libraries, the chapter also presents creative ideas for achieving cyber library marketing objectives. Highlighting a librarian/teacher collaborative unit, publicizing an author's appearance, promoting new materials or Internet sites, and making the SLMC's cyber library the default page on all public terminals are just a few of the ideas discussed in this chapter. The chapter closes with marketing ideas and suggestions about how to promote a cyber library in printed media such as professional library publications and local news venues within the school and community. A list of annotated Internet sites that can serve as excellent marketing examples and provide promotional techniques is also given.

Technical Assumptions

This book is written for SLMSs who are interested in designing a cyber library that will expand their conventional library collections, programs, and services by providing ideas, suggestions, and guidelines for content and its presentation. It is not a technical book that requires knowledge, for example, of HTML or Java script. It does make some assumptions, however, about the technical expertise of a SLMS. SLMSs or someone on their staff are expected to have a rudimentary knowledge of some turnkey Web editing software programs such as Microsoft FrontPage or NetObject Fusion. These user-friendly programs enable users to easily create a simple home page and make links from that page to other resources. The presence of at least one Web station in the library is also assumed. A Web station consists of a personal computer that is equipped with either Netscape Navigator or Microsoft Internet Explorer and a connection to the Internet through a modem or a T1 or T3 line.

Although there is a passing reference to cyber library mounting options in Chapter 1, it is assumed that SLMSs have a basic understanding that mounting options for a cyber library can be either on-site through a Web server or hosted off-site in a variety of ways. If SLMSs choose to host a site through an education portal, it is also understood that they understand the privacy implications for students and faculty when they register their site with this type of dot.com organization.

All of the Internet sites listed in this book are for reference and instructional purposes. The Internet, however, is not a stable electronic resource. It is possible that some Internet addresses will be unresponsive for a variety of technical, personal, financial, or commercial reasons. I have verified their availability as this book went to press. If an Internet address is inaccessible, please refer to the site title and enter the keywords in a search engine such as AltaVista. This site may still be retrievable even though it may have moved to a new address.

Technical Limitations

There are references to using a cyber library as a major resource in school districts that have distance education programs or high enrollments that necessitate the building of new schools. I wish SLMSs and administrators to understand that a cyber library is a poor substitute for a conventional school library media center. Books and other nonprint materials not in digital format form the essential core of what is needed by students for background material, understanding complex ideas, and acquiring knowledge. This book is about the need for the creation of a complementary electronic library comprising excellent, content-rich digital materials, because this format makes them more readily available and sharable.

The Internet tutorials in a cyber library, for example, cannot replicate spontaneous questions and answers or interaction among students in a conventional library class. A cyber reading room cannot replace the tables and comfortable chairs where faculty members can read the newspaper and students can receive one-to-one help, be tutored, finish homework, study for a test, research a term paper, or just read for pleasure.

A cyber library is, however, a wonderful cost-effective way to expand the programs and services of SLMSs so that students can realize their full potential. It is part of the future of SLMCs where there will be print and electronic communication, linear text and hypertext, assistance from librarians and access to librarians, ownership of materials and access to materials, and finally a SLMC that is both edifice and interface (Crawford 2001, 8).

References

Albee, Barbara, and Brenda Dingley. 2001. "U.S. Periodicals Prices—2001." *American Libraries* 32 (May): 72–78.

"Alexa Research Report Shows Inefficiencies of Web Users." 2001. *LJ Netconnect: Supplement to Library Journal and School Library Journal* (Spring): 5.

Arms, William Y. 2000. *Digital Libraries*. Cambridge: MIT Press.

Burnett, Tim. 2001. "Set up a Free Web Site This Summer." *Classroom Connect* 7 (Summer): 7–8.

Cox, Paul. 1997. "Cyberdegrees." *Wall Street Journal* (November 11): R26.

Crawford, Walt. 1998. "PaperPersists: Why Physical Collections Still Matter." http://www.Onlineinc.com/onlinemag/JanOL98/ (January 23, 2001).

Cummins, Julie. 2001. "Dead Trees and Wooden Nickels." *School Library Journal* 47 (March): 11.

Ensor, Pat., ed. 2000. *The Cybrarian's Manual 2*. Chicago: American Library Association.

"Falling through the Net: Toward Digital Inclusion: A Report on Americans Access to Technology Tools 2000." 2000. http://www.esa.doc.gov/fttn00.htm (October 10, 2000).

Garlock, Kristen L., and Sherry Pointek. 1996. *Building the Service-Based Library Web Site: A Step-by-Step Guide to Design and Options*. Chicago: American Library Association.

"Growing Pains: The Challenge of Overcrowded Schools Is Here to Stay." 2001. http://www.ed.gov/pubs/bbecho00/bbecho00.doc (March 23, 2001).

"Internet Access in U.S. Public Schools and Classrooms: 1994–2000." 2000. http://nces.ed.gov/pubsearch/pubsinfo.asp?pubid=2001071 (May 15, 2001).

Lubans, John, Jr. 1998. "Key Findings on Internet Use among Students." http://www.lib.duke.edu/lubans/docs/key/key.html (May 21, 2001).

Majka, David. 2001. "The Conqueror Bookworm." *American Libraries* 32 (June/July): 61–63.

Minkel, Walter. 2001. "Not So Elementary: How Young Is Too Young Online?" *School Library Journal* 47 (January): 41.

Rifkin, Jeremy. 2000. *The Age of Access*. New York: Putnam.

Roger, Eleanor Jo, et al. 2001. "The Public Library and the Internet: Is Peaceful Co-Existence Possible?" *American Libraries* 32 (May): 58–61.

Schumacher, Mary Louise. 1999. "The Struggle to Find Librarians." *Washington Post* (August 26): DC5.

Thomas, Karen. 2000. "One School's Quantum Leap in Florida: A Class of 2004 Will Do Its Learning Online." *USA Today* (April 6): 1A–5A.

Wiggins, Richard W. 2000. "Coping with the Trillion-Page Web." *LJ Netconnect: Supplement to Library Journal and School Library Journal* (Fall): 26–28.

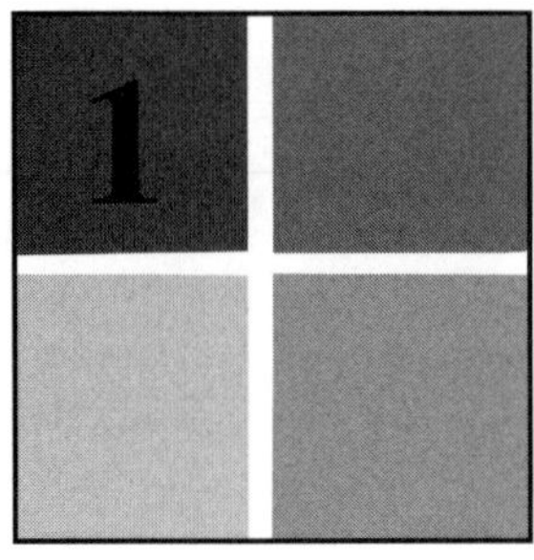

Cyber Library Guidelines

Mission Statement

Establishing a standard set of guidelines for constructing a cyber library is the first step in ensuring that its foundation is as strong as the one used to build a conventional library. Before designing a cyber site that may well rival a conventional library in collection size and scope, take the time to write a mission statement accompanied by specific goals. Plan to use it as a constant reference tool whenever decisions are necessary concerning cyber library contents, user population, collection development, and maintenance.

A mission statement is simply a one- or two-sentence description that articulates to future users the overall purpose for designing and maintaining a cyber library. It should appear somewhere on the cyber library's site, but need not be prominently displayed (Garlock and Pointek 1996, 14–15). The following are some general purposes that could be incorporated into a SLMC cyber library mission statement. A cyber library may exist to:

- Support the curricular, research, informational, and recreational needs of the students, faculty, and staff

- Inform, motivate, and inspire students, faculty, and staff members

- Provide skills for improving information literacy

- Supply programs, services, and information that improves the value of the Internet

- Serve as a supplemental research facility for students and faculty

- Provide links to other resources on the Internet

Cyber Library Specific Goals

After writing an acceptable mission statement, prepare a list of specific objectives that reflect the school's educational characteristics and the instructional needs of the SLMC. Although the investment of time to write these aims may seem wasteful in comparison to the creativity and fun involved in designing a cyber library, it will be worthwhile. Cyber libraries that lack specific construction guidelines, unlike conventional libraries, are easily recognizable on the Web. In one or two clicks of a mouse, users can easily appraise the content quality, searchabilty, and basic utility of a cyber library. In a conventional library, they would need to spend hours to evaluate the quality of the collection, the availability of materials, and their ease of use. Cyber libraries that lack specific goals are usually characterized by irrelevant sites, gaps in the collection, and poor navigation routes. A cyber library that is based on a series of goals should be easy to search, use, maintain, and expand (Kovacs and Kovacs 1997, 2–3).

While all of the following goals may not be appropriate for every cyber library's policies and procedures section, they are offered for possible consideration and adoption. The specific goals of a cyber library may be to:

- Supply online instruction to the Internet, licensed subscriptions databases, and the online catalog

- Provide additional online resources for printed materials class assignments

- Furnish sites that will enhance student learning and teach critical thinking skills

- Provide resources that will supplement the print collection

- Convey information about SLMC policies and procedures

- Communicate internal information to various members of the school community

- Generate positive publicity for the SLMC among its user population

- Create an image of future thinking and activity within the school community and profession for the purpose of attracting students, grants, awards, and quality personnel

- Provide remote access to library materials, services, and programs

- Facilitate use of licensed subscription databases such as Ebsco's Host, SIRS, and Wilson products through Web linkage to a specific Web address

- Build a collection of sites that reflects current national and state standards in language arts, math, and science

Cyber Library Users

Who is the primary audience for a cyber library is one of the most important questions to resolve before constructing one. It will help determine the types of materials that are collected, the programs and services that are provided, and how the information will be presented and displayed. It is crucial to decide between primary and secondary users. If a cyber library's primary users consist of students in grades 9–12, for example, the collection, language level, graphics, and site colors should be relevant and of interest to this age range (Carter 1999, 33; Weissman 2001, 42).

After establishing a primary user population, it is important to find out as much as possible about their needs and interests. They, in effect, have become the target market that Internet vendors so carefully research before mounting their products on the Web. Use some of the marketing techniques that dot.com companies traditionally employ to make their Web sites commercial successes. SLMSs actually have an advantage in this area because they do not have to pay for focus groups, surveys, and other marketing research. Much of it is either available within the school community or can be generated by the use of volunteers.

One of the best sources for information about students can be found in the school's most recent accreditation report. A copy is usually available in the SLMC. Look at the sections of the document that pertain to students and the community in which they live. Another source for this type of information is local census data. Information about population growth, cost of housing, number of people dwelling in one home, ethnic background, and more can be found at local census data Internet sites. Research the following demographic and educational information:

- Number of students in single-family homes

- Educational and economic levels of parent(s)

- Number of students/families relying on social services

- Special school programs (e.g., learning disabilities) and the number of enrollees

- Number of English as a second language–speaking students and families

- Access to local public and academic libraries

- Use of distance education or online courses

- Availability of home computers and access to the Internet

- Percentage of students holding after-school jobs

Use this information to not only design an appropriate cyber library for the primary audience but also to determine the characteristics of the secondary audience and the desire to serve them. If the majority of students live in single-family homes, for example, it may be important to include Internet sites about cooking and home safety. If many students have after-school jobs, a collection of Web sites about resume writing, interviewing, and even local job ads may be included in a cyber library collection.

The need to serve a secondary audience such as parents will depend not only on discoverable demographic information but also on what the public library is doing in this area. Be sure to check the Web sites of local public and academic libraries to see what services and programs they offer in the sections that are under additional consideration for a school cyber library. If local libraries offer sites and services that are more community based, plan to link to them rather than highlight these types of services in the school's cyber library.

The next source of information to consult is the school's course of study. Read through it to determine the number and types of courses offered in fields such as vocational and advanced placement. Note how many courses are available through distance learning or online via the school's Web site. Find out which courses require term papers or class assignments necessitating access to a library. Record this information for future reference in building the Web library portion of the site.

A third source of school-based information is the guidance department. Consult the guidance and college counselor, if the school has the latter. Ask him/her to provide general data concerning the types of social and psychological problems with which he/she deals. Has he/she counseled many students for abuse problems concerning substances, peers, or parents? Are there significant numbers of students receiving assistance with eating disorders or depression? Are there a significant number of teenage pregnancies?

If the school has a college counselor, inquire about the incidence of parental pressure to attend "Ivy League" institutions. Are many college-bound students at your school in need of financial aid? How do the majority of students study for the SAT? Do they enroll in prep courses or engage private tutors? How is information about colleges disseminated to the students?

The last school department to visit is the Study Skills Center or the faculty member who works with students with learning disabilities. Ask questions that will provide general information concerning the extent of problems with reading comprehension, writing essays, drafting thesis statements, completing mathematical problems, understanding scientific processes, and learning a foreign language.

The information that is collected from these excellent resources assists in identifying the needs and interests of the primary audience without too much effort on the part of SLMSs. They also provide the means for SLMSs to link to sites, databases, exhibits, and other resources that are relevant to the primary user population. Data collected from these types of resources enable SLMSs to customize cyber libraries by linking to age or subject-appropriate sites just as they have customized their conventional library collections. Cyber libraries also offer an additional benefit by providing anonymity to users who need information about sensitive topics or who need access to materials such as college directories that would normally not circulate from conventional SLMCs.

Focus groups and surveys are expensive methods that companies employ to determine the potential use of their products. They consider it a business necessity before they risk the time, personnel, and venture capital to launch a Web site. Focus groups give companies the opportunity to pose directed, but somewhat open-ended questions about their intended product or service. SLMSs have an advantage in this area. Students, with probably only the provision of some cookies and sodas, will readily contribute their opinions about the types of information that they would like to see in a school cyber library. Unfortunately, it is still the practice that children be seen and not heard in many aspects of our society. The majority of them will be flattered that an adult is seeking their advice regarding the design of a school cyber library. Student focus groups also give SLMSs the opportunity to inquire if students are willing to volunteer technical, advisory, or design assistance (Braun 1998, 26–29).

Although elementary students would probably enjoy this type of activity, their schedules and comprehension of this type of project probably preclude meaningful participation by students in grades 6 and lower. For seventh through twelfth graders, plan to invite them to the library by grade level in small groups of no more than twelve students. Compile a standard list of open-ended questions concerning:

- Academic research needs

- Homework assistance (particularly mathematics)

- Recreational reading interests, favorite authors, and so forth

- Local recreational interests (movies, museums, local theater, restaurants, and so forth)

- School problems (bullying, peer pressure, friendship, dating, and so forth)

- Parent problems (substance abuse, divorce, health concerns, and so forth)

- Study skills (tutoring needs, difficult courses)

- Vocational and career interests

- Favorite Web sites

- Cyber library design student opportunities (advisory board, technical and/or development assistance)

Convene several similar focus groups with faculty members. Ask them a series of questions regarding their:

- Curricular needs (particularly the need for interactive sites—the human circulation system, genetic probability scenarios, and so forth)

- Professional interests (continuing education, local colleges offering graduate programs, and so forth)

- Frequently visited Web sites (stock market, automobile purchasing, medical sites, and so forth)

- Potential use of a school cyber library

- Willingness to serve in an advisory capacity or to provide technical/design assistance

In addition to focus groups, companies also conduct surveys with potential consumers. In this area, they clearly have the advantage over SLMSs in terms of time, funding, and personnel. If there is no time to meet with students and faculty, design a survey based on the focus group question areas noted for each group. Obtain permission to have them distributed during a homeroom period. Explain the need for completion of the student surveys when you distribute surveys to teachers at a faculty meeting. If time is still a problem, cajole a teacher in the mathematics department, preferably a teacher of statistics, to have one class perform percentage summaries of the collected data as a math assignment. Add this information to the data collected from published school reports and interviews with specific faculty to form a composite view of cyber library primary and secondary users.

Proposing a Cyber Library

After preparing a mission statement, a set of specific goals, and a composite profile of primary and secondary users, draft a proposal that includes plans for the construction of a cyber library. Include in this proposal plans for: (1) soliciting administrative support; (2) deciding the approach (consortium versus single library); (3) assessing skill levels and training for designers; (4) equipment and technical needs; (5) budgeting; and (6) deadlines for testing and completion of the project.

Garnering Administrative Support

Local school administrators across the country are under pressure from parents, superintendents, and school boards to ensure that students are information literate and are keeping up with the latest technological advances. The creation of a cyber library by SLMSs that can serve as a place where students, faculty, and even parents can access full-text, content-rich materials on a 24/7 basis is a project that has great appeal for administrators. It is also the type of project that is easy to justify budget-wise.

Use the prepared mission statement, goals, and research on the intended audience to garner the support, encouragement, and funding you need from local administrators. Schedule sufficient time to meet and invite all of the appropriate decision-making personnel. If you have the technical assistance, prepare a one-screen mock-up of the proposed site to show them. The old adage "a picture is worth a thousand words" is true especially when it pertains to Internet sites. Listen carefully to administrators' comments and see if they articulate a vision of what a school cyber library should look like. Their vision will influence the approach, time, and funds that you request to complete the project. If the school employs a Web manager, master, or head of educational technology, make sure that this person attends the meeting. Ask his/her advice about blending a cyber library into the school's Web site. Seek this person's opinion, technical support, and design assistance. If the school resides in a district with several SLMCs, discuss the advantages and disadvantages of a team approach to the project. Observe administrators' reactions to collaboration. If they are in favor of it, this will not only effect funding but also the project deadline (Garlock and Pointek 1996, 13).

The goal is to leave the meeting with encouragement and assurance from all of the appropriate personnel that financial, technical, and staff support will be available on receipt of a detailed cyber library proposal that incorporates their vision, ideas, and suggestions wherever possible.

Planning the Approach

It is increasingly rare to find cyber libraries that have been created by one person. Yet Web-authoring software programs and off-campus Web-hosting sites make it possible for an individual SLMS to design a cyber library for a single SLMC. The added responsibilities for design and navigation expertise, however, combined with collection development and maintenance favor some sort of team approach even if it is within one school. The Internet is such an information maze that it is easy for one SLMS to omit critical subject areas or sites that are far superior to others. There are also several other factors that contribute to an outstanding cyber library for which most SLMSs lack proficiency. Simcox in *The*

Internet Public Library Handbook believes that there are four fundamental areas of expertise that librarians need to create a cyber library: (1) artistic vision and design expertise; (2) technological and programming expertise; (3) content expertise; and (4) organization and access expertise (1999, 103–106). While it is possible that a SLMS could embody all of these special talents, it is extremely unlikely. Cyber library construction loans itself nicely to a team approach either within a single school or among several schools. Forming a group of people creates a positive image of the project. Staff members, interested faculty, and students may feel more ownership and, as a result, may be more likely to contribute their time, skills, and suggestions. Different points of view can be accommodated and members of the group may network with others who could assist when technical or design problems are encountered.

Single School Team Approach: Advantages

Both types of team approaches have positive and negative aspects. In a single school team approach, the main advantage is the speed with which the site can be designed, materials collected, and the site mounted for public use. A small group within one school will not have to spend extra time, for example, drafting and resubmitting a mission statement and goals until consensus is reached. While there may be some gaps in a Web library collection, there will probably be few arguments concerning the classification and quality of chosen sites. A single school cyber library can also be customized more easily, whereas a cyber library serving several schools must necessarily reflect the educational needs and interests of different user groups. All SLMSs will want to place an online catalog, licensed electronic databases, and other commercial subscriptions on the first page of a cyber library for quick access. In a single school team approach, link placement to remote online databases is not a subject for discussion or voting. In a consortial approach, these types of decisions will have to be negotiated. A single school team approach also has the advantage of building a team of compatible members who are in agreement about content, access, design, and display. A consortial approach usually creates a climate of compromise rather than total agreement and members have to spend time maintaining good relationships with one another to ensure continued contributions. On-site hosting of a single school cyber library is an easy decision on the part of one SLMS. The responsibility for ensuring that the site is up or for taking it down can be done at that person's convenience. In a consortial team approach, several SLMSs have to be notified, and scheduling modifications to the site or downtimes become more complicated.

Consortial Approach: Advantages

While there are definitely downsides to several schools contributing to a cyber library, there are many advantages. Partnerships offer opportunities for SLMSs to share the expenses involved with creating and maintaining a cyber library. A group of SLMSs can share their subject expertise when constructing the Web library portion of a cyber library. Internet site collections can be larger because maintenance responsibilities can be evenly distributed. The cost of licensed subscription online databases can be reduced when consortium prices are negotiated. The talent pool for personnel with artistic, design, content, technological, programming, organization, and access expertise is much larger. Marketing and publicizing a consortial cyber library is sometimes easier because SLMSs feel that they are representing and promoting a team rather than just themselves. Updating a cyber library is a constant task given the changes that are taking place on the Internet with increased video and multimedia sites. Having several SLMSs responsible for monitoring and checking links reduces the workload. A consortium of SLMSs will always have members who are not satisfied with the status quo and who will push for necessary enhancements, additions, and changes. There is also a permanency to a consortial approach. SLMSs who spend time developing a cyber library will want to see it continue to improve. When there are several SLMSs involved from different schools, the departure of a member will not result in a cyber library's abandonment by an uninterested SLMS. Members of a consortium can usually obtain administrative support for negotiated agreements that help them maintain large collective projects (Smith et al. 2001, 18–20).

The decision to construct a cyber library independently or jointly can be difficult since there are significant advantages and disadvantages involved with either choice. Before making such a decision, it may be helpful to ask the following questions:

- What are the hosting problems?

- What are the deadlines for completion of the project?

- How much money can be saved by a consortial approach?

- Will the resources be much greater for my school's users?

- Will I be able to have a better cyber library because of greater expertise?

- Will sharing maintenance of the site reduce my workload?

- Will consortial members contribute fairly to the workload?

Building a Team

A cyber library has many components that a conventional library lacks. Conventional libraries can comprise rows of dusty shelves with poor lighting and ventilation, but if the shelves contain the materials that researchers or students need to complete an assignment or paper, then it has fulfilled its contract with the information seeker. Cyber libraries are much different in their requirements. The Internet is basically a visual medium. Sites must attract the eyes, especially those of children and teenagers, with bright colors. Access to sites must occur in less than thirty seconds and at only one or two clicks of a mouse or a user loses patience. Even though a student may take several minutes to walk up and down rows of shelves in a conventional library searching for books for their topics, cyber library searchers will never do the electronic equivalent. They expect instantaneous access to similar sources so that they can copy and paste appropriate passages right into their term papers and class assignments.

Designing a cyber library to meet the searching requirements of users accustomed to all types of electronic resources and equipment requires a team with specializations that most SLMSs lack. The first set of skills, artistic vision and design expertise, needs someone who understands how color, text, and white space work together. This person could be the art teacher at the school or even a talented art student. While he/she does not have to have the technical expertise to execute the design, he/she should have the ability to visualize the design in a hypertext setting so that it does not overtax users' eyes or dominate the content of the site.

The team member with this expertise should not be responsible for reinventing the design wheel. Other team members can help him/her by searching and printing the home pages of other cyber libraries that have won awards or are cited in books and articles as having attractive, well-designed sites. The artistic team member should be able to select a series of features and design layouts from these sites and either adapt or adopt them to fit the proposed cyber library.

The second member of the team should have technological and programming expertise. Make a list of the technological needs of the site before searching for an individual to perform these tasks. If the group decides that the cyber library will consist mainly of links to other searchable and interactive Web libraries and instructional tutorials, then the individual could be a member of the computer science or educational technology department or a student who is recommended by that department. A technological team member could also be a staff member in the library department who is willing to take a course in a chosen Web-authoring program so that the library staff can modify and maintain the site independently. If, however, the group decides to employ a great many "bells and whistles," meaning several different forms of Web-authoring software and a database search engine, the group leader may wish to budget for a company to assume this responsibility.

The third member of the team should be a librarian who can interpret the information from the focus groups and/or surveys and locate Internet content that can be adopted or adapted to a cyber library. Consulting with faculty and working with other librarians in a possible consortial approach should be a qualification for this position. This person should probably be the head of the group since he/she will need a high degree of subject expertise in many different areas (Simcox 1999, 105). Studies show that content-rich sites are the most valued on the Internet, and users are becoming increasingly savvy at distinguishing between sites that are just graphics and those filled with content (Bobicki 2001, 8). A librarian assigned to this part of the project will be responsible for providing the contents for a Web library, cyber reading room, and instructional tutorials.

The fourth member of the group should be an individual, possibly a librarian because of his/her training, who comprehends organization and access in a hypertext format. This person must understand how the primary user group would search a cyber library, how to place information in a hierarchy, what materials are going to be accessed most frequently, and where there need to be multiple access points. These skills are critical to making a cyber library seamlessly navigable to users (Simcox 1999, 105).

Technical Needs

The decision of where a cyber library is to reside will determine its collection size, design level, cost, and maintenance. A major trend is access rather than ownership of technology (Rifkin 2000, 44–45). Access to free Web-authoring software and a Web-hosting server is a simple solution to a large technical problem. This trend toward accessing technology rather than purchasing it is especially important for schools because of their financial inability to buy expensive hardware and to hire sufficient numbers of qualified technical support personnel to maintain it. The means to either freely or inexpensively maintain a cyber library on the Internet is the first technical option to explore unless the SLMC or school has a Web server.

Free Cyber Library Option:
Advantages and Disadvantages

Launching a cyber library at no technical cost can be accomplished by locating a nonprofit organization such as Red Rival (http://www.redrival.com) or Netscape Netcenter (http://www.netscape.com/Websites) or by using an education portal such as Bigchalk.com (http://www.bigchalk.com). The former organizations offer user-friendly software such as Microsoft FrontPage or Adobe GoLive that convert text into HTML, the language necessary for creating pages of text on the Internet. SLMSs can either edit and create a cyber library with the software and instructions provided at the nonprofit site or download some free Web page editing software to a school computer for building and uploading pages to the parent site.

The first advantage of this option is almost too good to be true. Free off-site hosting saves SLMSs the expense of purchasing, troubleshooting, and maintaining a Web file server, buying Web-authoring software, and learning a new program such as FrontPage or GoLive. The second advantage pertains to the speed with which a cyber library can be created. Once a cyber library design, organizational structure, and links are selected, it becomes a simple matter of entering the text through software provided and checking to ensure that such things as the design, hierarchy, appearance, font size, color, and graphics are correct and attractive to the users.

Are there any drawbacks to this technical option for a cyber library? Yes, there are a few. The first concerns space. Most nonprofit institutions and education portals limit a cyber library to between 10 and 20 MB of space. For a cyber library that consists mainly of links to other Web libraries, instructional tutorials, and cyber reading rooms, this is easily enough space. For a cyber library that contains a SLMS-designed Web library with a search engine, drop-down menu, and sophisticated graphics, the number of megabytes may not be sufficient.

The second disadvantage is advertising. For a free site, most organizations require that a small banner be placed on the cyber library that advertises the company name or logo. Red Rival, however, is an exception to this rather standard practice.

SLMSs may wish to think of the free option as an excellent way to mount a first-stage cyber library. With the use of free clip art sites, Web-authoring software, and hosting, it is an opportunity for showing administrators or grantors the need for a larger cyber library that will contain more interactivity, multimedia, and search engines. It is the desire to grow and add more content to a site that nonprofit organizations and education portals are predicting that SLMSs will do. They are trusting that when the free site space allotted is used up, SLMS will begin paying for additional space and services ("Building a School Web Site" 2001, 15).

Cyber Library Hosted Option: Advantages and Disadvantages

The second option for SLMSs is to search for a Web-hosting company and negotiate the cost of hosting and maintaining the cyber library on the company's Web server. There are, of course, advantages and disadvantages to this option as well. The advantages are that the company is responsible for ensuring that the cyber library is up all the time. This decision can ease the technical and financial burdens in a school that cannot afford to replace servers every three years, as recommended, load new networking software, as required, and troubleshoot server problems with minimal downtime.

While this option seems to clearly outweigh the purchase of a Web server and operating system software, there are some problem areas. The first concerns the same issue that the free hosting option has—that of space. The amount of space that a cyber library takes on a hosted Web server needs to be carefully estimated. There is a natural tendency, because of the excellent resources on the Internet, to increase a cyber library's collection just as there is in a conventional library. Web-hosting companies' charges are based on the amount of space (usually megabytes) that a cyber library takes up. Pricing space can sometimes be confusing, since companies have not yet developed standard practices that enable SLMSs to comparatively shop. If Web hosting is the chosen option for a cyber library, be sure to examine the pricing space structure carefully.

A second disadvantage is potential increases in "renting space" on the company's server. Many Web-hosting companies offer excellent leases the first year and the next year raise the prices substantially. If off-site hosting is an option for mounting the cyber library, try to negotiate a multiyear lease with some room for growth of the cyber library within that period.

When changes are made to a cyber library, SLMSs usually wish them to be spontaneous. In most cases, a cyber library that is hosted off-campus can be updated at any time. Some companies, however, have a level of service structure. They charge for changes or make them within a certain time period. Be sure to read and negotiate all of these details before signing a contract (Stielow 1999, 107–112).

Cyber Library On-Campus Option: Advantages and Disadvantages

While the trend for accessing a Web server rather than owning one is clearly the way of the future, SLMSs should investigate what is available on-site first. If the school has a Web site, owns a Web server, and maintains it, all a SLMS has to do is integrate the cyber library into it. One of the advantages is that the cyber library will be viewed as an integral part of the school community. The design, graphics, font, and color will not have to be experimented with because the cyber library will need to reflect the overall school Web site's design. The last advantage is the "trial and error" factor. With an on-campus Web server and Web-authoring software, there is opportunity and time for trying different information formats, graphics, and the like and previewing them in the school's browser before launching them into "cyberspace." An on-site system provides some flexibility and more time for learning and experimentation.

Although some of the disadvantages have already been noted in previous paragraphs, the one most likely to cause a problem is server downtime. As students and faculty come to rely on the outstanding contents of a cyber library that provides access to items such as class-related Internet sites and the SLMC's online catalog, they have little patience for the times when the server is down for maintenance or repairs. Their expectations for round-the-clock access can result in inquiring phone calls and e-mails if the Web server is down for undue amounts of time (Gregory 2000, 21–23).

Technical Design Options

Choosing one of the three mounting options is a decision that will impact the other technical needs of a cyber library. Deciding to rely on a nonprofit institution will confine a SLMS to a specified amount of storage space and will usually necessitate a site design level that excludes some options involving interactivity and multimedia formats.

Many academic and public cyber libraries are becoming more interactive by providing reference help, readers' advisory, art shows, and exhibits online. They are also using their online public access catalogs in new ways that allow users to place holds on materials, check whether they have overdues, and search for materials related to their reading interest profiles. This level of interactivity in a cyber library calls for programming and technical skills that go beyond the ability to use Web-authoring software and capture links from other sites. It will also take up more storage space on a Web server (Hughes 2001, 62–64).

A second technical decision concerning design level is the desire to go beyond text. Although there is nothing wrong with a cyber library that is totally text based, libraries have a history of providing information in a variety of formats ranging from maps and manuscripts to films and videos. Supplying materials in a multimedia format requires the use of plug-ins (i.e., software programs that allow various file types to be used through the same browser). The more common ones are Adobe Acrobat and Real Player. While plug-ins enable a library to make different information formats more readily available, they do require a higher level of HTML programming and technical expertise if the cyber library is going to be a content provider for multimedia sites (Benzing 2000, 77–81).

Budgeting for a Cyber Library

When preparing a budget for a cyber library, consider hardware, software, personnel, and training needs. Remember that the location of the cyber library and its design level will determine much of the project's cost (Simcox 1999, 102). The following ideas and suggestions are related to those decisions:

- Take the time to survey the school to determine what resources in the way of hardware, software, training, and personnel are already available.

- If a Web server is not available, explore free, nonprofit hosting sites and educational portals; commercial Web-hosting companies; and the purchase of a Web server.

- Determine the desired design level. If interactivity and multimedia formats are needed, budget for outside personnel to create the programming and provide the technical expertise.

- Check with personnel at the school to see if someone is willing to receive training in Web-authoring software programs such as FrontPage or GoLive.

- Request funding for managing and directing the project.

- Increase the annual budget to either pay staff to maintain the cyber library or subscribe to a commercial link-checking service.

Cyber Library Deadlines and Beta Testing

The establishment of a deadline and plan for beta testing a cyber library is different from conventional library projects because of the medium of the Internet. In a conventional library, the time to shift shelves can be easily estimated because of the number of available shelves and quantity of books. It is easy to do the math and plan for the number of staff and hours needed to complete the job in a specified number of days.

Working on the Internet is an accelerated process. The learning curve may be steep, for example, at the beginning of the project. Then it can move very quickly because the process for inputting or linking becomes rather routinized and repetitive. There is also a high degree of impermanence to the Internet that does not exist in a conventional library. Sites, unlike books, are there one minute and have either moved or disappeared the next. Shelves may be shifted only once a year in a conventional library, but the contents of an Internet site are moved sometimes daily.

For these reasons, it may help when getting a cyber library project launched if the contributors think of its debut as simply version 1.0. This thought process might discourage perfectionism, which can be the bane of cyber library development. On the Internet, almost every site is a "work in progress" because revisions can be made so easily and because constant change is so characteristic of working in cyberspace (Stielow 1999, 33–36).

Establish an early deadline and beta test date to accelerate the process. Complete a prototype of the project at the beginning that contains all the content headings and basic design features. As contributors input content or create links to various subject headings, there will always be room for more sites. Some can also be quickly deleted if they are not acceptable to team members. As the project advances, the prototype can be revised by simply moving the headings to different places on the screen, changing their titles, or deleting them altogether. Inculcate the idea among team members that a cyber library will change on a daily basis, with notices, publicity photos, new sites, and more information being added or edited. It will never be perfect or complete.

Ownership is always a problem in a conventional library, but it can be more of a problem in a cyber library. In meeting with other SLMSs, the phrase "in my library, we do such and such" is often heard at meetings and conventions. Sometimes the words convey a sense of pride and identification with an institution that gladden the hearts of administrators. On other occasions, the phrase connotes a sense of personal ownership that limits borrowing, implies undue vigilance, and makes an administrator wince. In a cyber library, ownership can be more obstructive because the nature of the site requires constant change, editing, revising, and deleting. It demands that contributors keep open minds, active imaginations, and maintain their tolerance for new ideas and information formats (Klein 2000, 37–38).

To reduce a sense of ownership and maintain the momentum so necessary for a cyber library project, suggest a rule that the team member conducting a beta test either with users or other team members not be the person responsible for the content being tested. When conducting a test of the site with users, make sure that the tester does not explain or justify the design to the test subject. The employment of students and faculty to test the navigation of a cyber library and specific parts of the site will introduce an element of objectivity that will make it easier to perform revisions.

Cyber Library Contents

The operation hours of a SLMC, collection size, and user population characteristics are the three main factors that help determine the contents of a cyber library. First, SLMCs are open less frequently than any other type of library. Students cannot access them after school for very long, in the evening, or on the weekend. The class time allotted for them to search for and retrieve information from them is also limited because of class attendance schedules.

Second, the collections of most SLMCs lack the depth in many subject areas to satisfy more than the superficial information needs of most students. Term papers, especially for eleventh and twelfth graders, can be a problem in a conventional SLMC because the collection is not deep enough in various subject areas. On the Internet, there are outstanding collections of materials, for example, in history, political science, and government that can supplement print collections.

The problem of citing primary sources is also a challenge for many SLMSs to solve, since SLMCs' collections have neither the room to store such materials nor the budget to acquire them. The Internet is replete with primary sources in all subject areas ranging from science and mathematics to history and literature.

Even when a SLMC collection is large enough to provide depth in various subject areas, its information formats usually consist of print and nonprint materials. The latter kinds are usually videos and CD-ROM programs. While all of these materials are necessary to a SLMC collection, they do not offer the enhanced learning experiences that some Internet sites do. Free, interactive sites abound on the Internet. Many sites take the form of simulations or interactive tutorials. The former are excellent for teaching complicated scientific principles or processes such as genetic probabilities or the circulation of the blood. Simulations in science can help students understand a scientific process, law, or syndrome much more easily than a print source can. Tutorials that permit users to work in the actual software they need to learn while receiving instruction are a much-improved form of instruction rather than referring to a book and then practicing the instructions on a computer.

Third, many types of materials, particularly reference and reserve materials, do not circulate from a SLMC. The wealth of reference materials such as almanacs, encyclopedias, dictionaries, and atlases on the Internet is absolutely free for them to use at any convenient time or day. Reserve materials such as periodical articles can sometimes be accessed remotely through an online database, thus making them available to many students and saving photocopying costs.

A second factor that influences the contents of a school cyber library is the information-seeking behavior of its user population. A SLMC's user population is characterized by its inability to delay gratification of information needs. Students, on the one hand, need information within shorter time periods because their teachers impose short deadlines for assignment completion. Much of student work is assigned and due within a twenty-four-hour period. Adults, on the other hand, are able to delay gratification of their information needs for long periods of time because they do not have many externally imposed assignment deadlines. Adults can also transport themselves to other places such as local libraries and conventional and online bookstores to obtain the information they need. Students, however, are dependent on an adult to transport them anywhere until the age of sixteen or older.

The last important characteristic of a SLMC's users is their need for instruction. Students require instruction not only in the use of a conventional SLMC but also in the use of the Internet and licensed subscription databases. In many cases, they do not even know what information is required to complete an assignment. They need instruction in searching, retrieving, and evaluating information in all of its diverse formats.

For these reasons, it is imperative that the contents of a school cyber library consist primarily of full-text materials and online tutorials. Providing students with access to citation databases and commercial sites that entice them with subject summaries of information is frustrating to students needing information within a short time period. Plan to provide full-text content that will complement and supplement the resources of a SLMC.

Students of all ages are becoming more educated about the Internet, and their information expectations are high. A recent analysis of the Internet traffic to the Colorado Southwest Regional Library Service System showed that the pages accessed the most were heavy in content and frequently updated (Bobicki 2001, 8). Searching and selecting well-reviewed sites that are rich in content should be the first content goal.

Cyber Library Content Categories

When planning the content of a cyber library, it is helpful to establish some categories for the content and also to determine the collection level. Stielow, in his book *Creating a Virtual Library*, divides cyber library content into four categories: (1) free Web sites; (2) internally developed content; (3) internally developed interactive services; and (4) private services/electronic resources library (1999, 76). A cyber library may consist of only one category, such as free Web sites, or it may feature content in all four areas. The divisions are provided to help formulate not only a content plan but also to enable a SLMS to plan for future enhancements to a school cyber library.

Free Web Sites

A cyber library consisting totally of free Web sites can be achieved easily by using a Web-editing program such as FrontPage or GoLive to identify a desired site, capture its URL address, and place it under a selected subject heading. At this time, a site annotation can be added too. This approach is one of the most efficient and least-costly methods to construct a cyber library. SLMSs without the time and funds to develop their own content can avail themselves of Internet sites that rival books in the richness of their coverage, presentation, and display features.

The free Web site category also loans itself easily to a choice between site adaptation and adoption. Adaptation involves capturing a selected number of sites from a large Web site and inserting them into a selected category within the school's cyber library. Adoption entails capturing the entire site and linking to it from the school's cyber library. The option to either adapt or adopt is important to consider when megasites are encountered that are multidisciplinary. It may be easier for students to search for a selection of science sites that exist within a large encyclopedic Internet site such as Britannica.com by linking to the science section address than it is to provide only one link to the entire encyclopedia (Carter 1999, 48–49).

While the list of potential Internet sites to stock a cyber library is endless, the following suggestions may be helpful as initial guidelines:

- Concentrate on collecting full-text sites

- Find age-appropriate reference sites

- Collect primary source materials when age appropriate

- Whenever possible, collect interactive sites such as the Gallery of Interactive Geometry (http://www.geom.umn.edu/apps/gallery.html) or The Soundry (http://www.library.thinkquest.org/19537/)

- Link to sites that provide instructional interactivity such as library tutorials and bibliographic citation creation sites

- Feature sites that target different learning styles (e.g., visual or auditory)

Internally Developed Content

Even though it is possible to confine a cyber library to free Web sites, it is most unlikely that a school cyber librarian will not have some internally developed content to include. This category consists of descriptive information, special databases, and digital archives. Descriptive information can encompass the conventional SLMC's opening and closing hours and its various SLMC polices and procedures. This type of information, if it is in a word processing program, can be easily converted to an HTML document and placed within a cyber library under an appropriate subject heading.

Special databases that have been designed specifically for a SLMC are also part of this category. If SLMSs have constructed their own database of curriculum-related Web sites by using a program such as Microsoft Access, it is considered to be internally developed content and links can be made from it to the cyber library. Any exhibit material such as pictures of the SLMC or a special photo collection that is in digital form is also internally developed content and could be linked to the cyber library.

Digital archives are materials such as backlists of bibliographies, pathfinders, and SLMS-designed Webquests that usually exist in word processing format. They are definitely the type of materials that should be considered part of a cyber library, because their Internet availability can save a SLMS time, endless photocopying, and provide 24/7 access to students and faculty.

Consider placing the following internally developed content in a cyber library:

- Introduction to both libraries (conventional and cyber) including hours of operations, staff members, calendar, user population, and brief collection description

- Policies and procedures concerning borrowing, overdues, acquisitions, gifts, controversial materials, Web content, archives, and collection development

- Descriptions of special programs and services such as a courier system, author visits, storytellers, reading contests, exhibits, and book displays

- Pathfinders, bibliographies, reading lists, and other subject-related guides

- Instructional design services such as Webquests and library skills units

- Services for faculty (e.g., requests for equipment, SLMC use by classes, library orientation and instruction, and booktalks)

- Reference services and term paper counseling

- List of subscribed periodicals and the years kept in hard copy

- Web-content and organizational assistance for student- and faculty-developed Web sites

Internally Developed Interactive Services

While most SLMSs can design a cyber library that consists of free Web sites and internally developed content without a high degree of difficulty, the category of interactive services must be considered carefully from a design, maintenance, and staff commitment standpoint. Internally developed interactive services include programs such as electronic reference or homework assistance that is currently so ably performed by the American Association of School Librarian's program called ICONnect (http://www.ala.org/ICONN/kidsconn.html). This type of service relies on e-mail and/or the inclusion of interactive forms as the communications medium.

Interactive services are excellent additions to a cyber library. They provide users with added convenience and services, enable SLMSs to better measure and evaluate some of their services, and are, in many cases, more efficient. They also offer SLMSs a wonderful opportunity to maintain a constant electronic presence in their schools that places them in the technological forefront.

There are also significant benefits if a cyber library is being constructed to serve several schools. In this scenario, the burdens of maintenance and monitoring can be shared among the group. In a school setting that has one SLMS, it may become an additional onus rather than an enhancement to a cyber library to host interactive services. Sometimes it is difficult for a sole practitioner to respond to the reference questions in a conventional SLMC. When that responsibility is combined with acquisitions, cataloging and processing new materials, teaching, instructional design, and a myriad of other tasks, checking e-mail for cyber reference and homework questions may be impossible.

A decision to provide internally developed interactive services must be carefully thought out lest it overwhelm its creators. Consider adding an interactive service that can be timesaving for the SLMS. A drop-down menu and e-mail form for multimedia services and equipment might be very helpful. Instead of answering faculty telephone calls all day or receiving numerous e-mails requesting that a video be ordered from a local video cooperative or equipment be delivered to a room, these tasks might be better organized and fulfilled with interactive request forms.

If a decision is made to include internally developed interactive services, consider using the e-mail system or designing interactive forms to provide:

- Electronic reference assistance

- Online request forms with drop-down menus for requesting multimedia equipment and services (videotaping of a class, delivery of a tape recorder, and so forth)

- Interlibrary loans

- Book and nonprint materials requests and holds

- Reservations to the conventional SLMC for a class or library instruction

- Requests for instructional design assistance for a Webquest or library skills unit or booktalk

- Multimedia booking services from a local video/film cooperative

After establishing an interactive service, conduct a quick user study to measure its effectiveness. Evaluate it for potential modification, dropping the service, or instituting another one. These types of services are time consuming for SLMSs. If they are not being utilized or faculty and students are experiencing difficulties when using them, you need to be able to make adjustments quickly to meet their needs and interests.

Private Services/Electronic Resources Library

The last content area to consider when constructing a cyber library consists of private services and electronic resources that are provided by an outside commercial source. These services and resources range from an online public access catalog to electronic databases such as Ebsco's Host, SIRS, and the Electric Library. They also include the new fee-based libraries, such as Ebrary.com, and education portals.

The advantages of including subscription and fee-based electronic resources in a cyber library are threefold. First, the companies are responsible for performing all of the maintenance and updating. SLMSs no longer have to load new updates onto a file server or onto local terminals. They do not have to have the latest version of an operating system on the server for the update to load successfully. If there is a connection problem, it can usually be resolved by a telephone call to either the database or Internet service provider, rather than internally troubleshooting the problem because of local hardware or software problems.

Second, Web-based databases also reduce the need for security in a SLMC by rendering the CD-ROM version of it redundant. SLMSs no longer have to be concerned about the potential for CDs being stolen or damaged.

The third benefit from accessing Web-based electronic resources is their flexibility in allowing customization of their home page to suit the individual needs of a SLMC. Online catalogs can be customized with individual school names and descriptions. Default screen choices between simple and advanced searching can be easily set for elementary and/or secondary school student use. Electronic magazine databases supply designations so that a SLMS can indicate if the SLMC owns the hard copy of a specific magazine, thus enabling students to determine whether an electronic article containing only an abstract is available in hard copy in the SLMC.

The cost benefits of some electronic databases are also measurable. There are a number of companies that issue monthly reports of use or feature a way for SLMSs to evaluate usage on-site. This last provision is an excellent assessment device for future acquisition and renewal decisions.

While some of the benefits of Web-accessible databases are designed clearly for the convenience of SLMSs, the best feature is the ability to provide remote access for all users. Almost all subscription databases have log-in and password structures for remote searching. SLMSs can list the log-ins and passwords in a password-protected area of the cyber library or distribute the necessary information in hard copy. Remote searching of subscription databases provides a SLMC with 24/7 capabilities for substantial information resources. Students, faculty, and even parents can search electronic databases for information in a variety of formats ranging from periodical and newspaper articles to primary sources. The panic experienced by so many students because they procrastinated completing an assignment or were overscheduled with school activities to use the SLMC during school hours is greatly reduced. It is also an excellent opportunity for parents to understand the wealth of information that SLMSs provide for future funding appeals, budget justifications, and general goodwill.

While all of the benefits appear to outweigh any disadvantage when linking subscription electronic resources to a cyber library, there is a major drawback. It is their high cost. Defraying that cost by purchasing access through a consortium of libraries is a strong reason for considering a multischool approach to constructing a cyber library. A consortial cyber library approach offers substantial savings when subscribing to various databases. The savings can also be used to purchase access to additional databases that a single school could never afford.

While a cyber library's contents will reflect the local curricular needs and interests of the students and faculty, there are several types of subscription electronic resources that should be considered. Some of the more recognizable vendors are cited in this list to serve as examples and not as purchase recommendations. These include:

- SLMC's online public access catalog

- Periodicals database (e.g., Ebsco's Host products, Lexis-Nexis, and ProQuest Platinum)

- Trial subscriptions

- Database search services (FirstSearch)

- Online encyclopedias (Britannica.com and Grolier's)

- Subject-specific databases (Gale, Wilson Web, CQ Quarterly, and so forth)

- Fee-based libraries (Ebrary.com)

- Education portals (Bigchalk.com and Blackboard.com)

Cyber Library Design and Style Guidelines

Cyber libraries provide unprecedented creative and instructional opportunities that few SLMSs will ever experience in a conventional library. Cyber libraries give SLMSs the chance to create a collection without a size limit or budget concerns. One has the pleasure of choosing the brightest colors from a spectrum of hundreds without requesting funding. Cyber libraries provide a place to work in a wall-less environment that supports constant changes, revisions, new programs and services, and forgives mistakes at the click of a mouse. Most SLMSs will spend their entire careers in SLMCs that will never be enlarged, remodeled, or repainted. If the administration grants a small increase in either the materials or equipment budget, it is usually the result of laborious budget justification in the form of memos, annual reports, and persuasive oral arguments.

Although a cyber library offers unlimited opportunities for design, color, and style, it is the wealth of options that also presents problems to professionals who did not major in art or graphic design. The combination of Web-authoring software with its feature options for twenty fonts, numerous free clip art sites, and software graphic programs can present the cyber library builder with a bewildering number of design and style options. Although most decisions of artistic exuberance can be ameliorated by the click of a mouse, no SLMS would like to see her/his cyber library featured on Web Pages That Suck.com (http://www.webpagesthatsuck.com).

Besides facing a myriad of options regarding fonts, color, graphics, icons, and the like, a SLMS cannot turn to a source for standards on Web design. While many books have been published on it that contain lists of dos and don'ts, there are no rules that apply to Web design. Leo Robert Klein, the "Web Design Luminary" at Slashdot.com, a popular news and discussion site for Web developers, believes that it is better to live with "more shades than black and white." His idea of a Web designer is someone who possesses visual coherence and the ability to arrange information in a manner that successfully expresses its purpose. According to Klein, these qualities can be developed just as easily from gazing critically at pictures in a local art museum as they can from attending a "dreary Web conference" (2000, 39).

Think of the Web as a place to build a library that fulfills its mission and specific goals and always reflects its primary user group. Rely on a team member who has organization and access expertise and a second member who has artistic vision and design expertise. Do not be overly concerned with design rules. They are not artistic commandments. Instead, read through some of the suggested guidelines and use them as signposts for cyber library progress checkpoints.

Organize the Information

SLMSs are experts at organizing information in a conventional library. Materials that are used frequently such as reference and reserve materials are usually shelved nearer to the SLMC information desk. In this way, a SLMS can access and refer to them quickly to assist students and faculty with their more immediate information needs. The shelves in a SLMC are arranged according to the Dewey decimal system and users can move up and down the rows by following a series of consecutive numbers to locate materials.

This overall pattern of organization is similar to the way a SLMS should construct a cyber library. The layout or structure of a cyber library should adhere to a pattern that permits ease of use for everyone. Consider the following suggestions when organizing cyber library content:

1. Begin with a list of all the major components to a cyber library. This list should include items such as library information, a Web library, cyber reading room, instructional assistance, and subscription electronic resources.

2. Under each of the selected components, list the contents. Within the category "subscription electronic resources," for example, include the SLMC's online catalog and other subscription electronic resources.

3. Rank the order of importance of each cyber library component according to its potential for frequency of use on a scale of one to three. Remember all decisions should be based on the searching behavior of the primary user group.

4. Within each component, rank the contents according to frequency of use based on the same scale. Under the category "library information," the mission statement might receive a three for low use while the operating hours of the SLMC might receive a one.

5. Draw screen-sized squares on three pieces of paper that are either 8×6 or 8×4 inches. These are the sizes of typical Web browsers depending on the number of toolbars, icons, and other features that are employed.

6. Each piece of paper is the Internet screen-sized equivalent to a level in a three-floored SLMC. The first floor contains the entrance to the SLMC. It should only contain the most frequently used materials, because users do not like to "climb stairs." In other words, they do not like to waste time clicking any further than they have to to obtain the information they want. Resist the temptation to place the mission statement and goals on the first floor of the cyber library. While they are necessary for the team to build a well-designed cyber library, students will never need to have this information and, frankly, could care less about it.

7. On the first floor, place doors or links that will take the user to the other less frequently used floors. The third floor, for example, should probably contain library policies and procedures, but they may be within a toolbar heading on the first floor entitled "Library Information." Users will not be able to read the actual policy until they click on the link on the third floor or screen.

8. After placing all the content categories on the appropriate pages based on frequency of use, it is time to consult other Web sites to choose a layout design that suits the user group.

Searching for a Physical Design and Navigation Routes

Good design and navigation routes are somewhat intertwined. An Internet site that is well designed is usually easy to navigate. The most important aspect of Web design is to remember that the medium is hypertext rather than single text. Bringing a "book mind-set" to Web design is flawed because of the way in which users access the Internet sites. Hypertext allows readers to scan information much more quickly because of the embedded links that highlight a word or term and then permit users to click on it and receive a quick definition or explanation that in single text would require the use of a dictionary or reference book. As a result, an Internet user's tolerance for several screens of text without a single hyperlink is low.

The intolerance for single text coincides with another user characteristic: information impatience. Internet users do not usually wish to click through more than three screens to find information. Reading a book employs a linear approach, but with hypertext, the eyes tend to move quickly to search for important clickable links or locate the information quickly on the screen. Hypertext may be responsible for a "point and click" generation that SLMS must accommodate by providing appropriate links and jumps to frequently used parts of the cyber library (Stielow 1999, 13–14).

When evaluating other library Web sites for design and navigation, keep these two factors in mind. There is still a tendency for librarians who have been trained to work primarily with print materials to neglect these two major design components, and many of their sites still show evidence of a book approach to Web design.

To shorten the search process, look for cyber libraries that have won awards. *School Library Journal*, for example, has a column written by Walter Minkel called "Web Site of the Month." It contains the description, address, and selection criteria for outstanding school cyber libraries or a specific aspect of them that he considers praiseworthy.

The design and navigation suggestions that follow are combined from Stielow's book *Creating a Virtual Library* (1999, 13–15) and the American Library Association's Children and Technology Committee's "Great Sites Selection Criteria" (http://www.ala.org/parentspage/greatsites/criterial.html):

1. Print the home page and several subsequent pages, if necessary, of cyber libraries that have appealing looks, feel, and function for the

primary user group. Ask test students or focus groups to evaluate them.

2. Test-drive the site to see how navigable it is. The links should follow a comprehensible hierarchy and no information should be more than three clicks away from the entry points. The user should not have to scroll through endless screens of text. Short paragraphs not exceeding one screen or approximately eighteen lines are the norm.

3. Examine the entry points and determine how easily a user can move back and forth within the site by clicking on appropriate hyperlinks and return to the home page. Look to see if each page can serve as an independent page and that there are links that allow the user to return easily to the home page and other frequently used parts of the site.

4. Evaluate the consistency in the design throughout the site. The navigational buttons, for example, should always be on the same side. Toolbars should be in the same place on every page. The writing style should be similar on each page and sections and subsections should follow a logical plan.

5. Search the Web library to determine if there are too many sites attached to each category. Does that part of the site need a search engine?

6. Read the text to assess its suitability for the primary user population. If the cyber library is designed for students in grades 6–8, are the writing style, vocabulary, and images age appropriate? Elementary students, for example, will appreciate short sentences and simple word choices.

7. Study the graphics on the site. Are they relevant, appealing, and appropriate to the content? Notice how graphics are used in the place of text to allow users to navigate more quickly through the site.

Building a Cyber Library Template

After evaluating other cyber libraries for design and navigation aspects, it is time to construct a prototype template that incorporates some of their feasible design and layout features. If the school already has a Web site, SLMSs will probably need to consult with the site's Web manager to determine the degree to which they will have to follow the school site design standards. Some schools, for example, permit departments to design their own Web sites regardless of the design, style, and layout of the school's home page. This trend seems to be waning, however, as schools see not only the marketing advantages of consistent presentation style and design but also become aware of the power of design to facilitate access and use of the site.

When preparing either an original or site-compliant template, remember that it is simply a prototype to help organize content and reflect the cyber library's mission and goals. Think of it as a working template that can be easily edited and rearranged and expect to change sections when previewing the cyber library in a Web browser. Refer to evaluation suggestions in the previous section and consider the following items when constructing the template:

1. Try to limit pages to no more than two and one-half screens in length. If more information is necessary, break it up into sections so that it will download quickly and navigate more easily.

2. Create a consistent structure for the site that is flexible enough to permit seamless additions and deletions. Make sure that frequently used information is not embedded on the second or third floors.

3. Each page of the template should identify the cyber library and have toolbars in place so that users will know exactly where they are in cyberspace.

4. Determine if there are aspects of the site that may be suitable for multimedia content. Experiment to see if graphics could convey the information more quickly and effectively than text.

5. Create appropriate cross-links to other sections of the cyber library. Think of them as the cross-references that are used in print indexes and online catalogs.

Cyber Library Artistic Guidelines

Remember that there are no artistic commandments for Internet design and display. When choosing design functions and options such as fonts, font sizes, and colors, always keep in mind the cyber library's mission, specific goals, and user population. Check frequently, if necessary, with students to evaluate their aesthetic responses to the site design and its navigability. Minkel and Feldman quote a librarian at the State University of New York who has observed that "the brighter the colors and the wilder the graphics, the more they liked it and the longer they stuck with it" (1999, 84). While it is possible to go overboard with font variety and color, the goal should be to have the most attractive and visually appealing site as possible.

Ryan, in *The Internet Public Library Handbook*, reminds cyber library designers that younger students find large type easier to read (1999, 128). Although users can set their Web browsers to display cyber library contents in their favorite font size, many do not know about this option. She recommends choosing a default font size that is age appropriate for the primary user group.

Graphics are another feature that must be used judiciously because they do not necessarily appear the same on all operating systems and Internet browsers. Consider compressing graphics to the smallest file size so that users will not become impatient waiting for them to download (Ryan 1999, 129–130). With these major guidelines in mind, consider the following artistic suggestions:

1.   If the team has no one with design expertise, consider employing the skills of a professional Web designer in exchange for site attribution or search for a student who may be willing to assist with this part of construction for an hourly pay rate.

2.   Search the conventional SLMC for any Web-appropriate colors, icons, symbols, emblems, or pictures that could link the two. If the SLMC has its own logo, place it on the home page as a clickable information icon. Users will more readily recognize that they are visiting a related SLMC because they will recognize similar SLMC colors or perhaps its library mascot.

3.   Work on designing an attractive façade to the cyber library. The first page is the entrance. Make it as attractive as possible through the use of color, movement (scrolling banner), graphics, and font style and size. This is the opportunity to show off everything that the cyber library has to offer.

4.   Create sufficient contrast between the text and the background. Remember that empty space between text and headings is visually appealing.

5.   Choose colors that can help translate the mission of the cyber library. Reds, oranges, and yellows indicate stress and danger while blues, grays, and greens convey a sense of coolness and relaxation. Too many colors are considered disturbing and stressful.

6.   Rely on a minimum number of font styles and sizes to avoid confusing users and to communicate the overall mission of the cyber library.

7.   To reduce the download time, try to limit the use of a visual to one per screen.

8.   Use hyperlinked tables if they will speed selection decisions. Rather than have a long list of scrolling options, place them in a one-screen table so that users can view all of them and chose accordingly.

9.   Use graphics and icons to navigate through the cyber library rather than as mere decoration. Users assume that pictures and icons are navigable links. Consider using the icons of subscription electronic databases as entry point links. Students will recognize the commercial site's colorful icon and will automatically click and open it.

10.   Movement attracts the eye and holds users' attention. Consider installing a scrolling banner to announce an author's visit, advertise the arrival of a new book, or announce that summer reading lists are available from the cyber library.

11.   Purchase a digital camera and a scanner to take pictures of the SLMC and students and scan them into the cyber library Web site. Make sure, however, to obtain parental permission before displaying pictures of students.

12.   Visit free clip art sites, but avoid the use of passé art such as apples and little red schoolhouses. Choose icons that pulsate or contain a minimal amount of animation. They add an element of interactivity to a cyber library.

Cyber Library Finishing Details

Before mounting the site on the Internet, there are a number of common-sense finishing details that should be part of a checklist. After you have previewed the site for its content, design, function, visual appeal, and navigability for the umpteenth time, check it for the following:

1.   Proofread every page of the cyber library to verify that spelling, punctuation, and grammar are correct.

2.   Search the cyber library in the two main browsers to make sure that information appears correctly in both systems.

3.   Check all links to confirm that they open.

4.   Click on any links with photos, icons, or visuals to confirm that they do not take more than thirty seconds to download. This is the patience limit that most users have for downloading nonprint items.

5. If plug-ins are used for audio or video sites, make sure that they are clearly identified and functional if the cyber library is supplying them.

Recommended Internet Sites

All of the following Internet sites have either been reviewed or recommended by librarians writing in professional journals such as *School Library Journal* or *Library Journal.* Several, where noted, have received awards for excellent design and presentation. They are organized according to the stages of cyber library construction presented in this chapter. Plan to visit them before beginning each cyber library building phase because they contain useful ideas and suggestions that can be adopted or adapted to your cyber library.

Mission Statement and Specific Goals

**Top Ten Reasons School Library Media Specialists
Should Connect to the Internet
http://ericir.syr.edu/ICONN/ihome.html**
> This site is useful for developing a mission statement and set of goals that coincides with one written by the American Association of School Librarians. It is a little less formal in tone than many of the college cyber library mission statements and is specifically suitable for school libraries.

Technical Needs

**Building the Web.com
http://www.buildingtheweb.com**
> Free Web page editing software and a tutorial for SLMSs who plan to develop and mount a cyber library through either a nonprofit institution or a subscription Web-hosting company are available at this user-friendly site.

**Davesite's Interactive HTML Tutorial
http://www.davesite.com/Webstation/html/**
> Provides a free, interactive tutorial that allows users to learn HTML processes and procedures while creating their pages in the actual software program.

**Netscape Netcenter
http://www.netscape.com/Websites**
> Furnishes a free, fast, visual online editor, 10 MB of space, a guest book, and hit counters to SLMSs who wish to create, mount, and maintain a free

cyber library. The only disadvantage is that the company requires a small, fixed banner advertisement for Netscape at the top of each page.

Page Tutor
http://www.pagetutor.com/pagetutor/makapage/

Librarians needing a free Web page tutorial will find this easy to use. It allows one to create cyber library pages on a local computer and upload them to either a Web-hosting company or nonprofit institution.

Red Rival
http://www.redrival.com

Red Rival gives SLMSs 20 MB, rather than the 10 MB of space provided by Netscape Netcenter, and does not require a banner or advertising. The disadvantage is that the company only provides a simple text editor. SLMSs must create pages with some of the free tutorial software and upload them to this site.

Whatis.com
http://whatis.techtarget.com/

Technical terms and Internet jargon are explained in noncomputerese at this Internet site. SLMSs who start encountering confusing terminology can type in a specific term and retrieve an understandable definition. It's useful when negotiating with sales representatives who sometimes overwhelm prospective customers with obfuscating technical terms during price negotiations.

Cyber Library Contents

Peter Milbury's Network of School Librarian Web Pages
http://www.school-libraries.net/

Check out the competition at this excellent directory site of school librarian-designed Web pages. It's organized by countries, and within the United States by states. There are also some links to recent school library research and reports and a useful link for the cyber library mission statement and specific goals section. Be aware that some of the SLMC pages are dedicated to professional associations and curriculum-related resources. Refer to it for content and design ideas.

Web Pages That Suck.com
http://www.webpagesthatsuck.com/

After looking at various school and SLMC Web sites, it is not a bad idea to perform an Internet prevention technique by visiting sites that are unfortunately notable for poor design or the latest madcap bell or whistle. The folks at this site have really done their homework by finding sites that illustrate all the don'ts on any Web site designer's checklist.

Web66: AK12 World Wide Web Project
http://web66.coled.umn.edu/

Visit this site and search its outstanding directory of "schools on the web." It is especially useful for ideas about how to integrate a school cyber library into a preexisting school site. This site could also be listed under "Cyber Library Design" because it has useful links on creating a Web site and setting up a Web server. It also contains lists of e-mail discussion groups for educators who manage Internet servers and wish to share questions, solve problems, and promote their ideas and successes.

Cyber Library Design

Best of the Web
http://www.botw.org/

Billing itself as "Headquarters for the Best of the Web Awards," this site is extremely useful to search for commercial and educational entities that have received awards for their design, content quality, and Web technicality. Although it is not dedicated to school cyber libraries, click on various years and view first-, second-, and third-generation award-winning sites plus all the latest design bells and whistles.

Yale Style Guide
http://info.med.yale.edu/caim/manual/contents.html

Considered a nicely outlined spin-off from the book *Web Style Guide* (1999) by Lynch and Horton, this site includes information about all aspects of Web design ranging from targeting the user group to the placement of text and graphics. If the SLMC's budget is tight, visit this site to obtain a textbook's worth of information at no cost.

Cyber Library Artistic Guidelines

Classroom Clipart
http://classroomclipart.com/cgi-bin/kids/imageFolio.cgi

The clip art that comes with various word processing programs is considered hackneyed and downright corny for use in a Web site. The thousands of free clip art images at this site offer a much better selection. Arranged in a user-friendly directory, the site also features a "Terms of Use" link so that users know how the images may be employed on their own sites.

Iconbrowser
http://www.ibiblio.org/gio/iconbrowser/icons/icons1-6.html

Obtaining copyright-free icons for a cyber library can be a problem, but not at this site. It contains six pages of downloadable icons and emblems that you can use on a school cyber library's page.

Ovid
http://www.ovid.com

How to use color, space, and graphics is tricky when space is limited to an 8×6-inch area of space. This interface for networked databases is a model for clean Web design and simplicity. It's easy to navigate and the icons are small and relevant. SLMSs who are searching for multischool cyber library design can learn a great deal from its uncomplicated style and layout.

References

Benzing, Matthew. 2000. "Browser Plug-Ins: Customization for Multimedia." In *The Cybrarians Manual 2*, ed. by Pat Ensor. Chicago: American Library Association.

Bobicki, Jeff. 2001. "All of the News, None of the Hassle." *LJ Netconnect: Supplement to Library and School Library Journal* (Winter): 8.

Braun, Linda W. 1998. "Building a Better Web Site." *School Library Journal* 44 (July): 24–27.

———. 2001. "Letting Teens Take the Lead." *LJ Netconnect: Supplement to Library and School Library Journal* (Winter): 26–29.

"Building a School Web Site." 2001. *Classroom Connect* 7 (April): 15.

Burnett, Tim. 2001. "Set up a Free Web Site This Summer." *Classroom Connect* 7 (Summer): 7.

Carter, David S. 1999. "Building Online Collections." In *The Internet Public Library Handbook*, ed. by Joseph Janes et al. New York: Neal-Schuman.

Garlock, Kristen L., and Sherry Pointek. 1996. *Building the Service-Based Library Web Site: A Step-by-Step Guide to Design and Options*. Chicago: American Library Association.

Gregory, Vicki L. 2000. *Selecting and Managing Electronic Resources*. New York: Neal-Schuman.

"How Can I Use Standards in My Classroom?" 2001. *Classroom Connect* 7 (March): 6.

Hughes, Jane E. 2001. "Access, Access, Access! The New OPAC Mantra." *American Libraries* 32 (May): 62–64.

Junion-Metz, Gail. 2001. "The Librarian's Internet Food for Thought: How Kids and Adults Learn." *School Library Journal* 47 (April): 33.

Klein, Leo Robert. 2000. "The Web Design and Sin." *LJ Netconnect: Supplement to Library and School Library Journal* (Summer): 37–39.

———. 2001. "The Web Is Not Your Library." *LJ Netconnect: Supplement to Library and School Library Journal* (Winter): 36–37.

Kovacs, Donald, and Michael Kovacs. 1997. *The Cybrarain's Guide to Developing Successful Internet Programs and Services*. New York: Neal-Schuman.

Lynch, Patrick, and Sarah Horton. 1999. *Web Style Guide: Basic Design Principles for Creating Web Sites*. New Haven, CT: Yale University Press.

Minkel, Walter, and Roxanne Hsu Feldman. 1999. *Delivering Web Reference Services to Young People*. Chicago: American Library Association.

Rifkin, Jeremy. 2000. *The Age of Access*. New York: Putnam.

Ryan, Sara. 1999. "Serving Young People—What You Can Do." In *The Internet Public Library Handbook*, ed. by Joseph Janes et al. New York: Neal-Schuman.

Simcox, Schelle. 1999. "Creating a Successful Web Site." In *The Internet Public Library Handbook*, ed. by Joseph Janes et al. New York: Neal-Schuman.

Smith, Susan, et al. 2001. "Make It a Team Approach." *LJ Netconnect: Supplement to Library and School Library Journal* (Winter): 18–20.

Stielow, Frederick, ed. 1999. *Creating a Virtual Library: A How-to-Do-It Manual for Librarians*. New York: Neal-Schuman.

Traw, Jeri L., comp. 2000. *Library Web Site Policies*. Chicago: American Library Association.

Weissman, Sara. 2001. "Know Your Audience." *LJ Netconnect: Supplement to Library and School Library Journal* (Spring): 42.

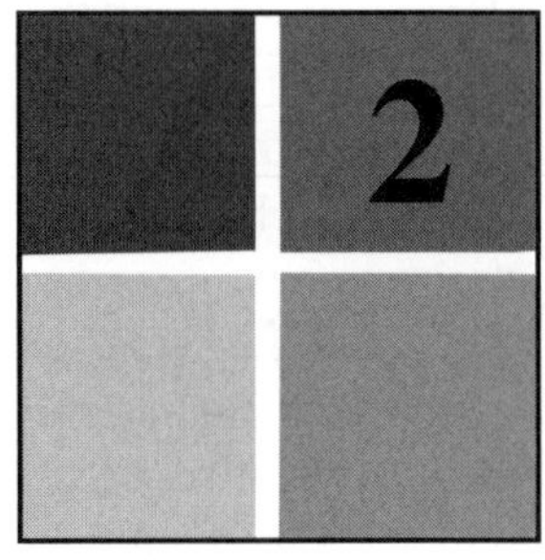

Cyber Library Policies

The Need for Policies

Providing library services and programs through an Internet cyber library is a natural extension of the responsibilities of SLMSs. Our job entails meeting our users' needs as much as possible and the Internet is an important source of information. The volume and flow of information on the Internet is a problem, however, because it increases our responsibilities and burdens. While we have more information available than ever before, our ability to search for it, organize it, and evaluate it is a constant challenge (Gorman 2001, 48).

For many years, SLMCs have been able to function successfully without a formal set of policies for accomplishing their goals and objectives concerning areas such as acquisitions, collection development, and copyright. The only policy that is considered mandatory is a controversial materials policy that most SLMSs keep on hand as a first-stage prophylactic device against a possible book banning. If SLMSs had the time to formulate some of the previous policies, it was a onetime task because no one, with the exception of the SLMS and a possible accreditation team member, ever had a need to refer to them.

Cyber libraries, however, present a different set of concerns that mandate a set of Web-accessible policies to focus collection development, facilitate their use, protect the privacy and confidentiality of students and faculty, and comply with recent copyright laws.

Legal and Ethical Concerns

Cyber libraries, unlike conventional SLMCs, are not only open when SLMSs are off duty but are also available to millions of users other than the school population. The electronic visibility of the programs and services of conventional SLMCs, particularly through our online catalogs and Web libraries, makes them much more vulnerable to justification and challenge from any virtual visitor. The collection of the online catalog is available for searching by anyone. If a SLMC, as it should, collects materials about controversial issues such as abortion, gun control, or euthanasia, it can easily become the target of a local watchdog group whose members may consist of school parents. Its Web library comprising SLMS-selected Internet sites is also searchable by anyone who has an Internet connection, including parents, school board members, and administrators. Any member of these constituencies may wish to question the reason for Internet sites in a particular information category or to recommend sites for a deliberately omitted subject area.

Our present legal climate also demands that SLMSs create cyber library policies because the Internet has made issues of intellectual freedom and privacy more complex. Every SLMS has watched students blithely cutting and pasting substantial passages from Internet documents into research assignments without citing the sources, let alone ever questioning their authenticity. The ability to capture an image of a famous work of art, enlarge it, and use it as the front cover of a report without giving any attribution is something that SLMSs witness daily in their SLMCs (Stielow 1999, 26).

Intrusions on privacy are also a problem for SLMS policymakers. Privacy threats come in two forms: visible and invisible. The former involves the possible risk to students from potential pornographers and abusers when their names and/or photos are placed on an Internet page. Minkel, in an article written about the need for photographs of students in a cyber library, mentions a recent lawsuit by parents of students at a New Jersey school that posted student photos accompanied by their full names on the Web. Although many schools have developed policies in this area since this 1999 lawsuit, it is a new policy area that school cyber librarians must address (Minkel 2001a, 38).

The invisible threat to privacy is more insidious. This area concerns the use of cookies and user profiles. Cookies (small text files that a Web site writes to the user's hard drive) and user individual log-in profiles provide owners of Web sites with information about a user's Internet searching proclivities. Purchasing three books from Amazon.com about golf is all it takes, for example, for Amazon.com to provide the buyer with a list of additional golf titles the next time he/she logs in.

Although computers can be configured to prevent cookies and enable a generic log-in to protect users' identities, most students do not know how to execute this option. In many schools, they are not permitted to employ a generic log-in because it would defeat the school's need to monitor student Internet use. The result can be targeted advertising toward a segment of the population that is most vulnerable to it and anger from parents who would like to avoid the problem altogether.

Ease of Use

"Ease of use" is a common evaluative library term that describes the searchability and accessibility of reference books. A reference book that receives high marks for ease of use is considered to be well indexed, organized, and imminently searchable. This term serves nicely as a criterion for a cyber library. Cyber libraries need to have polices that help keep them well organized and visually consistent. Conventional SLMCs are not as susceptible to disorganization and appearance problems as cyber libraries. The shelves and the classification system impose an easily maintained order that is not so easy to accomplish in a cyber library. Although cyber libraries do not require the labor of shelvers, they do need policies that maintain their design, layout, and organizational structure so that their users do not get lost in cyberspace. Web content and template policies are essential to the continued success of a cyber library.

Internet Use

A few years ago, schools developed a policy termed "acceptable use." It most often consisted of a one-page list of don'ts for students concerning the penalties for employment of the school's computers for accessing pornography, sending abusive e-mail, using others' passwords, and hacking. The policy also contained a form that required the student's and parent's signature before the student received computer access. The signed form was also stored in the student's folder at school.

Since that time, an increasing a number of other issues have arisen that encompass topics such as printing, downloading, use of workstations, and digital literacy skills. The policy, once termed "acceptable use," has been subsumed into a new one termed "Internet use." This new policy is helpful to cyber librarians because it gives them an opportunity to address some of the issues and potential problems that are unique to cyber libraries. SLMSs may also wish to include guidelines in the school's Internet use policy regarding student access to remote electronic databases and use of SLMC computers.

Internet Collection Development

Although the tremendous growth of the Internet makes a multitude of essentially free resources available, it also presents a series of issues concerning acquisitions, content quality, and evaluation. Internet sites do not lend themselves to easy classification. Most print materials, with the exception of some reference books, are about a subject area that corresponds to a related area of the collection. A book about the stars, for example, is shelved in the astronomy section of a conventional library. The Internet, however, is filled with excellent sites that sometimes encompass physical science and humanities subjects within one site. Does a cyber librarian choose links from within the larger site and place them in a Web library or create a single link to the entire Web site and place it in a category called "megasites"?

In a cyber library, cost and space restrictions do not apply. The scope of a cyber library collection can be limitless. A SLMS can easily spend significant amounts of time Web searching and building an enormous collection only to be overwhelmed by maintenance problems involving link disappearances and address and content alterations to the selected sites.

In a conventional library, SLMSs devote a considerable amount of time to reading acquisitions journals and purchasing print and multimedia materials based on professional reviews of them. This is really a second review stage since print materials have already undergone an editorial and copyediting review process before publication. Internet resources are not subject to an evaluative process before they are "published." There is no prepublication stage involving checking the contents for accuracy and verifying the authority of the author. Even when an Internet site is reviewed in a professional journal, it must be explored more thoroughly than a book, because its contents may have changed since the review's publication. The contents of a book, unless it is a new edition, remain the same.

Accountability and quality control are important elements in the education profession. An Internet collection development policy is basically an expression of accountability to primary and secondary users—students, faculty, and parents. All of them rely on SLMSs to abide by well-developed selection criteria for a cyber library just as we do for our conventional libraries.

The second element, quality control, is essential to a cyber library because of the vast size and scope of the Internet. SLMSs must have an Internet collection development policy that ensures quality control for site contents. Policies that govern the content, design, and potential use of a cyber library are essential for its success.

A Single Team
or Consortial Approach

There are two approaches to writing cyber library policies, the single team and the consortial approach, and each has advantages and disadvantages. Obviously, if one SLMS decides to build a cyber library there are no arguments regarding the collection size, scope, contents, and design or layout. A consortial approach, however, can reduce the workload of SLMSs by sharing knowledge and expertise that help determine which Internet sources will be included, what design template will be adopted, and how user groups will be protected. If a site is challenged or a legal concern arises, a consortium of SLMSs may be better able to withstand the pressure and receive more administrative support with a set of group-ratified policies.

Separate or Integrated Policies

After deciding to create site policies for a single school or consortium of schools, the next decision is whether to develop separate Internet policies or integrate them into existing ones. Gregory, in *Selecting and Managing Electronic Resources*, advocates an integrated approach because it allows for all types of resources to exist within an overall plan for future budget and funding considerations (2000, 12). Nonetheless, some policies, such as Web design, are new to SLMCs and will need to be separate. Others, such as a collection development policy, could be integrated into existing SLMC policies. Creating separate policies may be easier if they are to be available only at the cyber library site for informing, directing, and protecting purposes. Integrated policies, where suitable, publicly acknowledge that libraries strive to collect information on both sides of an issue and in diverse formats. Integrated policies indicate the continuum between the conventional and cyber libraries.

Flexibility and Boilerplate

Writing Internet policies, especially in an age of lawsuits and parental worries about pornographic sites, can be so daunting that many potential school cyber librarians may be tempted to procrastinate producing them. It may be helpful to think of policies as support to fulfill a cyber library's mission statement and achieve a set of specific goals. Refer to the cyber library mission statement and goals as you draft cyber library policies.

Once policies are written, view them as version 1.0. In conventional SLMCs, policies are usually written and filed away, only to be acknowledged in an accreditation report. The rapid changes taking place with all types of information technologies preclude a sense of permanence. A Web template policy, for example, could change in a manner of days if new graphics or a search engine is needed for the cyber reading room. The research and recreational reading needs of students change with the addition of new courses and societal trends. A collection development policy will need to be modified to reflect new subject collection areas. Draft policies give team members a trail to follow, but build in room to go outside the lines and to experiment with new designs, innovative technologies, programs, and services.

"Boilerplate" is a legal term for detailed, standard wording of a contract, warranty, or will. SLMSs need to avail themselves of this type of writing when it comes to preparing cyber library policies. Spending the time to laboriously write Internet policies will diminish the excitement, creativity, and plain fun that awaits a potential cyber librarian. Approach policy writing creatively. Refer to the various criteria listed in this chapter for each policy and visit the recommended Internet policy sites. Use the various policy criteria as a checklist for items that are to be included in your cyber library policies section. Print out copies of Internet policies and adopt or adapt desirable content. Obtain permission of the site authors if you adopt significant portions of the policy and give them full attribution on the cyber library site.

In most cases, SLMSs will find that the words and phrases within each site's policies are written in a rather standard writing style that could be termed "library boilerplate." Writing policies in this manner will save a considerable amount of time that can be devoted to other more creative pursuits.

Assessing Programs and Services

While cyber library policies reflect the mission statement and goals, they must also be determined by the types of programs and services that will be offered. Consider the following programs, content, technologies, and services questions to decide which policies might be applicable to your cyber library.

- Will the cyber library host and provide links to chat rooms or newsrooms and user groups?

- Will the cyber library offer readers' interactive advisory services, provide interactive reference assistance, or term paper counseling?

- If the library is consortial based, will there be professional services sites for SLMSs?

- Will there be associated outreach or distance education services?

- What is the focus of the Web library? Is it to be totally curriculum related or will it also encompass the recreational needs and interests of the primary user group?

- Will commercial sites offering product/ordering information be available?

- Will fee-based sites such as Questia.com be listed?

- What will be the library's position on sites that violate copyright laws?

- What is the design style and navigation structure of the cyber library?

- Will users be asked to contribute site suggestions to the library?

- Will there be sites that require a user to log in and have a password?

- What means will be used to protect the privacy of students and other users?

Types of Policies

With the exception of a library Web development policy for a consortial approach, it is recommended that cyber libraries have policies for Web design, collection development, copyright, and privacy. Within each of these policy areas, criteria are offered for inclusion.

Library Web Development Policy

Before developing a consortial-based cyber library, write a policy based on the consortium's discussion and responses to each of the areas and issues noted. Maintain the order as listed and you will have created a library Web development policy.

1. **Mission:** Decide the overall mission and goals of the consortium. It may differ from a single cyber library because it will need to meet the information needs of perhaps alternative, vocational, charter, and traditional schools.

2. **Primary Users:** Ask who the primary users are. They may be students with a wider range of grades, abilities, and aspirations than those in a single school cyber library. They may also include some faculty members.

3. **Cyber Library Scope:** Define the scope of the cyber library. Will it support just curriculum-related needs or include recreational and consumer information as well?

4. **System Administration:** Formulate a plan for administering the cyber library that includes group or individual responsibility for: (a) seeking and maintaining administrative support and funding; (b) site organization; (c) cyber library contents; (d) design and style; (e) collecting, reviewing, editing, and deleting Internet sites; (f) hosting the cyber library; (g) troubleshooting technical problems; (h) maintaining the site; and (i) promoting the cyber library.

Web Template Policy

Of all the types of cyber library policies, this one needs to remain the most flexible. There are too many advances and changes with technology that cyber librarians will need to adapt to in the future to develop a rigid policy in this area. Even though a Web content and template policy helps to concentrate and maintain a cyber library design and layout focus, always think of this policy as one that will require constant modification to reflect new ideas, formats, and technological innovations. Follow and respond to questions and text within the criteria in the order noted and you will have written a Web template policy.

1. **Purpose:** A Web template policy should provide cyber library designers with a standard set of visual cues that help users navigate through the pages that cyber librarians produce. It helps identify each page as part of a larger unit and can save time and effort by facilitating the addition and deletion of Internet sites and directional links.

2. **Design Elements:** After considering all of the following elements, write a sentence concerning the placement, size, or color of each one.

   - **Headers and Footers**—Choose the information to be included in the cyber library header. It usually contains the library logo and other identifying information. The footer should include the "last updated statement," an e-mail link to the responsible party, and appropriate return buttons or links to previous pages, home page, and so forth.

   - **Library Identifying Information**—Determine the size and placement of library identifying information such as a banner, logo, or library-related graphics that will be used on the home page and all subsequent pages.

   - **Toolbars**—Decide on the size and placement of toolbars on the home page and all subsequent pages.

   - **Navigation Devices**—State where layout devices such as icons, buttons, or identifying logos are to be placed on all pages. Verify that a place on either the banner or a button will always return users to the first page.

   - **Page Sizes**—Choose a page size (usually 640 × 480 pixels) for each screen.

   - **Fonts**—Select fonts that will be used throughout the site and state that they have been selected with the primary user group in mind. Remember that younger students will benefit from larger font sizes.

   - **Colors**—State which color will be used for the site background and the color that will be used for text. Provide a sufficient level of contrast but also make sure that they harmonize with one another.

- **Background Image**—If a background image is desired for any part of the site, state what it is. Verify that it has been checked on different browsers.

- **Images**—Decide on image sizes, how many colors will be permitted in an image, and how many images will be allowed on one screen.

- **Clip Art**—State the sources of any free clip art sites that are used regularly.

- **Text Delineations**—Choose text sizes for headings and text and decide where text is to be bolded, if at all.

- **Content Guidelines**—If links are to be annotated, decide on the length and whether to have a full sentence or fragment description.

- **Vocabulary**—Establish vocabulary standards for terms and phrases used frequently in the site (e.g., non-fiction versus nonfiction) and list them.

3. **Maintenance Elements**

- **Dates**—Include the date created and the date of the last revision of content or function.

- **Storage**—State where files for each page are to be stored. Bibliographies, for example, should be under a similar subject heading, and graphics files should be stored in an images folder to facilitate access.

- **Site Index**—Maintain an index of the site so that places for deletions, additions, and cross-links are easily understood.

Internet Use Policy

An Internet use policy should contain most of the components of the former acceptable use policy. At the risk of being repetitive, some of those components have been incorporated within the following criteria. They have been compiled from model Internet use policy sites that are available at the American Library Association's site (http://www.ala.org). By considering and responding to the following questions and issues in their preset order, you will have written an Internet use policy.

1. **Purpose**—What is the purpose of providing students with a cyber library? If necessary, refer to the mission and specific goals section in Chapter 1 for more detail.

2. **User Responsibilities**—Include the items that have been previously banned in acceptable use policies such as: (a) sending or displaying abusive messages or images; (b) using obscene language; (c) harassing, insulting, or flaming others; (d) vandalizing computers, computer systems, or computer networks; (e) violating copyright laws; (f) using others' passwords; (g) searching others' networked folders or files; (h) utilizing SLMC computers for commercial purposes; and (i) accessing pornographic sites.

3. **Student File/Folders**—If a cyber library allows students to save information on SLMC computers or its server, decide on a duration and warning system before the information, file, or folder will be deleted.

4. **Filter Presence**—The recent Children's Internet Protection Act (CIPA) declared that all public schools or schools accepting federal funds must install Internet filters. State that there is an operative software filter system installed on the cyber library in compliance with the new law.

5. **Disclaimer**—Offer a disclaimer stating that filtering software does not block all material users might find offensive and that the SLMS cannot be held responsible for a student encountering this type of site. State that not all sources on the Internet provide accurate, complete, or current information and that every attempt has been made to compile a Web library of resources that have been reviewed or recommended in professional journals.

6. **Access to Remote Databases**—Remind students that password access to subscription electronic databases is for their use and not the use of students at other schools.

7. **Printing**—Insert any applicable page-printing limit in this area and ask students to be judicious in their use of the printers. If there is a charge for the use of a color printer, for example, state it here.

8. **Downloading and Uploading**—If you allow students to download material to diskettes or their own e-mail accounts,

what responsibility do you wish the library staff to have for assisting them? Will the SLMC sell or offer free diskettes? Will the school allow students to save material to the hard drive of a library computer? What is the SLMC's policy on allowing a student to load his/her own software on a library terminal?

9. **Workstation Use**—Is there a limit on the number of students who may use one workstation? May a student reserve the use of a workstation at a particular time for a school-related project?

10. **Workstation Purpose**—What is the SLMC's position on downloading programs requiring large amounts of memory and the playing of computer games?

11. **Cyber Library Instruction**—Determine the priority, if any, that a class is to be given if there is an insufficient number of available terminals. Does a scheduled library class take precedence over a student finishing a term paper?

12. **E-Mail**—Are students allowed to access e-mail from a commercial site such as America Online from the library computers? If so, are they to be restricted to a certain time of day such as lunchtime or after school?

13. **Publishing of Student Work**—Would the library like to publish reviews of recent books by students for publication in a cyber reading room? If so, what are the rules concerning the printing of their names? Does the school allow first name and last initial only or is something additional more acceptable?

14. **Student Photographs**—Will the cyber library feature pictures of students at work in the library, reading, or winning a library contest? If yes, state the provisions for contacting parents, obtaining signed permission slips, and their previewing the pictures before publishing them on the Internet.

15. **Penalties**—Consult with school administrators to confirm that the penalties that you have formulated for the user responsibilities area are fair and enforceable. Make sure that you are allowed to withhold the computer privileges of a student who violates them before it is stated in the policy.

Internet Collection Development Policy

An Internet collection development policy is probably the most important policy to have because it assists a cyber librarian in staying focused when building a Web library or when adding Internet sites into an online catalog. A Web library consists of Internet sites that are classified under various subject headings. While it is similar to a conventional SLMC in many ways, Web libraries present a set of problems that call for some changes to a conventional collection development policy. Many sites, as mentioned earlier in the chapter, are megasites and are not easily classified under a specific subject heading. The sheer volume of sites can cause the selection process to be a full-time job, and the simple process of linking to them makes it easy to acquire too many. A Web library that is too large to efficiently maintain can result in numerous dead links and frustration on the part of users.

Write an Internet collection development policy by responding to the issues and questions raised in the following areas. Maintain the order as listed and you will have completed an Internet collection development policy.

1. **Mission**—A cyber library collection should reflect the mission statement and goals. If necessary, refer to the mission statement and goals in Chapter 1 for additional details. Choose only the goals that are relevant to collection development.

2. **Purpose of the Collection Development Policy**— State the reason for creating a policy such as the need to support the curricular and research needs of the students and faculty. Describe how SLMSs will use the policy to be critical and selective when recommending Web sites to the user population, seeking funding, receiving administrative support, and providing justification to users regarding the inclusion or exclusion of Internet sites. State its authority. Has it been approved, for example, by a consortium of SLMSs, building-level administrators, or the superintendent of schools?

3. **Audience**—Who are the primary and secondary user groups to be served by the policy? Do they have any special needs or interests that should be noted? For example, is the collection to focus on the needs of learning-disabled students because the school has many classes for them?

4. **Access**—Describe how the cyber library collection is to be accessed. Insert the Internet address for the cyber library site. If there are log-ins and passwords for remote access to electronic resources, place the information in this section.

5.   **Collection Background**—Outline the broad subject categories of the cyber library. Will the collection contain sites from history, science, literature, foreign language, and mathematics? If there are to be special collections of Internet sites devoted to local history or community affairs, state the reasons and provide brief descriptions.

6.   **Budget**—If you have received funds to search for Internet sites, to design a database, and to maintain it, state the amount and mention any appropriate individual line allocations.

7.   **Limitations**—Is there to be a limit on the number of sites in the Web library for maintenance or search engine purposes? If so, state it in this section and provide a reason. Are there categories of information that the cyber library will not collect? Some religious schools, for example, will not collect any Internet sites that portray the school's affiliated religion in a negative light.

8.   **Consortium Selection Responsibilities**—If you have chosen a consortial approach to collection development, outline the subject responsibility areas that each librarian has agreed to search for and maintain in the cyber library.

9.   **Collection Evaluation**—How often will the Web library be examined to determine if it reflects changes in the curriculum or an increase in class assignments in a particular subject area? Describe the process for doing it.

10.   **Maintenance**—Describe the procedure and frequency for checking links to determine site availability, change of address, or disappearance. What will be the time span for replacing, if at all, sites that have vanished? For example, if a site has been missing for three weeks, will you replace it with an equivalent site?

11.   **Weeding**—What criteria will be applied? What are the procedures for discarding a site? If a faculty member has requested a site for a class assignment, will he/she be notified before it is removed? How frequently will the Web library be weeded?

After completing the first stage of writing an Internet collection development policy, create criteria for site selection. In this section, refer to the following selection guidelines. The following selection criteria are used as part of National Cathedral School's Internet Collection Development Policy (http://ncs.cathedral .org/uslibrary/Library/Lib_Policies/Internet_Collection_Policy.htm). The sources from which they were compiled are listed at the site.

1. **Authority**—Include sites sponsored by universities, government, or professional associations that offer some commitment to authoritative information and perpetuation of their sites.

2. **Accuracy**—Select sites that contain information, seem error-free, and provide bibliographic information when appropriate.

3. **Diversity**—Choose sites that are representative of many different religious, ethnic, and cultural groups.

4. **Content**—Provide sites that are sound research sources with substantive content and that are written or compiled by scholars, professionals, government officials, librarians, or other experts. They should enrich and support the curriculum.

5. **Ease of Use**—Include sites that are easy to navigate, are presented in logical and reasonably sized units, do not require user registration, provide online help, and furnish Boolean logic and search engines when appropriate.

6. **Accessibility**—Select titles that are usually "active" or have accessible mirror sites and a fast response time.

7. **Objectivity**—Choose sites that do not reflect an evident bias and represent viewpoints that are important to understanding the subject matter.

8. **Currency/Timeliness**—Provide sites that are up-to-date and contain a publication date or last revised date. When appropriate, the site should be updated frequently and contain few "dead links."

9. **Costs and Copyright**—Exclude sites that charge fees or violate copyright restrictions.

Cyber Library Web Privacy Policy

Years ago this policy would seem a rather absurd addition to the arsenal of policies that are traditionally recommended to aspiring SLMSs. The Internet, however, has the ability to invade our privacy in ways that most of our users are totally unaware. The situation is so alarming that recent articles concerning issues of Web privacy are starting to recommend that courses be offered entitled "privacy literacy" (Coyle 2001, 17). The American Library Association has a long tradition of providing not only confidentiality for library information users but also for being at the forefront of notifying its members and the public when new issues about privacy arise. Their latest report, the "ALA Task Force Report on Privacy and Confidentiality in the Electronic Environment" (2000) is available at http://staffweb.library.vanderbilt.edu/ala_tf/Report.htm. A second outstanding source for information about Web privacy and other electronic legal issues is a site called Cyberspace Laws (http://www.cyberspacelaws.com). Both sites are excellent references to consult especially if a school district wishes to be more comprehensive in its approach to privacy issues.

The creation of a Web presence in the form of a cyber library compels SLMSs to write a privacy policy that contains guidelines and states the SLMC's position regarding library issues that may affect student confidentiality and their basic right to privacy. Since this area is just beginning to come to the notice of librarians, administrators, and parents, this section contains additional explanations in order to enlighten policymakers and assist SLMSs in shaping a future Web privacy policy. If the school already has a privacy policy, it may be possible to save time by incorporating the cyber library confidentiality and privacy issues into the current policy.

When writing it, be sure to give examples of the need for confidentiality that will be understandable to the age group. Tell them, for example, that when books are returned, their circulation record will be erased. Inform them of areas where identifiable information, such as e-mail addresses, is being gathered or logged.

1. **Student Confidentiality**—Students have a legitimate need for privacy. The SLMC should uphold the right of confidentiality and privacy of all its users. A student, for example, who is suffering from child abuse can find helpful, accurate materials online that can assist him/her to locate appropriate information and places that provide assistance and care.

2. **Privacy Protection Arrangements**—Many libraries arrange privacy screens or place terminals in discreet areas of the library to protect the confidentiality of users. While the potential for abuse of the Internet is a possibility with the age group, it is up to a SLMSs to consider

placing perhaps one terminal in a more private area to protect users' privacy and confidentiality.

3. **Library Records**—All but four states have laws specifically protecting library records. Some laws protect circulation records and not the general use of library materials. Consult these laws and see if they apply to your cyber library's online catalog.

4. **Library Logging Services**—Vendors are providing SLMSs with new record-keeping options for the online catalog. They feature automated transaction logs that can provide records of user activities, monitor students' borrowing patterns, create a profile, and apply that information to automatically offer related materials. Those records can be linked back to identifiable individuals. There are negative and positive aspects to automated logs. First, they can violate a user's right to confidentiality and privacy because they reveal the titles of the books that a student has borrowed. The positive aspect concerns the ability to personalize user services. A student who is interested in reading additional books about horses, for example, might appreciate a list of related titles the next time he/she logs in. A student, however, who may be searching for titles about AIDS because he/she is symptomatic may not wish to have his/her searching patterns tracked in the online catalog. Pose the following questions when writing this area of the policy. What will be the policy for keeping automated logs of patron use? If logs are to be maintained, what should be the time period before they are erased? Who should have access to them—only the SLMS or library staff members?

5. **Customized Services**—Many SLMC terminals encourage or require personal log-ins, so that student information can be reviewed if there is an acceptable use violation. Library systems allow users to set preferences and save them, and electronic databases let them e-mail search results to themselves. All of these features make use of personally identifiable information. Students should know how this collected information is protected from misuse.

6. **Privacy Literacy Issues**—As an educational service, SLMSs may wish to take the lead by demonstrating a few steps that users can execute to protect their privacy while online. These areas pertain to cookie control, customization, and data-gathering services. Cookies are small text files that a Web site writes to the user's hard drive. Once it attaches itself to the user's computer, it assigns a number that identifies the user's computer to the Web site. This number is stored and is employed to track the time a user visits the site and which pages and

areas of the site were accessed. A student can use browser settings to either accept or reject cookies. Customization allows users to sign up with a site so that only information in a certain area is sent to them. If, for example, a student wished to be notified only about new cloning sites at a Web service containing science sites, he/she must sign up and create an identity that usually must correspond to his/her real e-mail address.

For some of them, it may not be worth the potential loss of privacy to initiate customized information services. Data-gathering services are another area where students are vulnerable to invasions of privacy. Online postcards, options to mail an article to a friend, and free-trial services are examples of Web sites that are gathering data not only on the user but on other users as well.

7. **Student Photographs and Publications**—A cyber library that is filled with photographs of students working on terminals, reading, and completing class assignments is a welcoming site and an excellent way to promote library programs and services. Posting a student's name, picture, or class work on the Internet, however, is considered a violation of his/her privacy. The current trend in this area is for schools to determine what is safe, reasonable, and age appropriate. A parental form should be designed that contains levels of disclosure standards with a parental option for either approving or disapproving the entire set.

8. **Security**—Students have the right to know that the library is making an effort to secure the system from hackers and other undesirable technical intrusions. While it is not necessary to reveal the security software that is being used, a statement acknowledging that the cyber library contains a security system and maintains one is reassuring.

Copyright Policy

Copyright regarding the Web is an area that is undergoing scrutiny from a variety of governmental organizations and monitoring associations. While Congress found it easy to enact copyright laws for diverse information formats including computer software and CD-ROM products, recent copyright guidelines, especially involving the Web, have been much more difficult to formulate because of the development of new technologies for the distribution of information. The relationship between creators of works and the individual is also in flux. The Web has created a climate where self-publication is easy. Publishers who traditionally played a role in ensuring the quality of a work and its publication and dissemination are rendered redundant. All of these issues blur the distinctions that were so delineated in previous copyright laws. Stielow, in *Creating a Virtual Library* (1999), advises librarians to adhere to the same principles that are used for privacy issues: disclosure and openness. He considers these tenets to be the best defense against copyright violations (39).

In preparing a copyright policy for a cyber library, some basic areas relating to conventional library copyright policies are the same but other aspects may have to be monitored at a site such as the International Standards Copyright Office for Changes in the Law (http://lcweb.loc.gov/copyright/). SLMSs should continue to read announcements in this area that are regularly published in professional journals. Provide information to students and faculty in the following areas and site some of the recommended sites in this chapter as references if they wish additional information. The policy guidelines are compiled from the University of Oregon's Netizen Web site on copyright (http://www.netizen.uoregon.edu/document/copyright.html) and Stielow's *Creating a Virtual Library* (1999, 39–52).

1. **Library's Intention to Comply with Copyright Laws**—State that the library recognizes that it is illegal to duplicate copyrighted materials without the permission of the holder of the copyright, except for specific exempt purposes.

2. **Fair Use**—The SLMC abides by the "fair-use" doctrine that provides a limited basis by which students and faculty can use a copyrighted work without getting permission from the work's creator. Usually, this means that someone is not using the work in a manner that is, or has, the potential of diverting income from the work's creator.

3. **Publisher's Rights**—Publishers on the Web own the copyright to any original text and images that they create.

4. **Site Construction**—Copyright should be considered when borrowing design and code from other Web sites. This process may involve a request for permission and possibly payment.

5. **Digital Archives**—Physical possession of an item does not convey intellectual or creative rights. Unless each creator has consented, do not scan or download to the cyber library an exhibit of the student art show or class of student papers.

6. **Link Rights**—Although American libraries and archives remain free to provide complete access to most Web sites under the Fair Use Clause of the Copyright Act, there have been threats to copyright in this area. Some Web publishers are suggesting that others should agree to a license before linking to their page. In the future, some

publishers may charge for the right to link to their home page. In this area, it is advisable to adhere as much as possible to the following netiquette suggestions.

7. **Copyright Netiquette**—Talk to students about the value of creating something and the importance of protecting that right so that there are continued advancements for society. Use public domain sources whenever feasible. The National Aeronautics and Space Administration and the American Memory Project at the Library of Congress support thousands of educational links, projects, and activities. Consider forming a consortium of other SLMSs to create new public Web libraries or groups of sites that can be used without having to deal with a commercial publisher. If either you or a student is unsure about the status of a work, request permission to use it.

8. **Liability**—The greatest risk for liability by a cyber library is posting material on the Web site that is in violation of copyright. Agreeing to remove any copyrighted material promptly will usually satisfy most companies.

9. **User Permission**—Create a form that contains the following: name of student, school address, description of the material to be used, intended use, agreement to cite the creator, and a reply deadline.

Recommended Internet Sites

Visit the following sites for additional ideas, content areas, and templates for policies concerning Web content, Internet use, Internet collection development, privacy, and copyright. All of them have been cited in Webographies in various professional journals.

Web Template Policy

Guidelines for School Web Pages
http://macserver.stjohns.k12.fl.us/guidelines.html

Web template policies are sometimes hard to find on the Web because they are considered part of a collection of in-house documents. This source, however, provides a one-page series of guidelines concerning the site's style and appearance. It also includes a sample parent permission form that covers the publication of students' photographs and names.

Internet Use Policies

Guidelines and Considerations for Developing a
Public Library Internet Use Policy
http://www.ala.org/alaorg/oif/internet.html

The American Library Association (ALA) has an excellent site that discusses the need for an Internet use policy in all libraries. Most helpful are links to three public libraries' Internet use policies that serve as models for the guidelines that the ALA recommends.

Internet and Public Libraries . . . Issues and Opportunities
http://www.iage.com/rusa.shtm

Although this site targets public libraries, it is filled with up-to-date information about Internet use policies. The "Questions to Consider" when formulating an Internet use policy cover all the bases. Look at this site first before you develop a policy.

IUP Role-Play Exercise for School (Public) Library Staff
http://www.iage.com/roleplay.shtm

Role-playing exercises can help SLMSs and their staffs troubleshoot potential policy violations in a setting that encourages further discussion and clarification. These scenarios are realistic and helpful to make sure that everyone understands the policy and agrees on the means to enforce it.

A Legal and Educational Analysis of K–12 Internet
Acceptable Use Policies
http://www.ces.uoregon.edu/responsibilities/analysis.htm

If you require legal advice concerning policy development, visit this site. The author, Nancy Willard, is an attorney who possesses the rare legal ability of plain-speak. The legal background and liability issues for policies concerning privacy, student safety, district responsibilities, and intellectual freedom are easy to understand.

Internet Collection Development Policy

Australian Libraries Gateway—Guidelines for the Preparation
of a Collection Development Policy
http://www.nla.gov.au/libraries/resource/acliscdp.html

Prepared by the former Australian Council of Libraries and Information Services, this collection development policy, while suited primarily to printed material, can be easily adapted for the collection of Internet sites.

Under each category, it provides excellent questions to ensure that the policymaker has thought of all possible contingencies.

National Cathedral School Internet Collection Development Policy
http://ncs.cathedral.org/uslibrary/Library/Lib_Policies /Internet_Collection_Policy.htm

National Cathedral School SLMSs developed this policy as the start of a cooperative approach for collecting Internet sites for insertion into the MARC 856 field, an online catalog record, during the construction of a Web library. In addition to the selection criteria described in this chapter, this site also has useful subject scope guidelines that can be used for designing a Web library.

Privacy Issues

"ALA Task Force Report on Privacy and Confidentiality in the Electronic Environment"
http://staffweb.library.vanderbilt.edu/ala_tf/Report.htm

This report includes findings about the influence of new technologies and their possible impact on patron privacy and confidentiality. It discusses laws and legislation concerning privacy and the responsibilities that all libraries have to protect users' rights in the newly sensitive area.

American Library Association
http://www.ala.org/aasl/positions/ps_libraryrecords.html

ALA has a formal position on the right to confidentiality by all users of library information. Its position on it has been withheld in various court cases, and it would be easy to incorporate into a school's cyber library privacy policy.

Privacy
http://netizen.uoregon.edu/documents/privacy.html

While there are no privacy policies at this site, it is filled with issues related to privacy and more importantly their legal ramifications. SLMSs will have no trouble choosing categories for inclusion in an adapted policy.

Privacy Resources Electronic Information Privacy Center
http://www.eipc.org

The Electronic Information Privacy Center is a public interest research center that focuses attention on emerging civil liberties issues that can affect privacy and the First Amendment. The site has won numerous awards for maintaining well-organized, accessible pages that feature various publications, conference proceedings, newsgroups, and a privacy archive of online documents and articles.

Copyright

Copyright
http://www.netizen.uoregon.edu/documents/copyright.html

For a list of copyright issues and a simple legal explanation of the recent copyright law, this site is the best. SLMSs and even high school students will have no problem understanding the doctrine of fair use and the rationale behind copyright protection policies and laws.

Copyright Website
http://www.benedict.com/

If you wish to stay current with copyright laws and bleeding-edge issues concerning streaming audio and video, visit this award-winning site. It provides relevant, practical copyright information for SLMSs who need to remain current regarding copyright and the latest technologies. Be sure to click on the "Info" icon for an excellent summary of basic copyright law.

Copyright Policy

Bellingham School District 501 Copyright Compliance Instruction
http://www.bham.wednet.edu/copyrght.htm

This school district provides thorough copyright policies that you can examine for ideas to incorporate into a cyber library copyright policy. The site is an excellent one to use as a reference for specific copyright questions ranging from how many notes of a song a student may download to copyright issues involving the potential misuse of computer software. It also maintains the link District Copyright Web Publishing Rules (http://www .bham.wednet.edu/copyrule.htm), which furnishes users with guidelines for using Web information, graphics, and images and republishing them in their own publications.

References

"ALA Task Force Report on Privacy and Confidentiality in the Electronic Environment." 2000. http://staffweb.library.vanderbilt.edu/ala_tf/Report.htm (July 2, 2001).

Block, Marylaine. 1998. "Creating an Internet Collection Development Policy: Principles of Selection." *Knowledge Quest* 27 (September/October): 46–47.

Coyle, Karen. 2001. "Protecting Privacy." *LJ Netconnect: Supplement to Library and School Library Journal* (Winter): 14–17.

Gorman, Michael. 2001. "Technostress and Library Values." *Library Journal* 126 (April 15): 48–50.

Gregory, Vicki L. 2000. *Selecting and Managing Electronic Resources*. New York: Neal-Schuman.

Janes, Joseph, et al. 1999. *The Internet Public Library Handbook*. New York: Neal-Schuman.

Minkel, Walter. 2001a. "A Picture Is Worth . . ." *LJ Netconnect: Supplement to Library and School Library Journal* (Winter): 38–39.

———. 2001b. "Policy Discussion: Add Web Sites to Your Materials Selection Policy." *School Library Journal* 47 (March): 41.

Stielow, Frederick, ed. 1999. *Creating a Virtual Library: A How-to-Do-It Manual for Librarians*. New York: Neal-Schuman.

Traw, Jeri L., comp. 2000. *Library Web Site Policies*. Chicago: American Library Association.

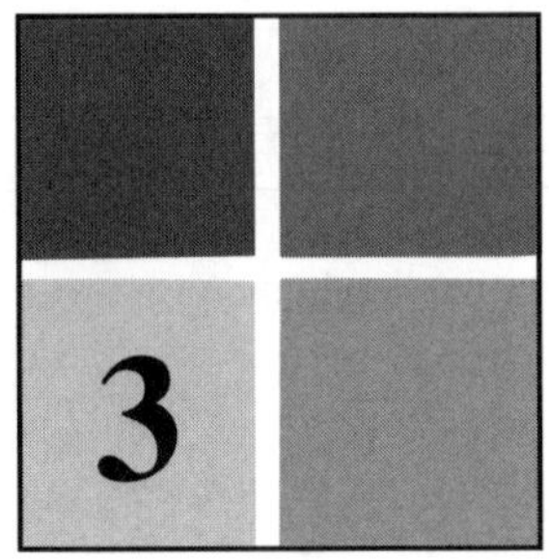# Constructing Web Libraries

Web Library Benefits

A Web library is probably the most significant component of a school cyber library because of what it offers students and faculty. It provides them with a second library consisting of free Web sites that are available on a 24/7 basis and enables SLMSs to support the mission and goals of their educational institutions in a way that was never possible prior to 1994. The multitude of materials for potential inclusion in a Web library is limitless because neither space nor cost is a consideration. Materials in formats that previously would require expensive new equipment to operate can be accessed right over the Web. Primary sources needing climate-controlled conditions and special storage can be acquired at the easy click of an HTML link-editing system. Resources are no longer limited to one user but can be accessed simultaneously by many students at any time of day or night. Unlike a textbook whose format is fixed in a sequential order, many Web resources can be uniquely adapted to fit the needs of the user (Gregory 2000, 14–15).

The framework for acquiring, organizing, and displaying the contents of a Web library is also readily obtainable. At present, there are a number of well-designed Web libraries such as KidsClick! (http://sunsite.berkeley.edu/KidsClick!) and Librarians' Index to the Internet (http://lii.org/) that offer not only superb ideas for organization, Web design, and access but also a host of content-rich Web sites in diverse information formats. SLMSs also work with a product in an organizational structure whose functions translate readily to a cyber library. The "library metaphor" of large subjects divided into narrower, related ones that help organize bodies of knowledge in the conventional SLMC are transferable to a cyber library (Stielow 1999, 53). SLMSs can even continue to use the Dewey classification system and Sears or the Library of Congress List of Subject Headings (LCSH) to achieve a workable Web library organizational design.

Web Library Disadvantages

While the benefits of a Web library clearly outweigh the disadvantages, there are some negative factors that SLMSs must consider when constructing one. With the millions of Web sites available for the capturing and cost no longer a factor, it is easy to construct a "Web warehouse" and subsequently have neither the time nor personnel to maintain it. Web libraries need some of the similar types of care that conventional SLMCs do. Time must be allocated for searching for Web sites, examining their contents, providing linkage, monitoring their availability, and deleting them when they are obsolete. While the contents of books remain static, Web site contents can change their focus overnight, necessitating a replacement if the new perspective no longer meets cyber library selection criteria.

There is also a reliability concern with a Web library that is not quite the problem in a conventional SLMC. In a SLMC, print materials can be collected ahead of time and placed on reserve for classes to use. In a Web library, there is no absolute guarantee that the site checked yesterday will be available and working tomorrow. For most sites that are in the public domain, this transience factor is not a significant problem. For sites hosted by companies and educational institutions, it can sometimes be a disadvantage.

Overcoming the Disadvantages

The Internet is one of the most tempting resources to SLMSs who love to do reference work, provide students with additional resources, and expand their collections. Time can pass so quickly when one is searching the Internet that it can truly become an information whirlpool to those who do not heed its temptations. Internet sites tend to be collected at the macrolevel and books at the microlevel (Gregory 2000, 24). Many times, parts of an Internet site contain information that is superfluous. SLMSs need to extract links, if they can, that are relevant. Arming SLMSs with the following policies and knowledge ensures success at taming this alluring cyber siren. Begin collecting sites or linking to sites only when you have:

- A cyber library mission statement and set of goals that explicitly reflect the overall purpose for collecting Web resources

- An Internet collection development policy containing selection criteria suited to the Internet

- A thorough awareness of the information needs and interests of primary and secondary user groups

- An intimate knowledge of the SLMC collection and the curriculum

Subject Scope Guidelines

Trying to adhere to a set of written policies is the first step in ensuring that a Web library is filled with useful materials. The second stage involves abiding by a set of subject guidelines that outline the range and types of materials to be collected. The following guidelines, while broad in scope, are helpful in focusing a SLMS's search for relevant materials. When searching for sites to include in a Web library, select sites from the following areas:

1. **Curriculum Related**—Search for sites that will expand the most frequently used areas of the curriculum. For example, if students are regularly writing reports about sharks, increase the collection by linking to sites about sharks.

2. **Collection Gaps**—Choose sites that fill gaps in the collection. Annual state and national government election sites provide more timely information that is usually not available in book format and is needed in American government courses every year.

3. **Full Text**—Collect reports, papers, periodical articles, statistics, and complete books when appropriate to the information needs and interests of the primary and secondary user groups.

4. **Indexes**—Provide links to indexes that outline a subject or discipline completely. Link to a timeline of the American civil rights movement if that is a topic of study within the history curriculum.

5. **Online Education**—Collect sites that contain multimedia texts, online tutorials, and techniques for enhancing teaching with technology. Provide a link to the Interactive Frog Dissection: An Online Tutorial (http://cury.eduschool.virginia.edu/go/frog) for the science department.

6. **Professional Associations**—Compile a set of links that contain lists of the most frequently referred to professional organizations that will serve students and faculty. Students writing reports about gun control will need information from the National Rifle Association. Faculty may need access to health maintenance organizations or state accreditation sites.

7. **Frequent Requests**—Search for sites that provide information about such topics as colleges, SAT deadlines, flags

of the world, maps of the Middle East, or photographs of giant pandas.

8. **Class Assignments**—Analyze class assignments and search for sites that will supplement the book collection. If a teacher always requires an oral report about the Mayans and Aztecs, provide a list of related Internet links as an additional resource.

9. **Library Reference Needs**—Compile a list of sites that are useful for completing daily library tasks such as acquisitions, cataloging, answering reference questions, and book reviewing.

10. **Reference**—Link to sites that provide a remote reference library for students and faculty. Include sites containing online encyclopedias, almanacs, and atlases.

11. **Special Materials**—Collect sites that offer materials that are difficult to physically access. Materials in this area include primary sources, rare books, and art gallery sites.

12. **Interactive Instructive Sites**—Find sites that add a multidimensional approach to learning in various disciplines. The Soundry (http://library.thinkquest.org/19537/), a site involving the physics of sound, contains sound-testing options with an audio player that greatly enhances learning about the physical phenomenon of sound waves.

13. **Critical Thinking Skills**—Search for sites that require students to interpret data, discover cause and effect, result in more than one solution, and employ multiple criteria from different perspectives.

Web Library Construction: Single Team versus Consortial Approach

Although it is feasible to construct a Web library using a single school team approach, the advantages of a consortial approach far outweigh the disadvantages. SLMSs who form either a district or a local area schools consortium can truly benefit from this approach by saving time, money, and sharing the workload. Web libraries are not going to vanish from the lexicon of new electronic programs and services that SLMSs are currently offering. Technology used in academic libraries and at Amazon.com, for example, is beginning to appear in school online catalog software making it possible to add Internet links into the MARC 856 field and catalog Internet sites into the collection as if they were books, videos, or CD-ROMs.

These same technologies will also make it easy to enhance Web libraries by enabling SLMSs, without much training, to customize them by adding metadata (i.e., visible author, title, and subject information about a site) and their own search engines when the collection becomes too large for scrolling. Technical enhancements that will be necessary to create second- and third-generation Web libraries can easily be accommodated by a consortial rather than a single school approach. At least one SLMS will usually have access to a technical support person who can provide advice and the expertise to advance a consortium to the next Web library developmental stage.

The Internet is indeed a cyber siren and it is difficult to resist the temptation to add a great interactive site, for example, on genetic simulation. Internet collections have the propensity for expanding at a faster rate than do print collections. New sites that are free for the linking and meet the selection criteria are almost irresistible to any professional SLMS. For SLMSs working within a consortium, the positive and negative aspects of future growth can be discussed. Written consortium plans for growth and development can provide the justification for hiring additional staff and payment for new technologies.

While the ability to share the collection development workload is an obvious advantage, tapping each SLMS's subject specialization areas for site selection is also a benefit. Although SLMSs are trained to be subject generalists, most have areas of interest that they feel more knowledgeable about than others. In a consortium, collectors can search for their area of subject expertise first and then jointly tackle some of the more obscure areas of collection development (Hughes 2001, 62–63).

Web Library Decisions: Adapt or Adopt

Both types of Web library building approaches, single school or consortium, necessitate decisions about whether to simply adopt an entire site by linking it to the cyber library's Web library page or adapt some parts of the site by selecting only specific links. Project Gutenberg (http://www.biblio.org/pub/docs /books/gutenberg/index.html), for example, is a huge Internet site containing hundreds of links to full-text books that are no longer covered under current copyright law. A SLMS may wish to place just one link to Project Gutenberg under the subject heading Literature. This means making a decision to adopt the entire site in its current form. Another SLMS may only wish to link to those full texts within Project Gutenberg that are either not in the SLMC collection or are being used as textbooks for various English courses. These links either fill a gap in the SLMC's print collection and/or provide online access for students who have either forgotten to take their textbook home or have misplaced it. In this scenario, a decision is made to adapt the site because only specific links fulfill the Web library selection criteria.

By noting the implications of this example, it is easy to see that there is no hard-and-fast rule concerning adoption versus adaptation. SLMSs who are building a single school Web library, however, may be able to proceed at a much faster pace if they choose to link to a site in its entirety and list it under a subject heading within the Web library.

Web Library Browsing Hierarchies

The decision to adopt or adapt a site can also be applied to selecting a browsing hierarchy for a Web library. Visit KidsClick! (http://sunsite.berkeley.edu /KidsClick!/) and the Librarians' Index to the Internet (http://lii.org/) and closely examine their browsing hierarchies. At the former site, SLMSs can link to a page entitled "What does this page look like through a Librarian's Eye?" Click on it and notice that the site architecture is transposed to reflect the broad hundreds of categories within the Dewey decimal system. The subject heading Science and Math, which is visible to the virtual visitor, contains sites that correspond to the conventional SLMC science and math collection that is shelved with the 500s section of the Dewey decimal system.

Look at the Librarian's Index to the Internet. Its broad subject hierarchies also correspond to the Dewey decimal system, but notice that it also features a list of subcategories directly beside the broad category. Under the category Arts, the first page of the site tells visitors that the broad subject term "arts" also contains links about the related subjects of "Architecture, Crafts, Performing, more. . . ." These additional subheadings are intended to provide users with the ability to make quick decisions the first time they view all the selections rather than clicking once more into Arts only to discover that the crafts sites are listed under the subject heading Recreation.

At this point in creating Web-browsing hierarchies, there is a tendency to adhere completely to one of the classification systems so ably designed by Melvil Dewey or the LCSH and apply it directly to Web library construction. Resist this temptation. Carter, in *The Internet Public Library Handbook* (1999), reminds librarians that browsing through an Internet subject hierarchy is a completely foreign experience for visitors than when they browse through books arranged on shelves within a conventional library. In a conventional library, users can look to the left or right or across the aisle for subject-related materials. Web library users, however, are confined to access points within the hierarchy at a given time. Their route is not serendipitous through the hierarchy as it is within stacks of books, and their tolerance for clicking into various levels of an Internet site is usually limited to three screens (46).

Subject Hierarchies Guidelines

Deciding on a browsing subject hierarchy is the first stage of building a Web library with a strong organizational architecture. Once this foundation is in place, it makes it much easier to add and delete links as the Web library becomes a dynamic resource. Online collection builders recommend that browsing hierarchies serve users best when they are no more than ten topics wide and three topics deep. Carter calls this building structure the "10-by-3 Rule." Web designers following this rule provide users with a maximum number of ten subtopics and only permit them to search within three screens' worth of information or sites within the subtopic. This rule defeats the strict application of the Dewey decimal classification (DDC) or LCSH to browsing hierarchies, because while they may adhere to a ten-subtopic list, they violate the advised rule of three for additional access. In the DDC system, a librarian can delineate hierarchies almost ad infinitum by assigning at least eleven subject delineating numbers past the decimal point.

Although the DDC is recommended as a browsing hierarchy for school cyber libraries because it enables students to mentally connect it with the organizational structure of their SLMCs, a strict adherence to it will lead SLMSs astray. DDC contains some areas that are counterintuitive to many users. Carter gives an example of calendars falling within the subheading of Horology under Astronomy as an example of placement that users would never logically comprehend. As a solution, their Internet Public Library (http://ipl.org/) designers added a Youth subject hierarchy that exists alongside the DDC headings (Carter 1999, 50–52).

If SLMSs do not wish to maintain coexisting browsing hierarchies for aesthetic and technical reasons, a better plan may be to adapt the DDC to particular subject hierarchies such as Mathematics or History. Remember, however, during this process to uphold the 10-by-3 Rule when further dividing and classifying sites.

Other than the previous rule and adapting parts of the DDC rather than adopting it whole cloth to the Web library, there are no firm rules for browsing hierarchies. The lack of rules is what makes them so challenging to design. Hierarchy development is considered more of an art than a science. The following guidelines can help with selection, but not supply the categories:

- Look at a variety of public and school library Web libraries to see which categories you can either adapt or adopt.

- Search the subject hierarchies at some of the more popular subject directories such as Yahoo and About.com for ideas and suggestions.

- Keep in mind the primary users and their interests and needs. Ask yourself what would make sense to them when they browse through the Web library.

- Design it and solicit the opinion and expertise of another SLMS.

- Select members of the user group to test the hierarchies even if they are only on paper. Watch for their reactions to see where they seem stymied or hesitant.

- Adopt either a flexible or strict system of hierarchies. The former allows SLMSs to immediately add a subcategory if a site does not fit within the existing ones while the latter would require a formal process and rationale for doing so.

- Scan for natural groupings—look at all the selected sites and determine if a natural grouping emerges that would fit a browsing hierarchy.

- Perfection is not a given in a subject hierarchy. Realize that dissatisfaction with part of it is a normal feeling. Since a Web library is online, it is easy to modifiy.

Web Library Content Descriptions

Subject hierarchies are the tools that users rely on to navigate a Web library, to click back and forth among areas of interest, and to focus on a finite collection of Internet sites. They do not tell the user, however, what information the site contains. For this part of the organizational structure, annotations are definitely in order. While there are some site titles that convey contents, most do not. The lack of an annotation affects user choice. Students looking for Internet sites about the physics of sound waves are much more likely to click on a site entitled Sound Waves than the ThinkQuest award-winning student-designed site called The Soundry, which covers the same topic.

Annotating sites can be accomplished by using the text-editing feature of any HTML software system such as Microsoft FrontPage or Claris Home Page. SLMSs can also annotate sites by using a text editor that is provided within the free Web-hosting sites mentioned in Chapter 1.

The writing of annotations, however, can be a timely process. Since they are essential and characteristic of any second-generation Web library, two approaches may be timesaving. Again, the choice is between adoption and adaptation. In many cases, the site has an excellent description in an About This Site section. By having one portion of the computer screen open to the desired Internet site and a second screen open to the Web library, SLMSs can cut and paste the annotation into their Web library and enclose the annotation in quotation marks. The second choice is to select descriptive keywords and phrases and convert them into two or three sentences and insert them by the site's title within the school's Web library. The procedure can move fairly quickly if two screens (Internet and Web library) are open simultaneously, thus facilitating the copying and pasting procedure. A last resort, of course, is to compose an original annotation.

Web Library Size

Although SLMSs cannot project how large a Web library will be with a high degree of accuracy, it is helpful to estimate it because collection size determines program and feature options and the project's initial deadline. Most Web library designers recommend that a Web library debut with 100 Internet sites. This number is also a cutoff point for deciding whether to select a database program to store item records in and to create additional access points. For a collection not exceeding 100 Internet sites, Web library designers advocate foregoing a database approach and creating a Web library by using programs similar to and including Microsoft FrontPage and Adobe GoLive. A Web library under 100 links can also probably be accommodated at a free Web-hosting site such as Red Rival or Netscape Netcenter.

Web Library Access Points

Web libraries with a projected growth of between 100 and 5,000 sites really benefit from a database approach because it permits not only the storage of data but also the ability to increase access to each Internet site. Programs including Microsoft Access and FileMaker Pro are user-friendly database programs that allow Web library designers to establish fields to collect metadata about each site. Metadata are information fields that relate to the title, author, date created, publisher, size, URL address, searchability, language(s), record number, and contents of the site. If information in all these fields is collected about a site, then it can be accessible to users when they search the Web library.

School cyber librarians need to make decisions about the metadata that are to be collected on each site because it will determine the size of the Web library and its subsequent monitoring and maintenance aspects. At present, there are no official rules for descriptive cataloging of Web sites that are similar to the *Anglo American Cataloging Rules, 2nd Edition*. The busy schedule and funding base for most SLMSs, however, precludes cataloging all the possible metadata levels. Instead, it is recommended that school cyber librarians make Web libraries searchable from either two or three access points. The first choice is to provide title and subject category access. The second choice is to include title, subject category, and keyword/subject access. The latter choice provides SLMSs with an attractive instructional option.

Search Engines

Most Web libraries that lack their own search engines permit searching by title within their existing subject hierarchies. They provide two access points. Students, if they are looking for a site about stars, scan the first page of the Web library, click on the Science hyperlink, and then click again on the subject Astronomy. They then begin scrolling through site titles and annotations for sites concerning the stars. The second option is to create a field for subject terms and keywords in one of the previously mentioned database creation programs and input an agreed-upon number of terms for each Web library Internet site. This additional access point means that users can search the Web library by entering a title, keyword, or subject term or click and/or scroll through the existing hierarchies. Providing subject/keyword capability, however, necessitates the use of a search engine.

Excite (http://www.excite.com), for example, produces a sophisticated and well-tested search engine with understandable installation instructions. If SLMSs are willing to display commercial advertisements on their Web library, the search software can be downloadable for free from Excite. There are other software programs such as Macromedia Cold Fusion and Perl Search Tools products that also provide search engine software.

Search Engine Benefits

A search engine gives SLMSs opportunities to customize their Web library to facilitate its use. This feature may be especially helpful to SLMSs who wish to limit students to a list of specified sites or types of sites.

In 1995, National Cathedral School (NCS) designed a Web library of approximately 2,000 keyworded sites using Cold Fusion search engine software. NCS librarians initially used Microsoft Access to build a database of sites that permitted the inputting of up to thirty-five keywords to describe a site. Since the field was open to any keyword, librarians were able to input a teacher's last name or a unique term as an identifier for a group of Internet sites regarding a class assignment. When the students were told to type the faculty member's name or a unique keyword in the search engine's search box, only the sites that were to be used by that class appeared on the students' computer screens. Faculty members found it easy to visually confirm that students were accessing only the permissible sites.

This keyword feature is also used in the NCS Web Library to retrieve sites that contain primary sources for the completion of the American history term paper. It can be employed to produce a list of sites that enhance critical thinking skills or feature online tutorials simply by adding a designated keyword in the subject area field of each site.

Search Engine Caveats

While a search engine can be an extremely useful application to a Web library, a decision to install one should be carefully considered. Although it is not that difficult to maintain, it does require sophisticated software, technical expertise, and a much higher level of understanding of Web protocols and HTML. A search engine implies the presence of either an in-house Web server or the leasing of one from a Web-hosting company (Stielow 1999, 150–153). SLMSs should definitely consult members of the educational technology department before deciding to proceed in this direction.

Web Library Wish List

Producing a Web library wish list is one of the most enjoyable parts of building an Internet collection. Think "out of the box" in this area. This is merely a wish list. It does not mean that every site on it will be included in the Web library. Let it be a list for present and future sites. There may be items that you can search for at a later date or that you will see reviewed in an issue of a professional journal. If you are working with a group of SLMSs, divide up the browsing categories and under each subject heading that you have selected, make a list of the types of materials and sites that would be useful to students and faculty and would fulfill the cyber library's mission and goals. Dare to dream a bit in this area. Remember that diverse information formats such as simulations, art galleries, virtual reality, audio programs, interviews, field trips, exhibits, and interactive tutorials are available for the linking. Refer to the demographic information that has been collected. How geographically distant are students and faculty to museums and art galleries? How many students have traveled abroad? What do they usually do for recreation? What types of social problems exist? How far are the nearest public and academic libraries? Plan to create a world of information and resources that will be theirs for the clicking.

The site ideas suggested in this section are to stimulate the imagination in some of the major areas of collection development. Collecting all of them would result in a substantial Web library. Under each subject area, consider linking to sites about:

1. **The Arts**—Keep the school's geographic location in mind plus all the types of arts and performing arts courses. Is there a drama club? Are school plays performed annually? Are there field trips undertaken to local museums and art galleries?

   ◆ Archaeology—Link to ancient sites and ongoing projects including the Perseus Project (http://www.perseus.tufts.edu/) and Jerusalem Mosaic (http://jeru.huji.ac.il/jerusalem.html), exhibits similar to the Dead Sea Scrolls (http://www.ibiblio.org/expo/deadsea.scrolls .exhibit/intro.html), and sites dealing with the science of archaeology.

- Architecture—Link to ask an architect, architectural styles, images, photographs, famous architects, architecture slide libraries, and virtual tour sites.

- Art—Link to multicultural exhibits and collections representing different cultural groups, for example, Hispanic, Asian, African American, and Native American art sites.

- Art Exhibits—Link to local and national virtual tours of current art exhibits.

- Art Galleries—Link to the National Gallery of Art (http://www.na.gov/), the Louvre (http://www.paris.org/Musees/Louvre/), and other famous gallery sites.

- Art History—Link to slides, images, pictures, museum links, art history glossaries, gateways to art history, period art, and timeline sites.

- Ask an Artist—Look for sites containing interviews with renowned artists as well as local ones.

- Crafts—Link to different types, how-to sites, craft shows, types of materials, and design idea sites.

- Dance—Link to performances, different dance formats, demonstrations, local studios, famous dancers, and dance directories sites.

- Drama—Link to costume pages, plays, performances, acting advice, local theater schedules, and historic theater sites including Shakespeare's Globe Theatre (http://www.rdg.ac.uk/globe/home .htm).

- Drawing—Link to tutorials, tips, guidelines, techniques, and supplies sites.

- Museums—Link to local and national museums—for example, the Smithsonian (http://www.si.edu/info/museums_research.htm), the Metropolitan Museum of Art (http://www.metmuseum.org/), and Chicago's Field Museum (http://www.fieldmuseum.org/).

- Music—Link to different types of music—for example, classical, rock 'n' roll, and folk, musical instruments, musicals, and music archives for songs and lyrics sites.

- Photography—Link to lessons, shows, tips, techniques, famous photographers, and contest sites.

2. **Colleges**—Where do the majority of students go to college (e.g., junior, state, or Ivy League)? How many of them require financial aid, need tutoring for the SATs, and receive help with the application essays?

   - Admission Support—Link to the College Board Online (http://www.collegeboard.com/), assistance with the admissions essay, free SAT prep, test-taking tips sites, and online tutoring contact sites.

   - Financial Aid—Link to financial aid sites that include online applications.

   - General Information—Link to campus tours, college and university home pages, college guides, and College and University Rankings (http://www.library.uiuc.edu/edx/rankings.htm), a site that includes ratings for college crime, majors, food, demographic mix, libraries, and more.

3. **Economics and Business**—What courses are offered in this curriculum area? Are there many students who are interested in business? Is there a stock or investment club at school? Are there companies in the area where a majority of the population is employed?

   - Business—Link to accounting, finance, and business resources, company information, stock-reporting services, and stock market interactive tutorial sites.

   - Economics—Link to famous economists, macroeconomics information, virtual economy interactive models, principles of economics, international trade information, resources for economists, and guides to economics.

4. **Education**—What are the backgrounds and research needs and interests of faculty members? How many are pursuing advanced degrees or courses for certification? For what subject areas would they be interested in obtaining online lesson plans?

- ◆ Lesson Plans—Subdivide this area further into sites that provide lesson plans for just the arts, foreign language, or science and include ones that incorporate use of technology.

- ◆ Professional Development—Link to subject-related organizations and associations, certification requirements, workshops, and educational conference sites.

5. **Foreign Languages and Cultures**—What foreign languages are offered at school? What are the ethnic backgrounds of the student body? Subdivide the category into, for example, Languages and Regions: France, Spain, Germany, Italy, Russia, and so forth, and consider a category called World Information for more generalized sites.

- ◆ Languages and Regions—Link to areas of historic or cultural interest, food sites including recipes characteristic of a region, common foreign phrases, holiday traditions, pictures of towns and regions, travel information, and translation assistance pages.

- ◆ World Information—Link to population, food, and health statistics, constitutions from around the world, an embassy directory, human rights reports, times around the world rulers, United Nations information, world flags, world conflicts, and country report sites.

6. **Geography**—How is geography taught at school? Is it offered as a separate course or is it integrated into history courses?

- ◆ Atlases and Maps—Link to atlases for specific curriculum needs, for example, the Great Lakes Atlas (http://www.epa.gov/grtlakes /atlas/intro.html), world atlases, map creation machines, historical, topical, outline maps, and map viewer sites.

- ◆ Geographic Data—Link to ask a census expert, state, local, and world populations, census data (current and historical), and national and local census data sites.

- ◆ Geographic Resources—Link to geographical encyclopedias, general geography resources, geography servers, national standards, discoveries, and famous geographers sites.

7. **Government and Politics**—How are American government and other related courses taught at school? Is there an active government or debate club?

- Government Information—Link to national, state, and local government sites and directories, state and national House of Representatives and Senate pages, the White House Virtual Tour (http://www.whitehouse.gov/), public papers of U.S. presidents, Thomas Legislative Information (http://thomas.loc.gov), and Federal Web Locator (http://www.inctr.edu/fwl/) sites.

- Legal Resources—Link to Amendments to the Constitution (http://cornell.edu/constitution/constitution.table.html#amendments), Core Documents of American Democracy (http://www.access.gpo.gov/su_docs/locators/coredocs/index.html), national election studies, American government outlines, Supreme Court Cases (http://supctlaw.cornell.edu/supct/), Famous American Trials (http://www.law.umkc.edu/faculty/projects/ftrials/ftrials.htm), free Web legal advice resources, county and city data books, and legal resources sites.

8. **Health, Medicine, and Family**—What types of courses are offered in this subject area? What kinds of information would be valuable for students concerning AIDS, sexually transmitted diseases, birth control, pregnancy, and drugs? Consider what types of materials would be valuable to parents or link to local public library pages that offer sites in this area.

   - Family—Link to child abuse, Alcoholics Anonymous and other drinking problem support sites, student-centered help with divorce sites, parenting advice, child development theory and practice sites, and Internet safety tips pages.

   - Health—Link to ask a nutritionist, nutritional information, eating disorder FAQs, planned parenthood, AIDS, suicide and drug information hot lines, health statistics, antismoking help, health search engine sites, street-smart safety tips, and sites about stress.

   - Medicine—Link to ask a doctor, cancer information, the Grateful Med Search Engine (http://igm.nlm.nih.gov/), Visible Human Project (http://www.nlm.nih.gov/research/visible/visible_human.html), history of medicine, pediatric resources, and disease database sites.

9. **History**—Consider all of the history courses that are taught including advanced placement courses. Make a list of all the history-related library instructional units that are taught during the year including ones for which pathfinders are distributed. Look for sites that transmit information orally, visually, and in written form.

    ◆ History—Link to full-text books, reports, documents, speeches, journals, letters, annals, eyewitness testimony, narratives, public records, newspapers, diaries, chronicles, manuscripts, laws, scrolls, sagas, oral histories, recordings, photographs, portraits, models, cartoons, posters, historical paintings, outlines, biographies, chronologies, interviews, and music characteristic of a historical period sites.

10. **Homework Help**—Review the types of reference questions that are homework related. Are students requesting help with algebra, French verbs, the process of photosynthesis, or building a Roman catapult?

    ◆ Homework Help—Link to ask an expert, general reference such as Kidsconnect Q & A Service (http://www.ala.org/ICONN/kids.com.html) sponsored by the American Association of School Librarians, the Internet Public Library (http://ipl.org/), B. J. Pinchbeck's Homework Help (http://www.bjpinchbeck.com), and the Math Forum (http://forum.swarthmore.edu/).

11. **Kids' Connections**—What is the age range of the student population? What is age appropriate for them on the Internet? For students in grades 6 or lower, it may be helpful to locate sites that are interactive and contain multimedia.

    ◆ Kids' Connections—Link to interactive coloring books, Dr. Seuss resources, Girl and Boy Scouts, global show and tell, comics and cartoons, hobbies, Web tales and stories, magazines, puzzles, flash cards, Disney resources, educational games, and puppetry sites.

12. **Library Links**—Remember that eleventh- and twelfth-grade students are expected to use local public and academic libraries for many research assignments. Creating links to these sites and others also furnishes a convenient professional resource for SLMSs.

    ◆ Library Links—Link to local public and academic libraries' online catalogs, the Library of Congress online catalog, and full-text digital libraries such as Project Gutenberg (http://www.ibiblio.org/pub/docs/books/gutenberg/index.html).

13. **Literature**—What courses are taught in this area including advanced placement? Compile a list of all relevant English-related pathfinders and units that are used during the year. Locate sites that expand the collection in this area.

- Literature—Link to megasites containing search engines, if possible, about periods of literature such as 19th Century British and American Authors (http://lang.nagoya-u.ac.jp/~matsuoka/19th-authors .html), literary criticism indexes such as Gale's Literary Criticism Index (http://www.galenet.com/servlet/LitIndex), author pages, author interviews, full-text books, literature guides, handbooks, literary awards, review sites, lecture notes, poetry, folklore, legends, epics, sagas, fairy tales, and literary periodical sites.

14. **Mathematics**—What courses are taught in mathematics? Is there a math club at school that would be interested in having a group of math-related links available to it?

    - Link to ask a math expert, online calculators, computer-animated graphics for complex analyses, math resources, problem and solutions archives and databases, mathematical FAQs, interactive geometry, mathematician biographies, math tables, interactive math lessons, math magic, math in daily life, math teasers and puzzles, and statistical sites.

15. **Media**—What types of media programs interest students? How much off-air taping is done in the SLMC? Do certain classes have a weekly current events assignment?

    - Movies, Television, and Radio—Link to television station home pages (commercial and educational) such as History Channel (http://www.historychannel.com/index.html), PBS Online (http://www .pbs.org/), C-Span (http://www.c-span.org/), A & E Television (http://www.aande.com/), Internet Movie Database (http://us.imdb .com/), National Public Radio (http://www.npr.org/), film history, virtual radio sites, and video company ordering sites.

    - Newspapers—Link to local and national newspapers and opinion and editorial pages from national newspapers and newspaper database sites such as Flying Inkpot's World Newspaper Links (http://www.inkpot.com/news/), Yahoo's Newspaper List (http://dir .yahoo.com/news/), and News Online (http://www.newspapers.com/).

16. **Reading, Writing, and Speaking**—Do most students read at grade level or above? Is a course offered in public speaking? Are there standardized tests that students must pass in these subject areas to be promoted or graduate?

* Reading—Link to reading assistance, speed-reading, and reading tips and techniques sites.

* Speaking—Link to sites that provide public speaking hints, ideas, and techniques; famous public speeches with audio; and public speaking online tutorials.

* Writing—Link to writing guides such as Common Errors in English Grammar (http://www.wsu.edu/~brians/errors/index.html), online writing tutorials and quizzes, grammar parsers, types of writing (prose, expository, and so forth), sentence craft, vocabulary test maker, and writing style sites.

17. **Reference**—This section is not only to assist students and teachers but also for SLMSs to use for quick referral when answering reference questions and providing information assistance.

* Bookstores—Link to commercial bookstores and textbook companies such as Adams Books Company (http://www2.adamsbook.com/adams/homepage.tmpl$Showpage), Alibris-Out-of-Print Books (http://www.alibris.com/), Amazon.com, Barnes and Noble (http://barnesandnoble.com/), Bookfinder.com (http://www.bookfinder.com/), efollett.com (http://www.efollett.com/), VarsityBooks (http://www.varsitybooks.com/), BigWords.com, and book jobber sites such as Ingram Book Company (http://www.ingrambook.com/) and Baker & Taylor (http://www.btol.com/index.cfm).

* Consumer Help—Link to consumer assistance sites such as Consumer Gateway for 40 Federal Agencies (http://www.consumer.gov/), Consumer Information Online (http://www.pueblo.gsa.gov/), and Consumer World (http://www.consumerworld.org/), computer and other electronic technologies buying advice and guidelines, and software evaluation sites.

* Copyright—Link to copyright FAQs and policy sites such as Copyright Act of 1976 (amended 1994) (http://www.4.law.cornell.edu/uscode/17/), Copyright and Fair Use (http://fairuse.stanford.edu/), and copyright Web publishing rules.

* Internet Resources—Link to megasite libraries such as Berkeley's Public Librarian's Index to the Internet (http://lii.org), Internet Public Library (http://ipl.org/), Internet Sites for Research (http://www.multnomah.lib.or.us/lib/homework/), Subject Guides (http://web.uflib.ufl.edu/subguide.html), WWW Virtual Library (http://www.vlib.org/Overview.html), educational portals such as

Blackboard.com and Bigchalk.com, and reference search engines such as the Web's Reference Search Engine (http://www.xrefer.com).

- Reference Tools—Link to megasite reference sites such as Fast Facts and Reference Sources (http://gwu.edu/~gprice/handbook .htm), all types of dictionaries including multilingual, quotations, biographical, and rhyming, thesauri, synonym finders, and almanacs such as Information Please Online (http://www.infoplease .com/), metric and currency converters, abstracts including statistical and historical, encyclopedias, and direction finder sites.

- Term Paper Assistance—Link to bibliographic citation interactive sites such as Noodletools.com (http://noodletools.com), research paper assistance sites, antiplagiarism pages such as Avoiding Plagiarism (http://www.careton.ca.wts/plagiarism.html), subject guides, and pathfinders.

18. **Religion and Mythology**—Refer to the school's course of study to see how these subjects are taught or incorporated into the curriculum.

    - Mythology—Link to all types of myths pages including creation, classic, and national, encyclopedias such as Encyclopedia Mythica (http://www.pantheon.org/mythica.html) and World Mythology Database (http://windows.vcar.edu/cgi-bin/tour_def/mythology /mythology.html), mythology dictionaries, and individual myths and legends sites.

    - Religion—Link to multifaiths and comparative pages such as Yahoo Religion Links (http://yahoo.com/society_and_culture/religion_and _spirituality/), Bible concordances and browsers, Bible names dictionaries, ethics resources, computer-assisted theology pages, philosophy and religion encyclopedias, and history of religions sites.

19. **Science**—Collect sites that stimulate critical thinking by analyzing cause and effect, by discussing patterns and structure among diverse concepts and ideas, by demonstrating the scientific process for determining causation (e.g., observation, formulation of hypotheses, testing of hypotheses in a pre- and postenvironment, and so forth), and by facilitating understanding of a difficult concept.

    - Astronomy—Link to ask an astronaut or space scientist pages, telescope sites such as Best of the Hubble Space Telescope (http://www.seds.rog/hst.html), cosmos theories such as Cosmology and the Big Bang (http://csep1.phy.ornl.gov/guidry/violence /cosmology.html), system sites including solar and planetary, phases of the moon, comets, observatory sites, encyclopedias and dictionaries, astronomical history sites such as Galileo Project (http://es.rice.edu/ES/humsoc/Galileo/), and interactive sites such as Bradford Robotic Telescope (http://baldrick.eia.brad.ac.uk/rti /index.html) and Solar System Simulator (http://space.jpl.nasa.gov/).

* Biology—Link to disease information, anatomical information such as Atlas of the Human Body (http://www.innerbody.com/htm /body.html), biodiversity, biology reference, system sites including reproduction, endocrine, skeletal, circulatory, excretory, digestive, and embryology, DNA, genetic simulation, evolution, botany, zoology, and individual animal site pages.

* Chemistry—Link to chemistry encyclopedias, chemical element charts such as Web Elements (http://www.shef.ac.uk/~chem/web -elements/) and Visual Interpretation of the Table of Elements (http://www.chemsoc.org/uiselements/pages/pertable_fla.htm), chemistry tutorials with practice problems, and chemistry education resources such as the Virtual Chemistry Textbook (http://library .thinkquest.org/3659/).

* Earth Science and Environment—Link to ask a geologist, earth history resources, earth sites such as Earth Viewer (http://www .fourmilab.ch/earthview/vplanet.html) and Earthshots: Satellite Images of Environmental Change (http://edcwww.cr.usgs.gov /earthshorts/slow/tableofcontents), flood, tornado, earthquake, hurricane, and typhoon sites, ocean links such as Ocean Sciences Education Teacher Resource (http://www.vims.edu/bridge), ocean reef, rain forest problems such as Rainforest Action Network Center (http://www.ran.org/), global warming, environmental picture sites, virtual tours such as Ozone Hole Tour (http://www.atm.ch.cam .ac.uk/tour/), and local environmental problems including garbage, urban sprawl, and pollution sites.

* General Science—Link to ask a science expert, science chronologies, dictionaries, and encyclopedias, biographies of famous scientists, science and standards, inventors, science tutorials such as Sensation and Perception Tutorials (http://psych.hanover.edu/Krantz .tutor.htm) and Circuit Builder Tutorial (http://www.jhu.edu/~virtlab /logic/log_cir.htm), full-text scientific articles such as High Wire Press (http://highwire.stanford.edu/), science fair project assistance such as Science Fair Project Resource Guide (http://www .ipl.org/youth/projectguide/), virtual exhibits such as Museum of Science's Virtual Exhibits (Boston) (http://www.mos.org/home.html),

controversial science such as Internet Public Library: Controversial Science (http://ipl.org/ref/RR/static/sci0800.00.html), and exploratory and causation sites such as WhyFiles (http://w.whyfiles.org) and Exploratorium (http://www.exploratorium.edu/).

- Geology—Link to rocks and minerals information sites, geological survey map and learning links, mineral and gem galleries such as the Mineral Gallery (http://mineralgalleries.com/) and Smithsonian Gem and Mineral Collection (http://www.150.si.edu/150trav /discover/evolve.htm), plate tectonics links such as Plate Tectonics Exhibit with Animations (http://www.ucmp.berkeley.edu/geology /tectonics.html), and geological reference sources.

- Physics—Link to physics signs, symbols, and formula links, famous physicists pages, particle, ocular, and other types of physics sites, and exemplary sites such as Aerodynamics of Bicycles (http://www.princeton.edu/~asmits/Bicycle_web/bicycle_aero.html), Amusement Park Physics (http://www.learner.org/exhibits /parkphysics/), Gravity Tutorials (http://www.curtin.edu.au/curtin /dept/phys-sci/gravity/contents.htm), Visual Physics (http://library .thinkquest.org/10170/main.htm), and the Linear Accelerator Center on Particle Physics (http://www2.slac.stanford.edu/vvc/home .html).

- Weather—Link to climate data link such as the El Niño and La Niña sites, climate prediction such as Experimental Climate Prediction Center (http://meteora.ucsd.edu/%7Epierce/elnino/en97/en97 .html), weather tracking links such as Tracking Hurricanes (http://www.miamisci.org/hurricane/instructions.html) and Chasing El Niño (http://www.pbs.org/wgbh/nova/elnino), weather reference sources such as WWW Virtual Library: Meteorology (http://dao.gsfc.nasa.gov/DAO_people/towens/VLM), drought study sites such as National Drought Center and Drought Science (http://enso.unl.edu/ndmc/), and national and weather forecast sites such as the Weather Channel (http://www.weather.com/), and Yahoo World and U.S. Weather (http://weather.yahoo.com).

20. **Sports and Recreation**—Include sports and recreational sites that are either played at school or engaged in locally. If kayaking, canoeing, rowing, and sailing are popular recreational activities, think about linking to sites that give local river conditions or ocean safety information.

- Recreation—Link to camping, hiking, ice skating (e.g., ice thickness report sites), skiing (snow fall/amount reports), soccer (local tournament sites), and baseball (Little League schedules and directions to games).

♦ Sports—Link to school sports site information that involves tips and techniques, safety precautions, rules, and schedules (if available at the school's site) for football, basketball, gymnastics, field hockey, tennis, soccer, Lacrosse, track and field, wrestling, and baseball.

21. **Search Engines**—While search engines should be included in a Web library, the links to them should not be buried. Display them prominently, since many users may wish to bypass the school's Web library and freestyle-search the Internet. Choose icons or links to three or four search engines that are taught in library skills or computer science skills classes. Having them readily available makes it easier for teaching purposes. The ones mentioned in this section are not inclusive, but they have received high ratings from expert searchers. A review of the most frequently used ones can be found at Choose the Best Engine for Your Purpose (http://www.nueva.pvt.k12.ca.us/~debbie/library/research /adviceengine.html).

♦ AltaVista (http://www.altavista.com) is a powerful search engine that contains many excellent features including image and audio searching and translation. It supports Boolean logic, contains a huge number of Internet sites, and is considered one of the best search engines for the Internet.

♦ Ask Jeeves for Kids (http://www.ajkids.com/) is a popular filtered search engine because it supports natural query language. Students can type in a question (e.g., what is the capital of Bolivia?) and receive acceptable results.

♦ Google (http://www.google.com) claims to be one of the largest search engines on the Web. It supports Boolean searches and seems to deliver sites that are more relevant to the entered search terms than do other search engines. Its response time is also fast.

♦ Yahooligans (http://www.yahooligans.com/), designed specifically with young people in mind, is a filtered site that is useful for elementary and middle school. The search engine supports Boolean logic and the site results are annotated. Yahooligans has six broad subject hierarchies that facilitate access by younger students.

22. **Student Opportunities**—This area can involve sites ranging from summer camps, vocational classes, internships, and workshops to

career information and sites to check for after-school or summer employment.

 • Student Opportunities—Link to camping sites such as Choosing a Summer Camp (http://www.bosbbb.org/prac18.htm) and Guide to Summer Camps: Summer 2002 (http://www.washingtonparent.com /guides/guide-camps.htm), things to do in the local area, internships (nationally and locally), volunteer opportunities, community service project sites, career information sites, career projection information, and links to local job listings for temporary and after-school employment.

23. **Travel**—Students travel with their parents and by senior year are sometimes college tripping by themselves. Many of their travel arrangements entail purchasing electronic airline tickets and making hotel reservations over the Internet. Faculty and students also have time to travel during the school vacation periods.

 • Travel—Link to airline sites that include reservation links such as Airlines of the Web (http://flyaow.com/), train travel links such as Amtrak Home Page (http://www.amtrak.com/), Rail Europe: Eurail Passes and More (http://www.raileurope.com/us/index.htm), popular destination links such as Disney World, Disneyland, and Visit Your National Parks (http://www.nps.gov/parks.htm), car rental and hotel links such as Travelocity.com and world travel information sites such as Virtual Tourist (http://www.virtualtourist .com/?s=1&) and World Travel Guide Online (http://www.wtgonline .com/navigate/world.asp).

Web Library Collection Mining: Print Resources

Before you rush off to search the previously recommended Internet sites, there are several excellent print sources that are worth consulting. *School Library Journal* features a column entitled "Web Site of the Month." Its author, Walter Minkel, selects a school or public library for its outstanding contribution to design, content, service, or some technical feature. The librarian's e-mail or contact address is also given should SLMSs wish to correspond with the librarian or ask questions. *Classroom Connect* is an inexpensive periodical that is filled with Web reviews and lesson plans that are built around a group of subject-related Internet sites or a general theme. It is well worth the subscription price.

Recommended Internet Sites

Visit the following sites to find ideas, suggestions, individual links, and entire sites to incorporate into a Web library. Some of the sites are useful for selecting subject hierarchies. Others provide hundreds of outstanding, well-reviewed links. The last category provides sites containing reviews of recent, recommended Internet sites.

Outstanding Subject Hierarchy and Collection Mining Sites

Berkeley Public Library for Kids
http://www.ci.berekeley.ca.us/bpl/kids/index.html
> Contains another set of excellent links for school cyber librarians to evaluate for their own Web libraries. Take time to look at their homework links and booklist sites for ideas in both of these categories.

IPL Especially for Librarians: Organizing the Web
http://www.ipl.org/svcs/organizing.html
> The information specialists and students at the University of Michigan School of Information have built an excellent site to study for ideas and to borrow links, but this part of their site features a series of links that describe methods for organizing the Web. It also provides brief comments and a link to each example. If you are still searching for ideas for organizing the contents of a Web library, this is the site to visit.

Kathy Schrock's Guide for Educators
http://www.capecod.net/schrockguide/
> Compiled by Kathy Schrock, well known cybrarian and educator, this is one of the best sources to assist cyber librarians in finding sites that help teachers with lessons plans and ideas for incorporating technology into their curricula. All of the sites are annotated.

KidsClick!
http://sunsite.berkeley.edu/KidsClick!
> Designed by Ramapo Catskill Library System, this Web library is an excellent example of design, subject hierarchies, color, and content. It has it all including 600 plus school-related Internet sites that are annotated. Click on the pages that describe the search engine and other features for ideas, advice, and consultation assistance.

Librarians' Index to the Internet
http://lii.org/
> Considered one of the best sites for subject hierarchies and descriptions, it also features a search engine with Boolean capacity. It's not only useful for obtaining subject hierarchies ideas but it's also a good place to check for reviews of new sites. Sponsored by the Library of California, SLMSs can subscribe to its listserv and receive summaries of new reviews and relevant technical information.

Multnomah County Library Homework Center
http://www.multnomah.lib.or.us/lib/kids/homework
> A public library that continues to be at the forefront for providing outstanding library services and programs to young people, this site is filled with school-related links that cyber librarians can site in their own Web libraries. It also contains one of the best sets of pro and con links for frequently debated topics such as gun control, evolution, and euthanasia.

700+ Great Sites!
http://www.ala.org/parentspage/greatsites/amazing.html
> Mine this site for ones that should be included in a school Web library and check out its design and subject hierarchies. Compiled by the Children and Technology Committee of the Association for Library Service to Children, it also features sites for parents and caregivers that could be incorporated into a Health and Family category. The annotations are informative and lively and contain age-appropriate suggestions.

Internet Review Sites

Bigchalk.com
http://www.bigchalk.com
> Although this site is an education portal that charges for use of its subject directories and other services, it contains an excellent listserv that cyber librarians can subscribe to for free. Every week, via e-mail, subscribers receive approximately eight sites that are recommended as "Top Web Sites of the Week" and several sites that are recommended as theme-oriented sites. The reviews are lengthy and cyber librarians can evaluate it themselves.

Scout Report
http://www.scout.cs.wisc.edu/scout/report/subscribe.html
> This weekly publication published by information specialists at the University of Wisconsin is highly selective in its listing of top new Web sites.

While the reviews run to one page single-spaced, their recommendations are really on target. Use the annotations to pull out keywords if your Web library has a search engine. The *Scout Report* also contains reviews of recent education and government reports that can be useful for faculty members.

Yahoo's What's New Listing
http://www.yahoo.com/new/

More useful to cyber librarians who are in a consortium, this list provides all the new sites that have been added to each of Yahoo's subject categories. Cyber librarians can easily divide up the subject categories and be responsible for checking their own subject divisions.

References

Block, Marylaine. 1998. "Creating an Internet Collection Development Policy: Principles of Selection." *Knowledge Quest* 27 (September/October): 46–47.

Carter, David S. 1999. "Building Online Collections." In *The Internet Public Library Handbook*, ed. Joseph Janes et al. New York: Neal-Schuman.

Gregory, Vicki L. 2000. *Selecting and Managing Electronic Resources*. New York: Neal-Schuman.

Hughes, Jane E. 2001. "Access, Access, Access! The New OPAC Mantra." *American Libraries* 32 (May): 62–64.

Stielow, Frederick, ed. 1999. *Creating a Virtual Library: A How-to-Do-It Manual for Librarians*. New York: Neal-Schuman.

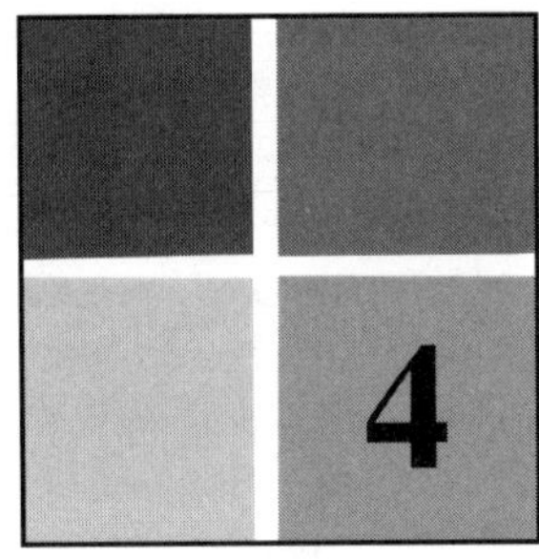

Using Portals

What Is a Portal?

Portals are neither new to the library profession nor the Internet. Libraries have been using online bibliographic service portals to provide a common command interface and to facilitate searching hundreds of commercial databases. Dialog and FirstSearch are examples of early portals. Yahoo's creation of subject directories and subject-related search engines is an example of an Internet portal that allows users to narrow searches to more well defined subject areas. After selecting the Yahoo subject directory Astronomy, for example, students can type the search term Milky Way and retrieve results that have excluded information about the candy bar by the same name.

With the explosive growth of Internet sites, generalized portals are becoming difficult to use since they still provide users with too many extraneous information matches. If a student performs a Boolean search in AltaVista and types the keywords "Jets and not New York," he/she will still retrieve hundreds of unwanted sites about the New York Jets because AltaVista allows companies to purchase the right for their name to override the AltaVista search command structure.

The solution to problems concerning the quantity and quality of Internet information results is to develop portals that are more vertical in structure and employ a one-stop shopping approach. Vertical portals, sometimes called vortals, are the latest Web trend in the growth and development of the Internet. Designers are trying to furnish users with a portal in their area of expertise that features the latest research, professional resources, e-mail, bulletin boards, and conference news. In some cases, they may also purchase products from subject-related online stores. A library portal, for example, may contain links to Amazon.com or Alibris-Out-of-Print Books to make book ordering more convenient (O'Leary 2000, 1).

The Purpose of Portals

The overall purpose of portals is to establish a specialized Internet community where users who share similar subject or professional interests can access all of the information they need at one Internet site. This concept of unifying all like-minded users by providing them with a virtual library of subject-related information is a huge challenge for commercial and nonprofit portal entities. Each one is striving to capture the portal market in its particular subject area. The proliferation of vertical portals or vortals rather than general portals like Yahoo is occurring rapidly. It is definitely the direction that the Internet is going to move as a solution to unsatisfactory Internet search results.

Types of Portals

With more than 100 million Web users in the United States, it is obvious that there is a need for portals in subject areas too numerous to mention. For SLMSs, however, there are two types of portals that should be considered: education and library. Education portals are designed to be the one site that everyone in the school community can click to obtain access to class assignments, grades, the latest school news, the school calendar, tests and quizzes, e-mail, and so forth. Parents can conference with teachers or administrators about their children's academic progress through a secure e-mail site. Students can log in and take a quiz they missed the day before. Syllabi and class assignments are online so that students and parents can check their homework assignments and confirm the date of a test or deadline for a term paper. The potential for a centralized homework retrieval site becomes a reality in an educational portal, thus reducing the need for telephone calls to individual teachers or the school secretary when students are absent (Meyer 2000, 20–21).

Besides providing a series of user-friendly templates for the creation of class assignments, Web sites, tests, syllabi, and the means to communicate with parents, many education portals also supply content in the form of Web libraries. The Web libraries range from a small series of curriculum-related links that are listed within a subject hierarchy to large and sophisticated ones featuring a search engine with Boolean capability.

The second type of portal that SLMSs need to consider is a library portal. This type of portal can connect SLMSs to Web libraries on all types of subjects including professional resources, librarianship-related articles, conference news and events, discussion lists, job announcements, and vendors of library-related products and services. While library portals are essential tools for the continuing education, current awareness, and vendor convenience of SLMSs, they differ significantly from education portals. The latter portals offer templates not only for faculty but also for SLMSs that enable them, without any prior knowledge of

HTML, to create their own Web sites, syllabi, course descriptions, class assignments, tests, and links to other resources.

Portal Advantages and Disadvantages

SLMSs are busier than ever managing conventional libraries with little or no library or technical support staff. In addition to teaching students print library skills, they have also assumed the responsibility for teaching them electronic searching skills with a new curriculum called information literacy. Educational portals can offer SLMSs who lack the time and technical assistance the means to establish a cyber library by simply linking to an education portal. Creating an additional link to a library portal can provide a connection to Web libraries of extraordinary quality and to publications and professionals that will enable future professional growth and development. Education portals have the following advantages for SLMSs.

1. They provide Web site templates that require no prior knowledge of Internet-authoring software. Some education portals state that the process of creating a Web site for either a school or cyber library will take only five minutes.

2. Many education portals are free in return for the placement of a small banner advertisement of the sponsoring portal on the cyber library's Web site.

3. Some educational portals allow schools to sell local banner advertisements and keep the profits, while others provide a fund-raising channel that gives a school a percentage of whatever school community members spend at the portal's retail sites.

4. Education portals offer Web libraries that can be adopted either in entirety or mined to acquire new links for the school's cyber library.

5. Many of the Web libraries contain search engines and metadata that allow users to search for sites by grade level.

6. Some education portals connect to electronic databases (e.g., Country Watch.com or Britannica.com) that a SLMC can employ at no cost.

7. Most educational portals offer filtered access to the Internet. Some allow users to search only their collections of links.

If a school does not have sufficient support personnel to create, maintain, and host a cyber library either on or off campus, the following list of disadvantages may be totally irrelevant. Educational portals definitely offer a chance to establish a residence on the Internet and provide students with 24/7 access to an expanded array of services and programs. If a SLMS has no other alternative to creating a cyber library, using an education portal to build one is probably the easiest method of doing so.

Education portals have several disadvantages, however, that must be weighed along with the advantages.

1. Web library contents can vary in quality and the total number of sites. Some educational portals offer a limited number of sites, and their quality can range from relevant to irrelevant to the school's curriculum.

2. Searching access can be limited to the education portal's site only. Users would need to log off the site and access a search engine to search the Internet.

3. Advertising is usually always the payment for the "free services" that are offered.

4. Sites built from template software have a characteristic uniform look. Many of the Web creation templates limit the ability to customize the cyber library to enable its design and navigation system to reflect the school's site pages.

5. There is always a potential for future charges as the company gains a market share of interested customers.

6. The education portal may go out of business, necessitating a transfer to another portal.

7. There is no ability to customize a portal's Web library to meet local curriculum needs, add temporary sites to the collection for teaching purposes, or add keyword sites to reflect special instructional needs.

Portal Pricing Arrangements

Portal pricing is still evolving. Pricing formats range from free and partially free to subscription. Free sites have corporate sponsors so that all of the users will see advertisements, banners, or logos as they search. Some sites, even if they are free, require users to become members before they allow SLMSs to evaluate the site. Membership usually involves providing the school name, address, and e-mail address of the SLMS. Access is almost instantaneous when the information is inputted. Other portals charge a subscription that is based on the selection of various tools and services, the number of students in the school, and the amount of megabytes that the site will take up on a server if the portal hosts it. Some sites, for example, do not charge for the use of templates to create a Web site, class descriptions, or syllabi, but they will charge for access and use of their Web library. Full subscription sites usually provide a user log-in and password system for a thirty-day free portal trial or access to a demo Web library. School library media specialists should take advantage of free-trial subscriptions to test and evaluate the efficacy of different portals.

Portal Selection Criteria

Vertical portals are flooding the Internet market right now. Many of them, in an attempt to be that one-stop shopping source, are acquiring or purchasing access to subscription electronic resources. For example, the education portal Bigchalk.com owns ProQuest Platinum, a company that produces electronic periodicals databases. Other portals are busy either merging or forming partnerships to gain and keep their market share (Meyer 2000, 21).

It is essential that SLMSs establish portal selection criteria to enable them to choose the most viable portal or to advise school administrators involved in the selection process about the library-related strengths and weaknesses of each. When evaluating educational and library portals, consider the following issues.

- What is the portal's primary user group? Is it administrators, faculty, students, or parents?

- What is the size and content quality of the portal's Web library?

- Does the Web library have a search engine? If so, does it search only the Web library or does it search the Internet as well?

- If Internet access is allowed through the portal, is it filtered?

- Are the Web library sites annotated and are they designated by grade levels?

- What is the pricing structure for future years? How is it calculated?

- Is the Web site creation template only suitable for teachers or can it be adapted for the programs and services offered by SLMSs?

- How flexible is the Web site creation template? If it allows links to other sites, will it support connection to the SLMC's online catalog, electronic resources, and Web library?

- What is the future for the portal? What are your plans for growth and development? Do you intend to increase the size of your Web library or are you going to emphasize lesson plans in more subject areas instead?

- If the portal is currently free, try to predict how long it will remain so by making inquiries among peers and portal contact people and by reading professional journal articles.

- What is the coverage of the portal? If it is a library portal, does it provide access to full-text publications, discussion lists, vendors, organizations, recent professional news and library standards, models, and studies?

Free Education Portals

The following portals are free because they are either sponsored by corporations or nonprofit organizations. Their future existence is dependent on many market factors. At the time this book went to press, all of them were still offering the services described in this section. There is no guarantee, however, that they will either discontinue or refrain from charging for their services in the future.

AOL@School.com
http://www.aol@school.com
Owned by America Online (AOL) and Time-Warner, this site will probably continue developing its services and resources. It offers free site creation templates, but does require the use of free AOL software. The audience consists of administrators, teachers, and students in grades K–12. It has its own site search engine called Gateway that supports simple searches and enables subject and keyword searches by grade level. It also permits filtered Internet searching through the search engine Ask Jeeves for Kids. "Research a Topic" is one of the best features for SLMSs because it contains a drop-down menu that guides students through the research process for any topic they choose. The site is also replete with lesson plans and offers online courses in a variety of technology tools such as FileMaker Pro and Microsoft PowerPoint.

Apple Learning Interchange
http://www.ali.apple.com
Apple Computer Inc. has a definite interest in education portals, since its primary hardware market targets schools. Its well-developed site is geared toward teachers and emphasizes learning resources in the way of lesson plans and units of practice and professional development involving Apple-sponsored classroom programs and activities. It has an excellent set of curriculum links that are tied to state and national standards. SLMSs should

use this site for collection mining of professional development and lesson plan sites for their own Web libraries.

Bigchalk.com
http://www.bigchalk.com

Designed specifically for librarians, administrators, teachers, parents, and K–12 students, this site is the only one to offer a Web creation site template that is designed for SLMCs. Among educational portal sites, this is also the only one to quickly become a comprehensive resource for lesson plans, library resources, and communication tools. While Bigchalk .com does not support Internet searching, it does offer access to thousands of curriculum-related and grade-level Web sites via a search engine and easy-to-navigate subject hierarchies. The company also offers subscription services to ProQuest Platinum, a periodicals database that contains citations and full-text documents from 2,000 magazines as well as the full text of the *New York Times* and *Wall Street Journal*; eLibrary.com Elementary, a database containing more than forty magazines, forty books, and 40,000 pictures suitable for elementary students; and Literature Online, a collection of American and English prose, poetry, and drama that numbers approximately 300,000 original works. Bigchalk.com also provides links to current assessment tools and standards. Be sure to evaluate this site not only for its current potential but also for its Web library contents and subject hierarchies.

EdNow.com
http://www.ednow.com

Sponsored by Sagebrush Corporation, producers of several online catalog systems, EdNow.com is geared toward SLMSs, administrators, and teachers. The first page consists of separate search engines for Ask Jeeves, lesson plans, books, and videos. The Web library is tucked on the left-hand side of the second page. It does have a search engine and is browsable by grade level, but the content is not robust. Use this site for its excellent librarian channel resource list. It contains a catalog of all the major library-related vendors that is useful in building a list of resources for SLMSs. EdNow.com does not offer Web site creation templates.

HighWired.com
http://www.highwired.com

This company's audience consists of teachers, parents, counselors, and students in grades 9–12. It provides interactive Web site creation software that is easy to use and allows schools to sell banner ads and retain the profit. The Web library is not content-rich even though it does permit unfiltered Internet searches. HighWired.com's strength lies in its Web site creation templates. It claims to have 14,500 schools using its Web site software. This company will need to enhance its offerings in collection depth, lesson plans, and professional resources to become a major portal player in the future.

Mindsurf Networks
http://www.mindsurfnetworks.com

The target groups for this library-oriented site are administrators, teachers, parents, and students in grades K–12. While it does not contain Web site creation templates, it does feature a good Web library that supports site and Internet searching. The Web Search Engines page comes complete with links to kid-friendly and metasearch engines plus a user-friendly lesson on search strategy. The Reference section of the Web library is replete with dictionaries, online encyclopedias, maps, atlases, thesauri, and translators. A Homework Helpers subject category is also filled with links to excellent homework assistance sites, and the College Planner site contains well-reviewed links concerning financial aid, test preparation, and college entrance exams. Mindsurf Networks is also filled with resource tools for teachers including quiz templates, lesson plan directories, communication with parents guides, and national standards sites.

SchoolCity
http://schoolcity.com

Teachers, parents, and students in grades K–12 are the audience for this education portal that provides site-building templates, lesson plans, and a Web library. Under a What Works heading, it also provides some excellent online courses. For techie teens, there is a Teen Talk section that contains information about Web site evaluation, the definition of cookies and how they work, and other recent technical developments. SchoolCity supports online shopping by providing access to numerous school-related vendors. Parents are urged to shop at the sites because the school will receive some of the proceeds.

Free and Subscription Education Portals

The following education portals charge for part of their site and offer other parts at no cost. Usually, Web creation site templates, scheduling, announcements, and chat features are free, while there is a subscription fee for use of the Web library and other electronic databases.

Classroom Connect
http://www.classroom.com

This site does not offer Web creation site templates, but it is one that may survive the competition in the education portal market. It is filled with lesson plans for teachers, virtual field trips, and information links about recent "hot topics" and contains an excellent professional collection of links related to standards, performance assessment, parents and community, and child development. Users can click on the Store button to learn more about their subscription services. Although Classroom Connect's audience is clearly teachers and students in grades K–12, its Web library is one of the best for content and high site quality. The search engine supports site searching by "connected lessons, Web units, pictures/sounds/movies, hot lists, spotlights and field trips." The Spotlight section features an interview with a subject-related expert. Classroom Connect is headed toward the goal of one-stop shopping for school and library resources. While it would be nice if it offered access to the Internet from its Web library, most users will be content to remain within the site. SLMSs may wish to search this site for links for their own Web library or investigate subscribing to it.

EdGate.com
http://www.edgate.com

Web site creation and quiz templates are readily available at this well-developed portal. It contains a Web library that is rich in content with well-annotated links. Its Web library, the "Copernicus Education Gateway," supports site and Web searches. The entrance, however, is a bit confusing. Users are confronted with a host of three-letter options before every subject hierarchy that requires clicking on either E for educators, S for students, or P for parents. While the contents in various subject hierarchies are excellent, the hierarchies themselves are confusing. Within the Research Center, users must search between broad-subject and specific-subject categories simultaneously. A user can click on History, for example, or click on Search Engines and Directories within the same hierarchy. The menu items are disparate and do not encourage intuitive browsing and selection. Nonetheless, these criticisms should not dissuade SLMSs from investigating and evaluating a site that may continue to be a major education portal in the future.

Electric Schoolhouse
http://www.eschoolhouse.com

Most of the services are free at this site, which contains Web creation, site, and quiz templates plus other educational tools such as bulletin boards, calendars, and chat rooms. The site building template also supports the addition of librarian- or teacher-selected links. Its audience consists of administrators, teachers, parents, and K–12 students. Electric Schoolhouse is concerned with safety and addresses parent concerns by providing a filtered Web library and Internet search engine. Users can choose to use search engines such as AltaVista, InfoSeek, or Yahoo, but the results are filtered to remove offensive results. Its Web library is robust and the sites are annotated and searchable by elementary, middle, and high school designations.

Lightspan, Inc.
http://www.lightspan.com

This company offers Web site creation templates, lesson plans, and an excellent Web library. The company's search engine covers its site plus the Internet. Lightspan's audience comprises teachers, administrators, and preK–12 students. The Web library is easy to find on the site, and the links are annotated and marked with appropriate grade levels. Users can also input search terms and opt to search from among encyclopedia articles, lesson plans, online activities, projects, themes, and Web site reviews. Most of the resources are free rather than subscription, including its Web library.

Library Portals

All of the library portals described in this section are free. Join, access, or subscribe to one that fulfills your portal selection criteria and meets your local professional needs and interests.

Internet Library for Librarians
http://www.itcompany.com/inforetriever

Sponsored by the Info Works Technology Company that designs quality control and productivity measurement software, this library portal is one of the oldest and best among the genre. Its collection of links is exhaustive in scope and subject depth. The subject hierarchies are well defined and easily searchable and promote searching within librarian specialization areas. All of the links are annotated and the collection contains a search engine. One of the site's best features is an excellent set of ready-reference links that should be browsed for possible addition to a school's Web library.

Internet Public Library Services for Librarians
http://www.ipl.org/svcs
Designed for librarians by information specialists and students at the University of Michigan's School of Library and Information Studies, this site contains probably the best reference portal on the Internet. Its scope and subject depth in reference sites are vast, and it even provides separate sections for adolescents and younger students. The annotations are also well written and accurately describe the contents of various sites. Access this portal for future online reference needs and browse it regularly for new reference sites. If a decision has been made to construct a school Web library, mine this collection for its outstanding reference sources for students.

LibraryHQ
http://libraryhq.com
When SLMSs need information concerning new library developments, they should visit this excellent site. It is sponsored by SIRSI, a library automation company. The site lacks a search engine, but it contains discussion lists, classified ads, a library speaker archive, and lists of book-related events. The articles reflect many of the current librarian concerns about issues involving filters, Z39.50 resources, and Web site evaluation. There are also links regarding library employment and choosing librarianship as a career. Its main component, however, is a database called Site Source. It is a subscription service that provides quick access to 40,000 plus high-quality cataloged Web sites in a variety of educational subject areas. Site Source is searchable by title, subject, author, and URL address.

LibraryLand
http://sunsite.berkeley.edu/LibraryLand
Considered one of the best library portals, even though its emphasis concerns public libraries, LibraryLand was built by the Berkeley Digital Library SunSITE that is sponsored by the Library of University of California at Berkeley and Sun Microsystems, Inc. If SLMSs are ever interested in designing a school library-related portal, this is the site to study. It contains twenty-four vertical portals that address areas involving library architecture, digital imaging, electronic reserves, and archives. LibraryLand is an excellent example for a consortial approach to portal construction because it has effectively employed the expertise of various librarians for each area. Its link collection is very thorough and well annotated and it contains a search engine. Professional areas that require specialization (e.g., Web

managers) also feature a special Resource Center with up-to-date information about all aspects of the topic.

LibrarySpot
http://www.libraryspot.com

StartSpot Mediaworks, a portal publisher, developed this easy-to-navigate site. One of its best features is the ability to search by type of library. This feature can definitely facilitate SLMSs' current awareness activities. Besides searching for articles, finding lesson plans, accessing grant links, and browsing digital collections, this site contains an outstanding Reference Desk Web library. Mine its collection for sites containing core reference items such as almanacs, acronyms, calculators, grammar style, statistics, thesauri, and zip code directories. LibrarySpot covers all the main topics of librarianship, but its collection is not as thorough as other library portals. The entries are annotated, but no search engine is available.

LIS News
http://lisnews.com

SLMSs can subscribe to this site via e-mail for daily, weekly, or monthly updates concerning the profession. Currently operated by volunteer librarians and information specialists, *LIS News* has a site search and an excellent set of subject hierarchies ranging from book news, intellectual property, legal issues, and library humor to school library news. The site also contains discussion lists on a variety of topics, library poll results, story archives, and a link to Suggest a Story. The ability to search just for school library news makes this a portal worth visiting often.

Recommended Internet Sites

Be sure to consult some of the previously described library portals for additional information about the fast-growing trend of vortals. The following sites also shed more light on the subject.

Portals

"Frequently Asked Questions about Portals."
2000. *LIS News* (July 7)
http://lisnews.com/article.php3?sid=20000707104903
(January 25, 2002)

Found on the library portal *LIS News*, this article provides simple answers to questions that other librarians and administrators may have about portals.

It also provides an excellent definition and derivation for the term and its current utility.

"Rating Educational Portals."
2001. *Beacon Learn North Carolina* **(Spring)**
http://www.learnnc.org/newlncs/beacon.nsf
/doc/9CAC871555C46AD485256A4C0064909B
(August 27, 2001)

> Published in the *Beacon Learn North Carolina*, an online newsletter of the North Carolina's Teachers Network, this article evaluates three sites—AOL@School, Lightspan, and Copernicus Education Gateway—for their lesson plans, activities, and reference materials. The authors, however, only evaluated the free resources at each portal rather than the entire range of their services. Despite this somewhat limited review, SLMSs can still obtain some additional information about three major portals that may be of future interest to a school or cyber library.

Robinson, Brian.
1999. "Leading Computer Companies Combine to Offer Education
'Portal' Services." CNN.com (August 18)
http://www.cnn.com/TECH/computing/9908/18/education.portal.idg
/index.html (July 17, 2001)

> Discusses the current and future technological, commercial, and educational trends concerning the use of portals within schools. Several companies believe that portals would enable schools to address 80 to 90 percent of their computing needs by employing them. Technology coordinators at several school districts that are currently using them are also quoted.

Smith, Harry K. "Educational Portals."
http://plato.ess.tntech.edu/foed334-02/Resources/ed_portals.htm
(August 27, 2001)

> Sponsored by the Tennessee Technological University, College of Education, this useful Web site discusses the evolution of education portals and their potential for becoming an integral part of the school community as a communications, course development, and electronic library resource. The site provides criteria for portal selection and reviews nine educational portals for their different offerings.

References

"Frequently Asked Questions about Portals." 2000. *LIS News* (July 7). http://lisnews.com/article.php3?sid=20000707104903. (January 25, 2002).

Meyer, Randy. 2000. "It Takes a Cybervillage." *LJ Netconnect: Supplement to Library and School Library Journal* (Fall): 20–25.

Minkel, Walter. 2001. "Great Expectations: Will Yourhomework.com Make Librarians' Dreams Come True?" *School Library Journal* 47 (April): 39.

O'Leary, Mick. 2000. "Grading the Library Portals." http://www.onlineinc.com/onlinemag/OL2000/oleary11.html (July 18, 2001).

"Rating Educational Portals." 2001. *Beacon Learn North Carolina* (Spring). http://www.learnnc.org/newlncs/beacon.nsf/doc/9CAC871555C46AD485256A4C0064909B (August 27, 2001).

Robinson, Brian. 1999. "Leading Computer Companies Combine to Offer Education 'Portal' Services." CNN.com (August 18). http://www.cnn.com/TECH/computing/9908/18/education.portal.idg/index.html (July 17, 2001).

Smith, Harry K. "Educational Portals." http://plato.ess.tntech.edu/foed334-02/Resources/ed_portals.htm (August 27, 2001).

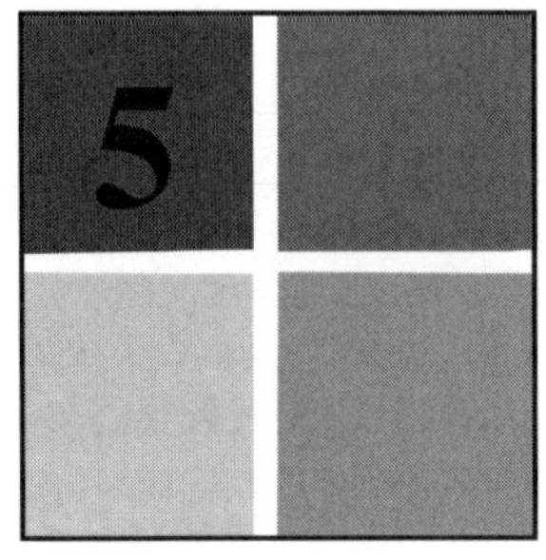

Acquiring Fee-Based Cyber Libraries

First-Generation Cyber Libraries

Cyber libraries are not new to the Internet. Most SLMSs are familiar with Project Gutenberg (http://www.ibiblio.org/pub/docs/books/gutenberg/index.html) and the On-Line Books Page (http://www.cs.cmu.edu/People/spok/aboutolbp.html). The former digital or cyber library consists of thousands of full-text books such as *Red Badge of Courage, The Scarlet Letter*, and *War of the Worlds* that have been converted from print to digital format and can be accessed for free. The scope of the Project Gutenberg collection tends to classics and books that were published prior to 1920. Books written before that time are no longer covered by existing copyright laws and are in the public domain. The collection's range of classics makes Project Gutenberg an excellent resource for a school's Web library because so many of the titles are used as textbooks in English and literature classes. The site also serves as a convenient backup for students who have either lost or forgotten to take their text home to complete a reading or an assignment.

The On-Line Books Page is another digital or cyber library that provides access to thousands of books that users can read while on the Internet. John Mark Ockerbloom, the owner of this site, has also added a serial archive. The free archive contains full-text articles of major serials subscribed to by most libraries. A site that gives free access to full-text articles from major periodicals makes another useful addition to a school's Web library (Benson and Fodemski 1999, 220–221).

Both of these cyber libraries are considered first-generation cyber libraries because of the following characteristics. First, they do not offer a search engine that supports multiple access points. Project Gutenberg allows users to search a title and author index to confirm if the book they wish to access is in the database, but it does not support Boolean or contents searching. Users cannot formulate a search strategy that would allow them to retrieve a specific passage from *The*

Scarlet Letter. They cannot search by a character's name or input a literary term, such as "irony," and receive a list of literary titles that contains examples of the term. Neither does Project Gutenberg nor the On-Line Books Page support searching by a book's index or table of contents.

A second characteristic of first-generation cyber libraries is the collection scope. To comply with current copyright laws, first-generation cyber libraries consist mainly of materials that were published before 1920 and more current materials that publishers have released into the public domain under fair-use guidelines.

First-generation cyber libraries are also limited by the types of materials they collect. Project Gutenberg and the On-Line Books Page contain the full texts of books and periodical articles. They do not provide access to government documents, diaries, letters, audio and video, pictures, and other multimedia formats. They consist totally of print text that has been converted to a computerized format so that it can be read in its entirety on a terminal screen.

Second-Generation Cyber Libraries

While Project Gutenberg and the On-Line Books Page are excellent resources to provide within a school's Web library, they lack many of the features that students and faculty have come to expect and appreciate with second-generation cyber libraries. These libraries do support searching by multiple access points, are more specialized in scope, and contain many different information formats including multimedia and digital. The latter format means that second-generation cyber libraries contain materials that were never published in printed form and only exist in electronic format. E-mail and faxes are examples of this type of format.

The most important aspect of second-generation cyber libraries, however, is one that they continue to share with their first-generation cousins. Most of them are still free to users. School Web library builders are already familiar with some of the second-generation cyber libraries. The American Memory Project (http://rs6.loc.gov/amhome.html), sponsored by the Library of Congress, is an excellent example of a second-generation cyber library. Users may browse freely through collections and exhibits of American history and culture containing the full texts of books, pamphlets, brochures, broadsides, diaries, letters, eyewitness accounts, songs, pictures, posters, movie clips, and much more. The collections are searchable by keyword, title, and subject. The search engine is powerful and supports Boolean logic.

There are a number of other second-generation cyber libraries that have been funded under a government-sponsored project called the Digital Library Initiative Program. They are at the University of Michigan (http://www.si.umich .edu/UMDL/), the University of Illinois (http://dli.grainger.uiuc.edu/idli/idli/htm), the University of California at Berkeley (http://elib.cs.berkeley.edu/), Carnegie-Mellon University (http://www.informedia.cs.cmu.edu/), Stanford University (http://diglib.stanford.edu/), and the University of California at Santa Barbara (http://www.alexandria.ucsb.edu/). All of these institutions are committed to developing multimedia collections of important primary sources in areas complementary to the Library of Congress in subject areas with regional and historical interest (Arms 2000, 146–150). For future reference, their Web addresses are included in the Links Citation List at the back of this book.

Other second-generation cyber libraries that may be of interest to school cyber librarians include:

- New York Public Library's Digital Library that features selections from various collections (http://digital.nypl.org).

- Indiana University's Digital Library Program that contains the Variations Digital Music Project (http://www.dlib.indiana.edu/).

- University of Virginia's William Blake Archive that includes searchable prints and scholarly annotations of Blake's artwork (http://www.iath.virginia.edu/blake/).

- Tufts University's Perseus Project that supplies collections of Greek and Roman texts, artifacts, and art articles (http://www.perseus.tufts.edu/).

- San Francisco's Fine Arts Museum that provides a searchable image database of a very complete fine arts collection (http://www.thinker.org/).

Third-Generation Cyber Libraries

Many third-generation cyber libraries share all of the elements and features of second-generation libraries with three exceptions. Third-generation cyber libraries charge a fee to access and print the contents, provide personal work space to highlight and annotate text, and automatically generate footnotes and bibliographies. The last two additions make a cyber library interactive, and this is the main distinguishing characteristic of a third-generation cyber library.

Within the last two years, three vendors and one educational institution have designed cyber libraries that offer collections containing full-text books, articles, documents, and primary sources in a variety of subject areas. Each library's collection is searchable from numerous access points including table of contents, keyword, subject, author, and title. Their search engines support sophisticated software that permits users to search the entire contents of an item by Boolean logic and uncontrolled vocabulary. They support online note taking within the text and readily loan themselves to transferring textual contents into a word processing document by using the cutting and pasting function.

Questia.com, Ebrary.com, e-Global Library, and netLibrary.com are the current leaders in a rapidly changing genre of cyber libraries. All of them have targeted college undergraduates as their primary audience, but secondary students, particularly the college bound, are also part of their potential user group. They have been developed in response to a growing need for full-text information on a 24/7 basis and for students taking courses online and enrolled in distance education programs. Ebrary.com and JonesKnowledge.com provide institutional subscription access, and Questia.com bypasses libraries by offering access to students via hourly, weekly, or monthly subscriptions.

Ebrary.com
http://ebrary.com

Ebrary.com allows a student to read as freely as he/she desires. One reviewer has compared it to "a book superstore minus the lattes and comfy chairs" (McCaffrey 2001, 22). The collection consists of full-text nonfiction books and journal and periodical articles in various subject areas.

When users desire to print, however, Ebrary.com charges a fee. Students may establish accounts containing as little as five dollars with a credit card. Each time they wish to print, copy, paste, or download a page, approximately twenty-five cents is deducted from their debit account. The revenue is shared between Ebrary.com and the respective publisher.

So far the company has amassed an impressive list of academic and public-oriented publishing houses ranging from Cambridge University, Massachusetts Institute of Technology, and California University Presses on the academic side to Random House, Penguin Putnam, and Macmillan on the public side. Since all publishers wish to increase awareness of their books, Yahoo, Excite, and Google have been granted permission by the publishers to freely index and search Ebrary.com. It also provides links to online booksellers so that users who wish to purchase the book or document may do so. The last commercial feature that Ebrary.com offers to publishers includes detailed reports and market feedback on how each title is used and the revenue it generates.

Students freely search Ebrary.com by a software program called Info Tools. It searches any word in any book or document within Ebrary.com's repository and permits the user to find related information by Web search engines such as AltaVista, Excite, Google, InfoSeek, and Yahoo. The search ware also allows users to choose a word or phrase in any book and instantly access a definition, explanation, or translation. Place-names can be located on maps and biographies quickly accessed for any person mentioned within a book or document. Info Tools also automatically generates footnotes and bibliographies in a variety of approved school- and university-supported formats.

e-Global Library
http://JonesKnowledge.com

Jones International University created a cyber library to support all of its students who are enrolled in distance education degree programs. Now it has decided to offer the cyber library to consumers on a broader scale. Fees are designed for library and/or individual access. The company, which employs approximately forty librarians, fourteen hours a day, can build a custom-tailored cyber library collection that will support any topic, curriculum, or program. It consists of research findings, academic papers, statistics, government reports, and conference proceedings. It is difficult to evaluate the size and quality of e-Global Library's collection. Rather than grappling with the copyright problem, e-Global Library has acquired 150,000 full-text government documents and links to 3,000 Internet sites. All of these resources are indexed within various subject areas. They also provide users with access to various online bibliographic databases. The databases, however, contain only the citation rather than the full text of the item.

While this part of its cyber library lacks access to full-text books and articles, e-Global Library has enhanced other aspects of the research process. It contains a significant number of online tutorials that guide users through searching the Internet, other libraries, and online bibliographic databases. Pathfinders, called research guides, are available in every major topic and describe key information sources for each. e-Global Library claims to verify the links daily and update the guides quarterly.

Besides all of these collection and instructional resources, e-Global Library offers a reference desk staffed by a team of librarians that is open from early morning until ten at night. The librarians guide students through the research process, provide additional information, and answer specific research questions via e-mail. A last resource, document delivery, connects users to fee-based sites where they may obtain copies of the articles they need to complete their assignment or paper.

Jones International University already has designed an educational portal that supports online courseware, test taking, and threaded class discussion groups. e-Global Library is a component of that portal that is being marketed to educational institutions.

netLibrary.com
http://www.netLibrary.com

OCLC (Online Computer Library Center, Inc.) has partnered with netLibrary.com to provide access to a collection of electronic books (e-books) that exceeds 30,000 and claims to be growing at the rate of approximately 1,000 titles per month. Libraries and individuals with accounts can purchase a collection set or individual titles that enable them to customize their collections to meet local needs and interests. Currently, netLibrary.com offers academic library-oriented collection sets in American history, business communication, commerce, computer science, economics, education, and other subject areas. Its public library collection sets consist of business, careers, Cliffs Notes, the Complete Idiot's Guides, computer how-to, cooking, fiction, literature, reference, study guides, sports, travel, and much more. Since netLibrary.com is partnered with 130 publishers, its collection of e-books will soon be attractive to SLMSs who have online catalogs within their cyber libraries.

Using netLibrary.com is a simple process once an account is established. SLMSs log on to the SLMC's extranet that has been established by a netLibrary.com account representative. They choose a Title*Select* home page and can search either the netLibrary.com catalog or its Special Collections. The system supports keyword, author, title, and subject searching. An advanced search option supports publication date and ISBN searches. Drop-down menus continue to appear that allow users to select or deselect additional titles, view a list of purchases, save titles, and finally submit the order.

SLMSs choose the appropriate circulation period for each title that allows them to control the checkout period for materials that are heavily used. At the close of the checkout period, the e-book is automatically "checked back in" to the school's online catalog and is available for another user.

All of netLibrary.com's e-books contain full MARC records cataloged in MARC 21 so that they integrate seamlessly within an existing online catalog system. Each book contains an embedded dictionary that also includes graphics and audio pronunciation of words to facilitate reading and text comprehension. Finally, the software provides citation, bookmarking, and personal notes functions to enable readers to customize their reading or research experience.

Questia.com
(http://questia.com)

Questia.com is the only third-generation cyber library to bypass libraries altogether and market its product directly to students through media channels such as radio, television, e-mail, and dormitory fliers at term paper time. Questia.com's collection goal is to provide a full-text, nonfiction library containing books and periodical and journal articles in a variety of subject fields. Unlike Ebrary.com that allows users to freely browse the full text of its collection and pay only on printing, Questia.com allows prospective users to browse only the collection's titles. Users who wish to access full-text materials must pay a fee. Questia.com provides subscription options that enable users to purchase access for forty-eight hours, one month, or one year. The cost for one month's access is approximately thirty dollars. Currently, Questia.com's cyber library collection consists of books and journals that are relevant to liberal arts majors. In the future, it plans to offer materials for the physical sciences as well.

The search function of Questia.com can be used free of charge to search for titles that students could then access in their own local school, public, or academic libraries. Users can search by subject, title, author, or keyword. Questia.com also offers an advanced relational search for words or phrases.

The degree of interactivity that characterizes third-generation cyber libraries is a major component of Questia.com's cyber library. The company provides students with file storage so that they can compose and save papers online. The prompts for cutting and pasting passages, quotes, and data from the original material to a student's document are signposted and occur regularly. Questia.com definitely targets students who are trying to make deadlines for completion of term papers or major research assignments.

Questia.com's library also features online citation software that seamlessly inserts footnotes and creates bibliographies in a variety of approved formats. A standard set of online reference tools (e.g., dictionary, thesaurus, and encyclopedia) is also included.

Rationale for
Fee-Based Cyber Libraries

Despite the availability of numerous free full-text cyber libraries, there are several factors supporting potential growth and development of fee-based libraries. The first factor concerns a change in the information-seeking behavior of users. SLMSs are already observing students' preference for obtaining all of their information sources, if possible, from the Web. Print materials, unless students are directed to them first, are not the information format of choice. When the Internet is the first option for content searching, there is an expectation that it will contain all the materials the searcher desires including full-text materials from books and periodicals. Currently, the Internet is not fulfilling this user need. Because of copyright law and uncontrolled distribution, many publishers are hesitant to make full-text materials available on the Internet.

This change in information-seeking behavior by users creates a market for businesses to provide what so many users want: fast, full-text access to information in multiformats. The market for full-text information is huge. More than 300 million Internet users worldwide conduct over 370 billion searches annually.

The business world knows that they are searching for authoritative content in a variety of subject areas because of the results of the Forrester Research study of 8,600 Web user households, which found that the number one reason 75 percent of consumers return to a Web site was high content quality ("Why Content?" 2001, 1–2).

A second factor is economic. The publishing market in the United States generates 32 billion dollars annually. A little more than 15 billion dollars of the market is for learning materials. Business rightly assumes that publishers would like to maximize their earnings for the content they provide. If they can sell their product in printed format and in a copyright-protected digital format, their profits should increase substantially (Albanese 2001, 126–128).

A third factor contributing to the creation of fee-based cyber libraries is educational. Although most secondary schools have not changed their transmission mode of education, college and universities are doing so at a fast pace. In the United States, colleges and universities increased their use of Web-based instruction from 22 percent of institutions in 1995 to 60 percent in 1998. The potential for online learning is alluring to many administrators faced with significant enrollment increases, insufficient classroom space, and a shortage of teachers because Web-based teaching is faster and less expensive. Web-based instruction also overcomes the traditional barriers imposed by time and distance. It can be available to students on a 24/7 basis (Reynolds 2000, 1–2).

While the companies described in the previous section are taking a risk that users will be able to locate sufficient free content on the Web to meet most of their information needs, they also assume that there will be an increase in Web-based learning and distance education at secondary levels. School districts that offer online courses and have distance education programs will want to provide their online students with facilities similar to SLMCs. The biggest advantage that a SLMC has over a cyber library is the ability to provide full-text materials in the form of books, reports, and documents. A school district's need to equalize online education with traditional education and provide both groups with expanded access will create a market for fee-based cyber libraries in secondary, and perhaps even elementary, schools.

Fee-Based Cyber Libraries: Benefits

The benefits of fee-based libraries can be considerable for SLMSs. They can save time, effort, and money for the following reasons:

- Materials in a cyber library do not get lost, stolen, or damaged.

- There are no expenses for cataloging, processing, and weeding the materials.

- With the exception of netLibrary.com's circulation rule of one book charged out to one user at a time, materials can be accessed by multiple users simultaneously.

- Materials could be purchased by a consortium of SLMSs within a cost-effective, coordinated collection development program.

- Materials are automatically returned. No overdue notices need to be generated.

- Materials are available on a 24/7 basis rather than just when the SLMC is open.

- Books having high theft potential can be purchased electronically.

- Books in high demand may be targeted for shorter circulation periods.

- Fee-based cyber libraries supplement conventional full-text collections and they do not require more physical space.

- Materials can be searched from multiple access points (e.g., individual passages, characters, table of contents, keywords, and so forth).

- Electronic full-text materials can be enhanced with audio, video, and other multimedia formats that cannot occur within a printed format.

- Fee-based cyber libraries may compensate for the inability of educational institutions to provide full-text materials to students enrolled in online courses and distance education programs.

- Collections can be instantaneously updated by purchase of collection genre sets in various subject fields such as history, literature, or computer science.

Fee-Based Cyber Libraries: Issues and Concerns

Although there are numerous benefits to fee-based cyber libraries, there are significant issues and concerns that SLMSs need to ponder and resolve before subscribing to any of them. Fairness and vendor stability are the two main problems. The fairness issue begins at home. Students who do not have a computer with Internet access are limited to using fee-based cyber libraries at school. Automatically, they are deprived of the 24/7 access that their home computer–equipped peers possess. What will or should schools do to ensure that students have home Internet-accessible computers? If courses are taught online, will technical equipment be a prerequisite for enrollment? What will the school do about students who cannot afford this type of equipment and wish to take a course online? Will they provide the necessary equipment and Internet connections for them?

Questia.com allows students to search their database freely for titles. It is possible for students to note the relevant titles and then search their respective school and public libraries to see if they contain the books they need. Ebrary.com provides an even better opportunity by allowing users to freely search the full text of its library collection. Students who are willing to employ the old-fashioned method of taking notes can make great use of Ebrary.com's collection at no charge.

Both Questia.com and Ebrary.com bypass SLMSs with their fee structure and by doing so raise another fairness issue. Questia.com allows students to pay graduated fees for forty-eight-hour, monthly, or yearly access. Is it fair that only students with sufficient funds have access to Questia.com to complete research and term paper assignments? Is their educational advantage significant enough that SLMSs need to budget funds to pay for those who cannot afford this cyber library? Should a school cyber library provide a link to Questia.com within its Web library and not be concerned with the payment issues?

Ebrary.com follows a debit account plan. As soon as students need to print a page, they are charged. Isn't this payment method analogous to paying to photocopy materials in a conventional SLMC? Are there any provisions made for students who lack funds to photocopy materials?

While the fairness issue concerning home access to an Internet-connected computer is difficult for a school system to resolve, payment for cyber libraries that offer license or subscription fees for libraries also generates some difficult questions. Questia.com's market research found that undergraduate students are willing to pay for the instant response and convenience of the company's research tools for cutting and pasting and citing sources. What will secondary school students, many of whom are on allowance and do not have the discretionary income of college students, do? It will be interesting to see if Questia.com and Ebrary.com develop some type of subscription or license fee structure for secondary schools so that the issue of fairness—at least while students are attending school—can be resolved.

Vendor stability is another issue to consider before subscribing to a fee-based library such as e-Global Library and netLibrary.com. The former cyber library may involve more risk, since it is subscribed to as a package. All of the Web links, online databases, research guides, pathfinders, and online reference assistance are provided. If e-Global Library were to encounter financial problems, a school's total cyber library could vanish into cyberspace. Although Jones International University is a thriving educational institution with a high projected growth rate of online courses and distance education programs, this scenario can be a major negative factor. It will be of real concern as competing companies that target school libraries begin to market similar products. The idea of purchasing a school cyber library complete with a Web library, access to full-text materials, instructional guides, tutorials, and lesson plans may be very appealing to school administrators or a school library consortium. The financial stability of the vendor, however, needs to be thoroughly researched before any license agreements are signed. The potential loss of a cyber library that is totally fee based during the time when school is in session makes reliance on fee-based libraries a risky endeavor.

There are also some vendor stability issues involving netLibrary.com and future companies like it that SLMSs need to consider before purchasing e-books for their collections. What means does an e-book company have to protect the existence of a book that a SLMS purchased since it resides on the company's server? What if the company goes out of business? What will happen to the electronic book that was acquired? In netLibrary.com's case, the company is owned by the Online Computer Library Center, Inc. (OCLC), which has agreed to escrow customer collections of owned e-books. SLMSs who negotiate with similar e-book companies need to verify that the company has an electronic insurance plan in the event of bankruptcy or closure.

Fee-Based Cyber Library Selection Criteria

Although SLMSs have developed selection criteria for electronic resources, there are some unique aspects to fee-based cyber libraries that merit different considerations. These factors involve issues concerning access, authority, preservation, and search capabilities. The following criteria can serve as a guideline to aid the acquisitions process:

- Consider the audience for a fee-based cyber library. Are the primary users to be high school students? If so, is the material age appropriate? Must all of the students read on grade level or above to comprehend it?

- Cross-check the contents of a fee-based cyber library with titles held in the conventional SLMC. What is the percentage of overlap? How frequently do these materials circulate? Is there a need for duplication?

- Look carefully at digital libraries created at universities and compare the contents against a fee-based cyber library's collection. The former collections are free and may supplement the SLMC's collection just as easily and at no cost.

- Consider purchasing items that would normally produce a SLMC storage or maintenance problem. A series of full-text pamphlets, for example, are harder to store, catalog, and maintain in a conventional SLMC than they would be in a cyber library.

- Examine the authority for fee-based cyber library collections. Does the collection reflect outstanding authors and writers who are experts in their subject areas?

- Investigate how much of the cyber library contents are enhanced by additional features such as audio, video, charts, maps, and diagrams.

- Ask about the life expectancy of an electronic work. Several studies have found that digital materials experience "format rot" at a very fast pace. What insurance will the company give with respect to replacement of compromised digital items?

- Question vendors about their archive policy should the company close. How will the school's cyber library acquisitions be protected?

- Evaluate the search capabilities of the cyber library. If it contains a million items, how easy is it for students to find the image or textual passage they want without retrieving thousands of irrelevant search matches?

- Compare prices of the printed and electronic item. Does the content of the electronic source and its accessibility outweigh the lesser cost of a printed copy?

- Identify collection subject areas that are in high demand and/or vulnerable to constant theft. Decide whether an electronic format would be preferable to print format in these areas.

Future Fee-Based Cyber Library Developments

Initially, all of these fee-based cyber libraries targeted undergraduates as their primary audience, because this research-driven part of the population held the most potential for profit. As company product developers read articles documenting the poor quality and small size of most SLMC collections, they will begin to produce collection sets for the K–12 market. netLibrary.com, for example, is already marketing its product to school districts around the country. Although most of its K–12 collection consists of nonfiction books, it is a matter of time before fiction titles will be offered as well (Minkel 2001, 35).

Many school administrators will undoubtedly realize the cost benefits to a school system for acquiring a full-text cyber library collection. They may even find solutions to the fairness issues raised in the previous section. Challenged by traditional budget constraints, some may ask why there is a need for a conventional

SLMC. School districts with booming enrollments or dilapidated buildings may be tempted to either design cyber libraries or replace obsolete SLMCs with electronic ones.

SLMSs have to monitor the growth and development of fee-based cyber libraries and continue to educate administrators about the need for both types of facilities. Never before have SLMSs been so essential to their parent institutions. SLMC programs and services are educationally imperative if schools are to supply students with the information-seeking skills, training, and knowledge they must have to prosper in twenty-first-century America. SLMSs need conventional SLMCs as teaching laboratories for information access, dissemination, and instruction. Although cyber libraries are necessary to the educational mission of a school, there is an absolute need for conventional SLMCs that can provide students and faculty with the instruction to enable them to successfully use both types (Craver 1997, 2).

Recommended Internet Sites

The Internet sites in this section provide information concerning the current status and future developments of digital libraries and fee-based cyber libraries.

Digital Libraries
http://www.bookwire.com/LJDigital/diglibs.articles

One of the foremost experts on digital libraries is Roy Tennant, a professor at the University of California's School of Information at Berkeley. Professor Tennant writes articles on this subject that are published regularly in *Library Journal*. Most of the articles focus on current problems and concerns that large universities face in creating digital libraries, but he also attempts to extrapolate those findings and update readers on developments with respect to their commercial counterparts.

Gibbons, Susan. "Some Emerging eBook Business Models: netLibrary, Questia and ebrary"
http://www.lib.rochester.edu/main/ebooks/
newsletter1-2/vol2-business_models.htm
(January 25, 2002)

This article appeared in an online newsletter about e-books sponsored by New York State Library. It provides an excellent comparison of the target market, number and types of documents, extent of access, number of users, records provided for a library's online catalog, and the method of purchased access among netLibrary.com, Questia.com, and Ebrary.com. SLMSs who are considering providing links to a fee-based library or purchasing access should definitely read this article to obtain more information.

References

Albanese, Andrew Richard. 2001. "The E-Book Enterprise netLibrary's Digital Mission." *Library Journal* (February 15): 126–128.

American Memory Project. http://lcweb.gov (July 20, 2001).

Arms, William Y. 2000. *Digital Libraries*. Cambridge: MIT Press.

Benson, Allen C., and Linda M. Fodemski. 1999. *Connecting Kids and the Internet*. 2nd ed. New York: Neal-Schuman.

Craver, Kathleen W. 1997. *Teaching Electronic Literacy: A Concepts-Based Approach for School Library Media Specialists*. Westport, CT: Greenwood, 1997.

Ebrary.com. http://ebrary.com (July 20, 2001).

e-Global Library. http://JonesKnowledge.com (July 20, 2001).

Gibbons, Susan. 2000. "Some Emerging eBook Business Models: netLibrary, Questia and Ebrary." Rochester Regional Library Council (December). http:www/lib.rochester.edu/main/ebooks/newsletter1-2/vol2-business_models.htm (January 25, 2002).

McCaffrey, Meg. 2001. "One-Stop Reading." *School Library Journal* 47 (July): 22.

Minkel, Walter. 2001. "Dot-Coms Offer Libraries for a Fee." *School Library Journal* 47 (January): 35.

———. 2000. "E-Book Anxieties." *School Library Journal* 46 (February): 29.

netLibrary.com. http://www.netLibrary.com (July 20, 2001).

On-Line Books Page. http://www.cs.cmu.edu/People/spok/aboutolbp.html (July 19, 2001).

Project Gutenberg. http://www.ibiblio.org/pub/docs/books/gutenberg/index.html (July 21, 2001).

Questia.com. http://questia.com (July 20, 2001).

Reynolds, Janice. 2000. "Distributive Learning Evolves to Meet Needs of Lifelong Learners." *e-Education Advisor* 1 (Fall): 1–15.

"Why Content? The Unassailable Argument for Why You Need Website Content." 2001. ScreeningMedia Inc. http://www01.screamingmedia.com/en/content_services/why_content/data.php (August 27, 2001).

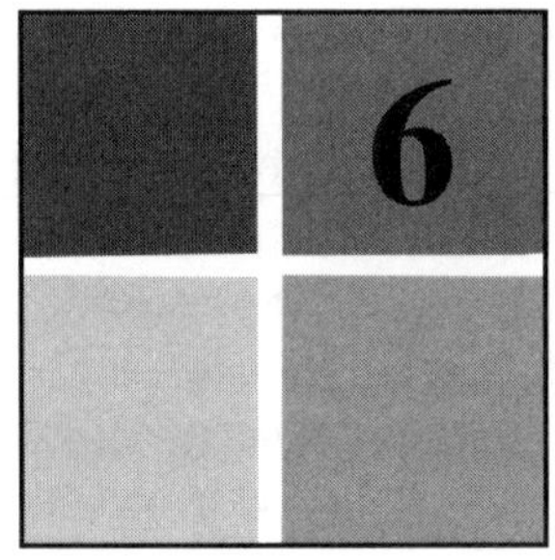

Establishing Remote Access to Subscription Resources

Expanding Access to Subscription Resources

While students and teachers will appreciate access to a Web library and fee-based libraries such as Ebrary.com and netLibrary.com, they will also expect to have access to subscription Web-based SLMC resources from home or other remote locations. Databases including Electric Library, Britannica.com, Ebsco's Host, ProQuest Platinum, SIRS, and Wilson Biographies Plus are examples of Web-accessible databases that many SLMCs subscribe to.

Providing remote access to subscription resources will be a direct response to a growing demand as more schools incorporate Web-based instruction units into the curriculum, offer online courses, and host distance education programs. A Web library, however, will not provide students and faculty with the full-text information they will need to complete regular research assignments and daily homework. Giving students access to the SLMC's current subscription databases on a 24/7 basis can provide them a great deal of information with a limited amount of expenditure (Stielow 1999, 141).

Licensing Arrangements

Establishing remote access is a contractual matter involving access licensing. This type of licensing is different from software licenses, sometimes called "shrink-wrap" licenses, that librarians agree to by clicking "OK" while installing and being prompted by the software. Access licenses are not standardized and predictable. Unlike software licenses that grant the user ownership of the product within various replication restrictions, access licenses entail ongoing obligations concerning the ability to pay for services as received, renewal of contracts, and possible increase in prices. Since each vendor's license agreement many be different in some of these areas, it is important that SLMSs read them carefully, especially the parts pertaining to remote access.

Reading a single-spaced, multipage agreement does not require legal expertise, but it does call for patience and knowledge of terms in context. The following vendor questions can be used to review the remote access section of a company's license (Gregory 2000, 51–53). If the agreement is still confusing in this area, contact a vendor representative and ask for further explanations.

- Read the agreement to understand the vendor's definition of the terms "site" and "user." Sometimes a site can be restricted to a particular terminal, building, or campus. A user may be restricted to presently employed faculty and enrolled students or it may be anyone who can access the school's cyber library through the Internet.

- Study the agreement to determine if off-site users can access the product. If the SLMC is a member of a library consortium, does the license cover all of the schools?

- Examine the agreement to find out what happens if there are unauthorized uses of the resource. Is the school to be held accountable? Usually, access agreements do not hold the school responsible as long as the SLMS has provided users with appropriate notice of the product's restrictions. If a violation occurs, the company should be required to give the SLMS sufficient time to solve the problem and take remedial action.

- Read the license agreement to determine what type and level of security the school must have in place before remote access is provided.

Technical Concerns

To link the SLMC's Web-based subscription resources to its cyber library requires some time and patience. All of the linking methods described in this section have some advantages and disadvantages. From time to time, they will require contacting the vendor and personal troubleshooting because of problems involving user log-ins and multiple access. For example, if the database uses the log-in and password access method, it may, for a variety of technical reasons, not accept it. Even though the license agreement supports more than a thousand users, it sometimes refuses to admit some users if there is high use. Frequently, the issues are easily resolved. As a management technique, however, it is helpful to maintain an alphabetized list of vendors with the following information: (1) their technical support telephone number; (2) school library media center vendor invoice number; (3) date the access license expires; (4) IP (Internet Protocol) address ranges, if being used; and (5) any special user log-ins and passwords. These are the information items that are usually requested before technical support staff can begin to render assistance.

User Authentication

The biggest challenge to establishing remote access to subscription databases is authentication. This word is a term that defines the process by which the identity of a user accessing a subscription database is verified and subsequently authorized to use the product. All subscription resources require some form of controlled access, because if everyone were allowed to type in the database Internet address and click on its contents, the vendor would soon be out of business. Controlling access is a two-step process. First, the system must have a way of authenticating or identifying the user. Second, it must have a method for knowing that the authenticated user is allowed access to, for example, Scribner's Writers. This process is called authorization.

Resolving authentication issues helps SLMSs decide among three standard options for the provision of remote access for students and faculty. The following authentication questions can assist you in choosing the best method for providing remote access:

- Who will have access to SLMC Web-based subscription resources?

- Is the set of users well defined? Do you wish, for example, to include parents or allow them to use their children's authentication process?

- Are there other schools either in the district or in the local area where users will need access to these resources?

- If you have cooperative agreements with other libraries, may their users access your resources without renegotiating the site license?

Authentication functions on a number of different levels. It can consist of a name, a library identification number, or some other school-assigned student number. In other situations, the computer maintains an internal list of authenticated users and the student is admitted by simply clicking on the database title. Once a user has been authenticated, the computer network can be programmed to make a select set of resources available. In this scenario, students who log in as such would receive access to all of the SLMC's subscription databases, but not the school's database where their grade reports reside.

School-Based Authentication Approach

Authenticating school-based users entails collecting detailed information for each authorized user group. The computer will most often store each user's name, address, a unique identifying number, the year of graduation, and specific information concerning the resources that each student is allowed to access. A school-based system must be scaled to cope with the number of users. If the user group consists of thousands of students, for example, it can become unwieldy and require a different approach.

There are a number of companies that allow for school-based authentication including Kerberos for Unix-oriented schools, Windows NT domains, and Novell Directory Services. They also provide a level of security that will satisfy vendors who are justifiably concerned about supporting remote access because of copyright and commercial concerns.

Consortial and Multischool Authentication Approach

SLMSs are fast discovering that the most economical way to subscribe to Web-accessible resources is through a consortium. It can save all of the members a considerable amount of money and provide all of the member schools with the opportunity to expand their offerings in different subject areas. A second plan may involve one SLMC providing Web-accessible resources to other SLMCs within the district. When more than one school wishes to share Web-accessible resources in a controlled access manner, the number of users can increase substantially. If four schools consisting of 2,000 students in each, for example, formed a consortium to purchase access to six subscription databases, the number of users and the scale and complexity of authenticating them in each database could easily overwhelm a local area network. For these reasons, consortial and multischool authentication systems establish a trust relationship among each SLMC. Instead of executing the authentication process for each individual, the system trusts each SLMC to have a school-based authentication system in place. The system is programmed to authorize each member SLMC as a single user, eliminating the need to authenticate each student, faculty member, or administrator in the consortium's user community (Breeding 2000, 223–224).

Authentication Choices

There are three approaches to solving the authentication problems associated with the establishment of remote access to subscription resources: IP address verification, proxy servers, and user account-based systems. Each approach possesses benefits and limitations. Choosing the best one for your cyber library will depend on a number of local factors. If, for example, a small SLMC wishes to provide remote access to a user group with a fairly stable population, then IP address verification may be the first authentication option. If you are a member of a consortium consisting of several large schools with a substantial population of students who graduate each year and faculty with regular turnover, you may wish to set up a proxy server to allow remote access to subscription resources. It should also be noted that it is not unusual to find different options being employed in the same system based on classes or location of users. Students at SLMC terminals, for example, might be authenticated by an IP address but when they try to access the same database from home are prompted to supply a user name and password to gain admission (Gregory 2000, 53–54).

IP Address Verification

A network is defined as several computers linked together. The Internet is simply many networks linked together with all of them using the same network protocol called Transmission Control Protocol/Internet Protocol (TCP/IP). In order to be part of the Internet, each computer must have its own Internet address that consists of a thirty-two bit binary number represented by four numbers in dotted decimal formation. An IP address, (e.g., 165.32.59.156) will be assigned to terminal number one in the SLMC and another IP address (e.g., 165.32.59.157) can be assigned to terminal number two. The use of these addresses serves as a practical mechanism for a general system of authentication. Once the SLMS supplies the vendor with a list of all the IP addresses, the vendor places them within an access control list so that only those SLMC terminals will provide access to their subscription database. IP address verification is the method most preferred by vendors and probably the one that is easiest to execute for SLMCs. With this choice, the vendor's database server is configured to accept requests from specific IP addresses or ranges of addresses that are supplied by the SLMS.

The benefits for SLMSs are twofold. First, SLMSs are not responsible for configuring a system that can involve a greater degree of technical expertise than they possess. Second, all of the security mechanisms rest with the vendor. Students can gain access by using either Internet Explorer or Netscape Navigator with no additional intervention.

IP Address Verification Limitations

While IP address verification is the dominant access method in libraries right now, it does have some disadvantages. IP addresses are of two types: static and dynamic. Static addresses mean that a specific IP address is always associated with, for example, library terminal number one. A dynamic IP address structure means that the unique identifying address number may change for each terminal because the system is configured to borrow one temporarily only when that terminal is being used. IP address verification does not work as smoothly when a dynamic address structure is employed. Many vendors, for example, only support static IP addresses.

This problem also affects the provision of remote access to Web-accessible subscription resources. Since most Internet service providers (ISPs) do not assign the same IP address to users each time they connect, it makes it impossible for SLMSs to provide vendors with a list of IP addresses for students and faculty who are using other ISPs from home or other locations to connect to the cyber library's subscription resources (Breeding 2000, 226–227).

Some SLMCs have found a solution to this problem, but it is not as elegant as some of the other authentication alternatives. All vendors that support remote access will supply SLMSs with a user log-in and password to their databases. SLMSs can provide a link to their cyber library home page that requires the student to log on and produce a general school-assigned password. A student, for example, at Northwood High School would click on a link entitled "Home Database Access—Use your student log-in and password." After providing the correct information, a page appears that contains the title of each database along with its Internet address, required user name, and password. Users can print the page and refer to it whenever they need to access SLMC subscription resources from remote locations.

Proxy Servers

To surmount the disadvantages of IP address verification, many libraries are choosing a proxy server-based approach. This option still requires the SLMC to maintain an internal list of user names and passwords. Proxy server software runs on an Internet server and is generally available at no additional cost. With this method, a computer not in the school's network can acquire an IP address from the school's network. The SLMS configures the proxy server to prompt the student for a user name and password. When this information is entered correctly, it is checked against a database of valid users and the student is able to access the desired subscription resource from home or any other off-campus location.

Proxy servers remediate remote access problems because the proxy server makes the IP address of an off-site computer the same as that of the school's network. No additional effort is required by the vendor when a SLMC uses a proxy server for remote access. The only possible problem concerns the contractual one of the vendor granting remote access to an agreed upon number of users within the license agreement.

Proxy Server Limitations

There are three proxy server types: manual, automatic, and reverse. A manual proxy server requires that students edit their browser settings. Once these browser settings are changed, the browser routes all student Web requests through the SLMC's Internet server. When students no longer wish to access a cyber library subscription resource, they must remember to reset the browser settings. Failure to do so can result in a substantial buildup of Internet traffic on the SLMC's server causing a potential bottleneck. An automatic proxy can eliminate the extra traffic through the proxy server by allowing the student's browser to control which requests are actually forwarded to the proxy server. A reverse proxy can also be used as an additional means of security since it resides outside a firewall. The subscription databases can be placed behind the firewall and the reverse proxy acts as a device to send and receive student or faculty requests to the Internet server.

Although the latter two proxies, automatic and reverse, offer a solution to the potential network traffic problem, proxy servers still require the creation of a user authentication database and managing passwords. Both are time-consuming and technically challenging tasks to a SLMS with no prior expertise with Internet servers.

User-Account Authentication

The last method employs a combined approach to providing remote access. In this case, students provide some specific information about their right to have access to the electronic resource such as the school's name or a subscription number from an institutional subscription. Students then create their own user identification and password for future use. The vendor may subsequently base access on the identification and password and may also support IP address detection. The advantage of this system is that the passwords cannot be known or guessed by another computer user. It is a means of providing strong security. Using the same method, accounts can also be institutional. For example, all users within a specified group or even the entire school population can be given the same user name and password.

User-Account Limitations

This method is somewhat limited by the number of users. As the number increases, so does the potential for compromising the passwords. If a password becomes compromised, it must be changed and all of the users informed of the new one. If individual user accounts are established, managing them and notifying all the users of the individual passwords can also be time consuming (Breeding 2000, 225–229; Gregory 2000, 53–54).

Security Issues

Security is not an absolute guarantee with any of the previously discussed authentication methods. Right now, there are no security systems that are failsafe against persistent hackers. Most vendors that rely on IP address verification are well aware of the ease with which such a system can be compromised. By recommending a specific system, they have, in effect, assumed a great deal of responsibility for security. As the search continues for a more comprehensive solution to authentication and security problems, vendors must accept some degree of unauthorized use of their resources. Monitoring for security breeches seems to consist of searching for violators of site licenses and other forms of obvious misuse.

If a vendor notifies a SLMC that its subscription resource is being seriously compromised, the vendor will usually work with the SLMC to establish a better authentication method rather than lose a potential client.

Recommended Internet Sites

The following sites are recommended to SLMSs before they contact a vendor to contract for its services. Most of them deal with licensing while others provide information about authentication methods.

Ariel, Glen, and David Millman. 1998.
"Access Management of Web-Based Services." *D-Lib Magazine* **(September)**
http://www.dlib.org/dlib/September98/millman/09millman.html
(January 25, 2002)

> This article is extremely thorough in scope and comes complete with helpful diagrams of the transactions that take place between a Web server and a user's computers. SLMSs who wish to understand the technical aspects of how a server authenticates users for authorized remote access will find it helpful. It does, however, require some technical expertise and background in Web server functions and applications.

**Definitions of Words and Phrases Commonly Found in
Licensing Agreements**
http://www.library.yale.edu/~llicense/definiti.shtml

Before you turn to reading a vendors single-spaced license agreement, familiarize yourself with the terms that you will encounter by visiting this excellent Yale University site of license agreement definitions. Written without any legalese, this six-page list contains all of the latest computer terms that vendors are using in their agreements. If you need to know the difference between "authorized use" and an "authorized user," this site will more than meet your expectations.

Goerwitz, David. 1998.
**"Pass-through Proxying as a Solution to the Off-Site Web Access
Problem."** *D-Lib Magazine* **(June)**
http://www.dlib.org/dlib/June98/stg/06goerwitz.html
(January 25, 2002)

David Goerwitz of Brown University's Scholarly Technology Group discusses all of the existing authentication methods that are used for remote access to subscription electronic databases and provides understandable explanations of the problems involved when proxy servers are used. School cyber librarians may need some technical expertise and background with Web servers to understand all of the implications, but they should be able to grasp the economical solutions that proxy servers can offer a school that is trying to provide remote access to subscription online databases.

International Coalition of Library Consortia
http://www.library.yale.edu/consortia/statement.html

Yale University has produced a ten-page statement of the current perspectives and practices for the selection and purchase of electronic information. It includes a dictionary of terms, budgeting guidelines, pricing strategies, and criteria for content and management of electronic resources. Written primarily for academic libraries, SLMSs will still find this a useful source because of its comprehensiveness and well-organized approach to electronic resource acquisitions.

Licensing Digital Information
http://www.library.yale.edu/~llicense/intro.shtml

Licensing agreements will no longer be complex, legal documents filled with computerese terminology once you read this annotated "Liblicense." Each section of a simulated vendor license is explained and the pros and cons of specific language are discussed at this user-friendly license site. Print a copy and use it to cross-check the vendor license that you may be about to sign.

Licensing Resources
http://www.library.yale.edu/~llicense/liclinks.html

Sponsored by Yale University, this site provides a list of well-annotated resources that contain information about licensing agreements. The American Library Association site is included as well as that of the Art Museum Consortium. Refer to this site if you are thinking of signing an agreement with a vendor that sells access to esoteric subject matter. You can also confirm more readily what is the accepted licensing norm for science or humanities electronic databases by referring to an official organization's site such as the Modern Language Association or American Medical Association.

References

Ariel, Glen, and David Millman. 1998. "Access Management of Web-Based Services." *D-Lib Magazine* (September). http://www.dlib.org/dlib/September98/millman/09millman.html (January 25, 2002).

Breeding, Marshall. 2000. "Security and Authentication Issues." In *Cybrarian's Manual 2,* ed. Pat Ensor. Chicago: American Library Association.

Goerwitz, David. 1998. "Pass-through Proxying as a Solution to the Off-Site Web Access Problem." *D-Lib Magazine* (June). http://www.dlib.org/dlib/June98/stg/06goerwitz.html (January 25, 2002).

Gregory, Vicki L. 2000. *Selecting and Managing Electronic Resources.* New York: Neal-Schuman.

Parker, Kimberley. 2000. "Collecting Electronic Resources: What You Don't Know You Can Learn." In *Cybrarian's Manual 2*, ed. Pat Ensor. Chicago: American Library Association.

Stielow, Frederick, ed. 1999. *Creating a Virtual Library: A How-to-Do-It Manual for Librarians.* New York: Neal-Schuman.

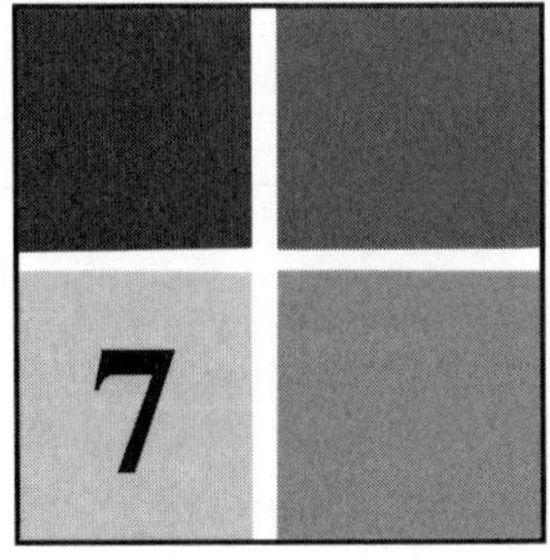# Creating Cyber Reading Rooms

What Is a Cyber Reading Room?

A cyber reading room is similar to the area of a conventional SLMC where students can go to visit with a friend, read a newspaper, relax with an issue of *Seventeen Magazine* or *Sports Illustrated*, practice reading for school play try-outs, meet with an author, participate in a library contest, pick up a bibliography, listen to a booktalk or story being read, and much more. It is also place where students and faculty can receive personalized service in the form of reading guidance and suggestions for research assignments. Whether it is the fiction room or the section where fiction books are shelved, this part of the SLMC usually features brightly colored posters, some art prints, a theme-oriented bulletin board/book display, and some comfortable chairs. Its purpose is to provide our users with a nonevaluative environment where they feel thoroughly at ease to ask questions, enjoy themselves, and perhaps take advantage of some special library services and programs.

The introduction of the Internet allows SLMSs to extend the atmosphere, color, services, and programs of the conventional SLMC into cyberspace. For semantic reasons, this area of a school cyber library is called a cyber reading room, but you may wish to call it the Cyber Café, Kid's Room, Cyberia, or sponsor a contest and have the students choose their favorite name for it. Think of it as a place where the programs, services, images, sounds, and sights change frequently. Unlike the Web section of a cyber library that contains links to educational sites, a cyber reading room should furnish links to places that may give a student the "aha!" experience. Make it a site that students will wish to visit more than once and will recommend to their friends.

The Purpose of a Cyber Reading Room

SLMSs and even some administrators may question the need for a school cyber reading room. Is it not the providence of a public library, they may ask? The answer is yes and no. Yes, the local public library should meet some needs of the students in this area, but it cannot personalize its services to the degree that SLMSs can. Unlike public librarians, SLMSs have a more intimate knowledge of the needs and interests of their user population. SLMSs know when a popular teacher is teaching a unit about dinosaurs or reading *Charlotte's Web* to fourth graders. They can respond more quickly to a heightened subject interest by placing links to dinosaur and/or spider-related sites and read-alike titles for E. B. White's children's classic in a cyber reading room. While public librarians can also provide these activities, they do not have the knowledge of the curriculum and syllabi that enable SLMSs to capitalize on "teachable moments" and the spontaneous enthusiasm that may be generated by an instructional unit or lesson plan.

Most SLMC mission statements contain sentences stating that one of our goals is to meet the educational and recreational reading needs of our students and faculty. Underlying this specific objective is the subliminal message that SLMSs are really attempting to expose students to literature rather than potboilers, to provide them with information in areas that they may be too embarrassed to ask for, and to teach them to be critical users and evaluators of information. Our last unstated, but most important goal is to provide students with such a warm, educationally supportive environment that they will continue to fund, assist, and promote school and public library programs and services in the future. Creating a cyber reading room gives SLMSs an expanded opportunity to fulfill our mission in two important areas.

Cyber Reading Room Opportunity

Before the Internet, if SLMSs were asked to name their biggest competitor for market share of their services, most of us would respond "the television." Students spend an inordinate amount of time watching television—more than they do reading. Children ages twelve through seventeen average about 22.4 hours a week of television compared with 5.1 hours for reading outside of school. Students watch television more than they play with friends and interact with their parents (Louv 1990, 90). But now a second competitor to SLMC services and programs has emerged to rival even television for students' time for reading. This competitor is the Internet. Studies show that students are spending more time on the Internet and that it competes with television as a source of recreation. Internet usage studies on the members of the high school class of 2001 found that Internet use has doubled since they were freshmen, from an average of six to eleven hours per week (Pastore 2001, 1–3).

Television continues to be a fierce competitor for SLMSs because we do not have access to it. It is an expensive medium in which to create a product and is funded by advertising revenues. SLMSs cannot afford to televise a story hour, host a booktalk, interview an author, or promote new videos or books in this medium because the costs are prohibitive. The medium of the Internet, however, is a different story. This is a medium in which we have, with the exception of the costs of an Internet service provider and a minimal amount of equipment, free access. SLMSs do not have to pay anyone to feature an interview with an author, to link to a new books page, or announce a new library contest or program. We have the unprecedented opportunity to generate content within a medium rivaling our archenemy, television, for students' attention.

Experience Economy

In recent years, economists have emphasized that our economy is service based. The majority of Americans work in jobs that provide a service such as teaching, food delivery, or health care rather than manufacturing something like steel, automobiles, or refrigerators. Economists are beginning to notice a shift from a service economy to one that features experiences. Experience services are distinct from services that individuals purchase when they pick up their dry cleaning or car after it has been repaired. Theatergoers buy an experience when they pay to spend time enjoying a play that a company stages to engage them in a personal way.

Experiences are usually considered the core of the entertainment sector and include drama, concerts, movies, and television shows. In the past twenty years, however, the number of entertainment choices has increased substantially to include many new experiences such as virtual reality, synchronized sound, three-dimensional backgrounds, audio-animatronics, and much more. One of the first people to capitalize on this human desire for experiences was Walt Disney who succeeded in creating a living, experiential cartoon world in California. Disney created the first theme park that not only entertains customers with rides but also immerses them in an unfolding story involving a complete production of sights, sounds, tastes, aromas, and textures. Restaurants are another example of businesses that are part of the experience economy when they not only serve food but also layer on additional sensations with sound, costumed servers, props, and artwork. Children love to visit restaurants such as the Rainforest Café, because they also experience the sights and sounds of rain forests through the use of tropical music and the appearance of live indigenous birds.

While SLMSs can readily identify with the entertainment aspect of the experience economy, we may justifiably question why purchasing a car or even a hamburger needs to be an entertaining experience. Yet publishers have been trying to enhance the reading of our primary product, books, for years through the use of bright book covers, embossed lettering, dramatic photographs, designer fonts, and pop-out art. Preschoolers, for example, have books with pages that simulate a father's beard through the use of sandpaper.

Companies believe that they stage experiences when they engage customers in a memorable way. They are beginning to purposefully use their services as the stage and their goods as props to engage an individual for the following reasons. They know that buyers of experiences, if they are memorable ones, will become repeat customers. If they can make purchasing a car a memorable experience, they hope that you will return to their dealership to purchase another one (Pine and Gilmore 1999, 2–19).

As companies begin to recognize and respond to this subset of the economy, SLMSs have a chance to capitalize on it too by building cyber reading rooms. Our stage is the Internet, our props are books and other information formats, and the experience that we are marketing is reading. Unlike a conventional library that confines many of our goods to a linear format, the Internet provides SLMSs with the opportunity for students to have a sensory reaction to many of our goods and services. Reading a biography of an author can be greatly enhanced by an interview experience with that writer through the Internet. Gazing at the colored plates of famous paintings in an art book can be much more memorable if it is accompanied by a virtual tour of the gallery that actually houses them. Understanding the oral, persuasive powers of Adolf Hitler can be facilitated by viewing a video clip of one of his huge World War II rallies.

Certainly, all of these enhancements could be accomplished in a conventional library, but they would all involve considerably more time, effort, and money to achieve the same effect. Arranging for an author interview entails setting up equipment, class interruptions, rescheduling classes, and an expensive author honorarium. The visit to an art gallery, depending on its location, could involve an overseas visit or, at the very least, a field trip on school buses. With the Internet, it takes only minutes to insert a link to an author interview, art gallery, or historical video clip footage site.

Since we SLMSs have a captive audience for our goods and services for approximately six hours per day, five days per week, many may question the need for making reading more of an experience. Most of us believe that our product—in the form of books, videos, and CDs—is sufficiently attractive to hold student interests and to provide them with memorable experiences. Unfortunately, with the Internet and television claiming much of student free time, this reasoning is complacent and dangerous. While our products are of high quality and content, ours is a service-based profession that needs to offer students and faculty experiences that are memorable or they will search for stimulation elsewhere.

Experience Economy Divisions

Pine and Gilmore, in their book *The Experience Economy* (1999), divide this new economy into four realms, all of which should, whenever possible, overlap. The first division involves the educational aspect of an experience. What do you want students or faculty to learn from the experience that you are providing them? By supplying them with a Webography about dinosaurs, do you want them to acquire more knowledge about dinosaurs' evolution, eating habits, and causes for extinction? What information or activities do the sites provide that might help induce them to explore and learn more about these fascinating creatures?

The second division is the entertainment aspect of the experience. When students are entertained, they are not really doing anything but responding to or enjoying the experience. They may, for example, squeal with delight when they hear a simulation of a dinosaur roar. This part of the site makes the experience more enjoyable so that students will remain at the site to experience the rest of what it has to offer.

The third division is the escapist aspect of the experience and one that SLMSs may consider unnecessary in a cyber reading room. All of us, however, engage in escapist activities. Any SLMS who flies to a professional conference has witnessed hundreds of adults using their laptops to wile away their flight time by playing solitaire. Many others are busy reading the latest formulaic legal thriller by a best-selling author. Students also need escapist experiences. The solution is to choose ones for the cyber reading room that stimulate critical and strategic thinking skills, such as chess or brainteasers, rather than an unchallenging online card game.

The last division concerns the esthetic aspects of an experience. What is it about a cyber reading room that makes students wish to click on it and pass the time away visiting its sites? What can a SLMS do to make the environment student friendly, attractive, interesting, and comfortable? What types of sites in this area would students be most likely to click on again just to experience its contents? For some students, it may be art, for others motorcycles or natural wonders. This is an area where SLMSs have the opportunity to thrill students with something that they have never seen or experienced before.

Cyber Reading Room
Content Questions

Although there are a number of standard suggestions and ideas for creating a cyber reading room, each school is in a different location, has unique demographics, and faces diverse technical capabilities. The time and effort that SLMSs spend in designing a cyber reading room also has to be proportional to the other important tasks of operating a SLMC. Before constructing this section of a cyber library, it can be helpful to answer the following questions or pose them to groups of students throughout the school's grade levels.

- For what grade levels will you need to provide sites? Is the age range broad enough that you will need a Children's Room and a Teen Room to attract students?

- Will you provide access to and information about chat rooms?

- Where is the school located? Are there many opportunities for enrichment activities such as field trips to museums, art galleries, foreign travel, live theater productions, and so forth?

- Are there any clubs that could use supporting game sites such as chess or bridge?

- Do you sponsor a conventional book club that could be enhanced by on-line features?

- What are you technically equipped to provide support for? Can you provide listservs, e-mail activities, multiple-user domains/dimensions, newsgroups, and bulletin boards?

- What do students do for local recreation? Are they close to national parks or outdoor recreational areas?

- How might you address their social interests and possible problems involving dating, friendship, and substance abuse?

- How much of the cyber reading room creation would you be willing to supervise if students indicate that they would like to be more heavily involved in its development?

- When students use the SLMC's terminals in their free time, what sites, games, and other activities hold their attention and interest?

- Is there a population demographic for which a cyber reading room could perform an outreach type of service? Are there students, for example, who leave school early for jobs, have to assume responsibilities for siblings after school, or are not "connected" to the school community?

Cyber Reading Room Size and Scope

While there are no official guidelines concerning the size of a cyber reading room, keep in mind that this is a section of the cyber library that should be responsive to fads, the seasons, current events, and student interests. Sites in this area may be ephemeral in nature because of the subject matter. During the highly contested 2000 presidential election, a cyber reading room may have featured up-to-the-minute news sites about the current status of vote counting in Florida. The second after a winner was declared, those sites should have been deleted.

A cyber reading room is different from a Web library. The latter should be filled with content-rich sites that may not be entertaining but do provide full text about a school-related topic. If there is room, a Web library can expand its collection as long as there is sufficient computer space to store sites and time to maintain them. Although cyber reading rooms do not have a site limit, they should not be an electronic resource that requires multiple subject hierarchies. It should be a place that students and faculty can access quickly for an item or information that is of recent interest.

Subjects within a cyber reading room can reflect the breadth of the fiction area of a conventional library while simultaneously covering student-related interests such as dress and style, the latest music group, and local sports team results. The "quest for the best" is a good motto to follow with a cyber reading room. When Halloween is coming, include only the sites that feature the best costume ideas and pumpkin carving rather than mediocre sites under the rubric "Halloween."

Language in a cyber reading room needs to be hip and informal. Do not be afraid to use the latest student expressions when annotating the sites. The objective is to attract and maintain their interest. Solicit student opinions before choosing a name for this area of a cyber library. If students give it a cool-sounding name, they are more likely to promote it among their peers.

Suggestions for Educational Experiences

While the perfect site contains educational, escapist, entertainment, and esthetic qualities, it is difficult and challenging to find ones that contain all of them. Consider some of these ideas for educational cyber reading room sites. For many students, they will also be entertaining and esthetically pleasing.

1. **Bibliographies**—Bibliography sites can range from a list of new, conventional SLMC acquisitions to theme-related, annotated lists for either students or teachers. Spark them up with graphics and relevant hyperlinks to other Internet sites for a more sophisticated look. If the school has a color printer,

make copies and distribute and display them with the physical books in the SLMC. Keep the last several months in a linked archive for readers who may find time later on to consult them.

2. **Webographies**—Similar to bibliographies, Webographies consist of lists of links that may be really hot for some technical bell and whistle or are subject or theme related. To ensure that students or faculty visit the site, write a catchy annotation to accompany each one. Webographies, unlike bibliographies, provide instant information gratification because users just click to see the contents. If you have prepared one just for faculty members, it may be worth printing and distributing it so that they can bookmark the sites on their own computers.

3. **Book Awards**—Many readers whose time is limited like to read only books that have received some officially recognized form of literary merit. Consider including a book awards site that contains an archive for the Newbery, Caldecott, Booker, Pulitzer, Nobel, and National Book Awards.

4. **Book Discussion Groups**—If students are too heavily scheduled to participate in the SLMC's book club, place some links in the cyber reading room to online book discussion groups. Consider placing links to Books@Random Library (http://www.randomhouse.com/library/rgg.html), HarperCollins Reader Resources (http://www.harpercollins.com/readers/reader.resources.htm), or Reading Group Choices (http://www.readinggroupchoices.com/). Perhaps they will have time to join in after school or on the weekends.

5. **Book Reviewers**—Studies have found that students are more likely to seek the advice of a peer than an adult when they need information or have a problem. This same pattern may be true for book recommendations. Consider forming an online book reviewers club of students who are willing to write online reviews for recent, popular fiction. Contact their English teachers to see if they can receive extra credit and the local school newspaper to see if it will advertise the service and publicize the link address.

6. **Book Reviews**—Students and teachers like to read reviews of books. Many third-generation online catalogs provide links to reviews from professional journals in addition to

the annotation to assist readers in choosing titles. You may wish to provide links to the major sites that review materials such as Amazon.com as an extra service.

7. **Booktalks**—These are a wonderful way to promote new titles or introduce students to books that are theme related. They are an integral part of a conventional SLMC's reading appreciation program. Why not provide students with links to some online booktalk sites? There are some excellent ones such as Nancy Keane's Booktalks (http://nancykeane .com/booktalks) that furnish more than mere reviews. These sites can serve as an online readers' advisory site by not only providing additional titles about the same topic but also additional information about the book that is usually not included in typical reviews. SLMSs who have the time may wish to publish their own booktalks online and, if there is some technical support, record them so that students could listen when they click on the titles.

8. **Readers' Advisory**—This is one of the most personalized services that SLMSs offer in conventional SLMCs. It requires that SLMSs read widely in all areas of the collection and be able to retain author and character names, plots, subjects, and themes in the most amazing memory bank: their brains. From all of this mentally categorized reading, they reliably produce books on request about time travel and twins, horses that talk, and kids who run with gangs. While there is no replacement for this type of one-to-one interactive service, some cyber libraries are beginning to establish a similar service via e-mail. Establishing this type of service can be as simple as contacting SLMSs with a written request or posting a form with drop-down menus that help narrow students' choices. Within the Readers' Advisory section, libraries also maintain lists of read-alikes for some of the more popular titles and refer readers to listservs and newsgroups that specialize in historical fiction, romance, or fantasy. Fiction Mailing Lists (http://www.fictional.org/ralists.html) contains an overview of six popular fiction lists. Students using these lists can lurk until they feel comfortable participating or join in when they want to comment or assist someone else with information. Publishers are also becoming part of readers' advisories by furnishing links to sample chapters, book discussion guides, author interviews, and fan chat rooms. For additional

Readers' Advisory links, refer to Morton Grove's Webrary (http://www.webrary.org?RS/Rsmenu.html) and Overbooked (http://freenet.vcu.edu/educaton/literature/bklink.html) (Johnson 2001, 913).

9. **Reading Programs**—Participating in a yearly reading program can be not only educational for students but entertaining as well. If you decide to establish a reading program, this is one area where you need some bells and whistles. Use some reading puzzles, brainteasers, cool graphics, fonts, and bright colors to attract students. Since a reading program takes some time to set up and monitor, be sure to enlist the support of the key school personnel who can help you promote it. Public library sites are more advanced than school cyber library sites in this area because they have historically taken responsibility for summer reading programs. Two programs worth visiting are Oklahoma 2000 Summer Reading Program (http://www.connectok.com/summerfunsite) and Chapter a Day (http://www.chapteraday.com). The former is cosponsored by the Oklahoma Department of Libraries and the *Daily Oklahoman* newspaper. Its bells and whistles feature audible "mouseovers." Running the mouse over some of the illustrations such as the frog, clock, and snake will produce a croak, tick, and giggle in that order. The site is robust with loads of book lists, book awards, things to do, and more importantly a question-and-answer contest that runs throughout the summer (Minkel 2000b, 30). Chapter a Day is used by 2,700 public and school libraries. It costs approximately 150 dollars for a onetime setup fee. Each weekday, adolescents who enroll in the Chapter a Day Teen Book Club receive, via e-mail, a few pages from the beginning of a popular fiction or nonfiction book followed the next day by additional pages. Each day's section requires about five minutes to complete answers. By the end of the week, teens will have read about two or three chapters of the book. The following week, they receive a similar amount of content for another book (Minkel 2001, 31–32). If you are still debating the idea of a reading program, visit the Florida Library Youth Program (http://dlis.dos .state.fl.us/flyp200) and download a copy of its manual (http://dlis.dos.state.fl.us/bld/FLYP2000).

10. **Relationships**—One of the areas where students, especially teens, need information from reliable sources concerns dating, friendship, and family issues. Within this section, SLMSs may wish to include evaluated links to sites about substance abuse and sex education. The Internet Public Library: Issues and Conflicts (http://ipl.sils.umich.edu/) has an outstanding site under the subject headings Dating and Stuff and Issues and Conflicts that can be mined for ideas and site addresses.

11. **Writing and Publishing Opportunities**—Encouraging students to write and publish their writing has always been one of the most rewarding aspects of a SLMS's job. Many students, however, are either too shy or unfamiliar with our services to request assistance in this area. An online Writing Corner for prose, poetry, and expository writing is a helpful addition to a cyber reading room. The Association for Library Services to Children 700+ Great Sites (http://www.ala.org /parentspage/greatsites/amazing.html) has an excellent resource of eighteen sites under the heading Writing by Children that is worth considering for a cyber reading room.

Suggestions for Entertainment Experiences

Making a cyber reading room an enjoyable area to visit is one of the main reasons for creating it. The competition is stiff for students' viewing hours, and you want students to visit this area of the cyber library as often as possible. Consider linking to sites within these subject areas.

1. **Audio Materials**—Children love to hear SLMSs read and tell stories. Newer computers have the capacity to allow downloading of fairly large audio files without crashing. SLMSs may wish to record story hours and download them into their cyber reading rooms. If the SLMC's computers can support it, install an audio plug-in so that students can listen to stories during their free time. For ideas, take a look at Toronto Public Library (Canada) (http://www.tpl.toronto.on.ca /KidsSpace/SRC). Its site has an audio file called Books for Me that children can download and sing to because the lyrics are provided on the screen.

2. **Author Interviews and Question Sessions**—Honoraria for authors, even when the costs of their visits are shared among schools, can still be prohibitively expensive. As a policy matter, many authors do not even visit schools. Their publishers, however, are providing Internet sites where they can visit schools electronically. Searching literature portals under an author's name can also yield interviews that have been published on the Internet. Consider creating links to these interviews when students are reading their works as part of a class assignment or just for enjoyment. Investigate the idea of a question-and-answer session with a popular author. Although the publisher may charge for this service and it will never be as personal as a visit, it is not an unworthy substitute.

3. **Cyber Library Contests**—Children like to test themselves, especially when they are in nonthreatening situations. While a conventional SLMC may be just the place to host literary or other genre trivia contests, placing it concurrently in a cyber reading room can broaden the audience. If you design a literary contest about famous fictional lovers for St. Valentine's Day, for example, make the game available in the cyber reading room and create a link so that students can send you the answers via e-mail.

4. **Game**—Many SLMCs allow students to play games during the lunch period or after school as long as they are considered educational. For a cyber reading room, you may wish to provide links to similar games that are played in the SLMC such as chess. WebChess (http://www .june29.com/Chess/), for example, is an excellent site that provides students with the opportunity to graduate to increasingly more challenging gambits and opponents. Mamamedia (http://www.mamamedia .com), however, is the megasite for games. It contains more than 2,000 safe Web sites, 200 of which are replayable activities, including a digital sandbox.

5. **Movies**—On Monday mornings, it is not unusual for SLMSs to overhear students complaining about the poor acting, weak plot, or implausible stunts in a recent movie they paid to see. Students love to go to the movies, but much of their decision to attend is based on television advertising and the recommendations of peers. Why not include in a cyber reading room some links to movie review sites that give them an opportunity to critically evaluate a movie before they part with their money? The Internet Movie Database (http://www.imdb.com/) is one of the best film resources to place in a cyber reading room. It lets students search by title, actor, director, and producer. The plot

summaries are lengthy, and movies are classified so that students who liked the latest submarine techno-thriller can find similar ones to rent at their local video rental stores.

6.　**Reading Games**—Child development experts are constantly preaching to parents about the need to let children play. Although most of them strongly advocate multidimensional play for children under the age of ten, many children and teens are drawn to computers for play purposes. Providing them with games that involve reading is a much better alternative to having them click on sites that do not stimulate their brains and engage their curiosity. A children's librarian for the Toronto Public Library has observed that games are the most popular part of the library's Web site (http://www.tpl.toronto.on.ca/KidsSpace /SRC). As a result, it has added plenty of them in the form of puzzles and interactive reading stories. Check out its Games and Activities portal site for site addresses, graphics, and other ideas. There are two additional Canadian public libraries with excellent reading games that are worth visiting. Calgary's "Electronic Reading Game" (http://www.public-librar.calgary.ab.ca/wra2000/wra2000.htm) features a multipart Internet game with puzzles and trivia pages about famous Canadians. Students may also search for images in a "Midnight at the Museum" game and keep score on printable score sheets. Interactivity is an important ingredient for reading games because it engages students' minds. Edmonton Public Library sponsors Bugs in Space/Rocket into Reading that contains an ongoing story about two bug mascots. Players can add new paragraphs, and the best ones are chosen to continue the story's development (Minkel 2000a, 42–43).

7.　**Things to Do**—In this area of a cyber reading room, you may wish to provide visitors with links to events, sites, activities, and happenings within students' more immediate surroundings. If the local newspaper publishes a Weekend Section, this is a good place to start looking for ideas. While you may not find an event's site address, you will probably see a notice giving details as to place, time, price of admission, and so forth. Create a link within the cyber reading room to this information by copying a suitable graphic that expresses the idea of the activity and writing an appropriate blurb about it. If the school is hosting a fall festival, find images or graphics of autumn leaves or pumpkins, create a link to the image, and write a description of the event beside it. Before vacation times, branch out to include sites that students might wish to visit with their parents or relatives including local museums, historic houses, state and national parks, and/or amusement and theme parks.

Suggestions for Escapist Experiences

There is a thin line between entertainment and escapist experiences, but there are differences. Escapist activities usually involve greater immersion than education or entertainment experiences. All of us recognize the signs of an escapist experience when we have to rouse students to run to their next class because they were so engrossed in magazine articles that they forgot the time. One telltale sign of people having escape experiences is the concentration that seems to overcome those persons as they become more immersed in an activity. While all of us dream of this phenomenon occurring with books in the conventional school library, there are many Internet sites that provide a similar experience and are educational in nature.

1. **Cyber Connections**—One of the biggest enticements on the Internet are chat rooms. It's also one of the first Internet activities that was considered unacceptable for students to engage in during the school day. Students love to talk, share experiences, commiserate, and celebrate with one another. Unfortunately, this Internet activity is such an escapist experience for them that it distracts from learning and completing assignments. Keypals Club, however, which was one of the first telecomputing activities tested online, may be a more acceptable use of the Internet that still allows students to connect with one another in a safe environment. Sites that connect students to one another in foreign countries can assist in sharpening students' reading and writing skills in a foreign language. Geography becomes relevant when students converse with a student who lives in the land they are studying, and everyone benefits from learning what it is really like in a country other than the United States. Keypals Club is available for students of all ages. In some cases, a group of students may correspond with a similar group in a foreign country. Other sites put "penfriends" in touch with one another. EPals (http://www.eplas.com/) is one of the largest sites providing the ability to connect a teacher's classroom with classrooms from ninety countries speaking eighty-seven languages. Its purpose is to arrange for a teacher-monitored opportunity for students to correspond with other students throughout the world. For students desiring a one-to-one exchange, provide them with access to the Keypals Club (http://www.mightymedia.com/keypals/) and show students how to complete the registration instructions.

2. **Interactive Sites**—Sites that provide escapist experiences usually offer a degree of interactivity to engage user interest by allowing them to manipulate information, images, or data and observe the effect it has with other aspects of the site. The site, Amusement Park Physics

(http://www.learner.org/exhibits/parkphysics/), for example, lets students move various amusement park rides in certain directions to illustrate different physics principles. Students interested in music would enjoy the Symphony Interactive Guide (http://library.thinkquest .org/22673/index.html) that teaches the components of a symphony by allowing them "to play" different instruments. The census data site Historical United States Census Data 1790–1970 (http://fisher.lib .virginia.edu/census/) allows students to select ten-year intervals from 1790 to 1970 for each state and county. They may choose up to fifteen variables and request that the data be displayed in various graphs. Another site called Personality: What Makes Us What We Are? (http://www.learner.org/exhibits/personality) gives students the opportunity to take a personality test that helps determine how other people may view them. Highlighting an interactive site within a cyber reading room gives students the opportunity to experiment with it and learn something that might not be part of the curriculum.

3. **Virtual Field Trips**—The world of children can be so narrow because of their geographic location, lack of independence, transportation, and family income. Although they can escape to different countries and even worlds through fiction and nonfiction books, the Internet introduces a level of reality that enhances the experience and makes it more memorable. Discovery sites give students a chance to click on objects, images, and graphics at their own pace and to explore them in more depth. These sites can supplement the book they may be reading on the topic. Parts of the world that are now unsafe or environmentally hazardous can be explored. Places that students have never gone and probably never will can be visited. Highlighting a discovery site in a cyber reading room provides an enriching experience for children and perhaps their parents. Virtual field trips have the potential to inspire students or give them ideas for possible careers. Some virtual field trips are designed to describe particular topics such as how sound waves travel, while others explore sites including ancient Mayan ruins, the Galapagos Islands, and outer space. When inserting a link to a virtual field trip into a cyber reading room, check to see if a teacher is doing a unit in the subject to increase its relevancy and broaden the potential audience. Educational Web Adventures (http://www.eduweb.com/adventure.html) has designed several interactive Internet sites that contain learning modules and Web adventures including Colonial Williamsburg, Weisman Art Museum, the JASON Projects (live satellite and Internet broadcasts of underwater expeditions including the wreck of the Titanic), and the Bell Museum of Natural History. Virtual School Bus (http://www.field-guides.com/)

takes students to places such as field marshes and volcanoes and contains subject-expert selected sites and pre-cache mechanisms that allow students to download the entire site to their computers and move through at their own pace (Benson and Fodemski 1999, 79–80).

Suggestions for Esthetic Experiences

While an escapist experience is usually characterized by immersion in a site because its offerings are unique and often interactive, an esthetic experience is quite different. Students who have an esthetic experience with a site have little or no effect on it. They leave the site untouched. In a strict educational experience, students learn from entertaining sites they enjoy, escapist sites they visit, and esthetic sites they sense. In the real world, an esthetic experience might consist of gazing at the Mona Lisa or El Capitan in Yosemite National Park or listening to the night sounds in a tropical rain forest. While books can help students imagine some of these places, the old adage "A picture is worth a thousand words" is more applicable. The Internet is filled with sites that give students esthetic experiences. Some of them are sufficiently memorable that they may wish to revisit them.

1. **Art Galleries**—Art galleries abound on the Internet. Almost all of the world's major museums provide gallerylike tours of some of their more famous paintings, sculptures, and artifacts. Create a site within the cyber reading room called Painters and Palettes. Insert links to a selected group of paintings from one museum and pose questions about their style, painter, theme, and composition. Tell students what is so remarkable about the work and why it probably came to be displayed in a museum. If time is a factor, just place the site within the cyber reading room, give its details by using a hover button, and have students look at it. Visit the site Art History Sources on the Web (http://witcombe.sbc.edu/ARTHLinks.html) and draw on it for buildings, photographs, and archaeological finds to display.

2. **Exhibits**—Many museums have "blockbuster exhibits" of art, furniture, rare objects, drawings, paintings, scrolls, and so forth that have been collected from various owners and other museums to form touring collections. Years ago, students only had the opportunity to view these exhibits if their parents took them or if they actually lived close enough to transport themselves to a host city's museum exhibit. Fortunately, this is no longer the case with regard to many exhibits. Through generous funding, many museums mount their big exhibits on the Web. The Dead Sea Scrolls (http://www.ibiblio.org/expo/deadsea.scrolls.exhibit/intro.html) and Vatican Museum Exhibit

(http://metalab.unc.edu/expo/vaticanexhibit/Vatican.exhibit.html) can still be viewed on the Internet even though the exhibits have been dismantled and returned to their respective owners and curators. Visit the site WWW Virtual Library: Museums (http://vlmp.museophile.com/) to find ones that are age appropriate and interesting for students to have an esthetic experience that will be truly memorable.

3. **Nature Sites**—Showing students pictures of some endangered species and the world's natural wonders may not only evoke their awe and curiosity but also help maintain their presence on the earth. Without taking the side of the environmentalist or the oil producers, show them pictures, for example, of the Brooks Range and Denali National Park in Alaska. Pose questions that expose them to both sides of the oil drilling issue, or just present them with pictures of Alaskan wildlife, mountains, and valleys to inspire them to take a trip there someday and see it for themselves. Michigan State University has a site called the Children's Garden (http://commtechlab.msu.edu/sites /garden/index.html) that features more than fifty-six individual theme areas that create a place of wonder and enchantment for students of any age. If your school is in a cold climate, why not link to the site in February when almost everyone has grown a little tired of winter and is awaiting spring?

4. **Web Cameras**—Thousands of Web cameras operate daily on the Internet, but most of us do not associate them with esthetic encounters. Yet these tiny cameras attached to a Web server and automated by software can provide students with many memorable experiences. They can visit a watering hole in Namibia, Africa, through Noah's Ark at About.com's List of Animal Cams (http://biology.about.com /science/biology/cs/animalcams/index.htm) and watch for antelope and lions to show up. If nothing is going on, they can go underwater to look at the reef in Coral Gables, Florida, or soar to outer space through the satellite images compiled at WebCamVideo.com (http://webcamvideo.com/domi/satel/en.htm). If you wish to access the megasite of web cameras, have them visit Earth Cam (http://www.earthcam.com) for a listing of thousands of cameras grouped into fourteen categories, each with its own subsections. Choices range from gazing at the Acropolis in Greece to searching for killer whales off the coast of Washington State with the orca (killer whale) camera. A second megasite entitled Tony's List of Live Cam Worldwide (http://chili.rt66.com/ozone/cam.htm) provides SLMSs with thousands of possible Web cameras to view and place on exhibit in a cyber reading room (Hodge 2001, 88–90).

Recommended Internet Sites

There are three general sites that you may wish to scan occasionally for sites to place in a cyber reading room.

KIDS Report
http://scout.cs.wisc.edu/scout/KIDS/index.html

This site will show you what sites are popular with students in grades K–12. Sponsored by two classrooms in the Metropolitan School District in Madison, Wisconsin, and two classrooms in the Boulder Valley School District in Boulder, Colorado, it contains a list of annotated sites written by students. Visitors can browse past issues or search their archives.

Public Library of Charlotte and Mecklenburg County (North Carolina)
http://www.plmc.lib.nc.us/

For ideas and suggestions for a well-developed cyber reading room, this site is one of the best. It has separate "rooms." One is called the For Teens Library and the other is entitled For Kids. Click on the one that is more appropriate for your student audience. The teen room contains: (1) an excellent Homework Help center that is filled with relevant links concerning content that students need for information to complete class assignments; (2) a College and Career Center that provides outstanding links to college megasites; (3) a Books and Reading room that features interviews with young adult authors and a Reader's Club; and (4) a Just for Fun section that furnishes links to local library programs and various library events designed for young adults. The For Kids site provides storytelling links and stories that children can listen to in English or Spanish. It also contains a Book Hive that provides children up to twelve years old with outstanding bibliographies, reading lists, and links to children's authors and novelists.

Yahooligans
http://www.yahooligans.com/

Students love to check out this site to see what's new by clicking on the New icon located at the top of their home page. Click there and you will find a link to a Web page listing recent additions for the last week. While you are viewing it, click on the button labeled Net Events to learn about live events that take place on the Internet weekly. This is where students go to find out about live chat sessions with famous authors or sports figures.

References

Benson, Allen C., and Linda M. Fodemski. 1999. *Connecting Kids and the Internet*. 2nd ed. New York: Neal-Schuman.

Hodge, Brian. 2001. "Windows on the World." *Smart Computing* 12 (September): 88–90.

Johnson, Roberta. 2001. "Global Conversation: Readers' Advisory on the Web." *Booklist* 97 (January 1 and 15): 912–913.

Louv, Richard. 1990. *Childhood's Future*. Boston: Houghton Mifflin.

Minkel, Walter. 2001. "A Chapter a Day." *School Library Journal* 47 (May): 31–32.

———. 2000a. "Life's a Beach." *LJ Netconnect: Supplement to Library and School Library Journal* (Fall): 42–43.

———. 2000b. "Web Site of the Month." *School Library Journal* 46 (July): 30.

Pastore, Michael. 2001. "Internet Use Continues to Pervade U.S. Life." http://cyberatlas .internet.com/big_picture/demographics/article/0,,5901_775401,00.html (August 27, 2001).

Pine, B. Joseph II, and James H. Gilmore. 1999. *The Experience Economy: Work Is Theatre and Every Business a Stage*. Boston: Harvard Business School Press.

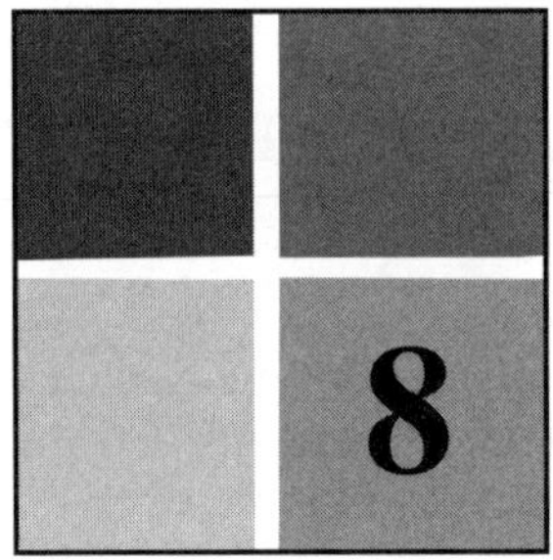

Providing Cyber Library Instructional Services

Internet Instructional Challenges

The availability of the Internet, with its millions of Web sites and numerous Web-accessible subscription resources, provides SLMSs with an opportunity to simultaneously improve teaching methods and the mode of knowledge delivery. SLMC access to the Internet came just in time as our students are facing an explosion of information choices that have both positive and negative aspects. The fact that students can choose from a multitude of print and nonprint resources requires not only a tolerance for many alternatives but also the ability to choose correctly to fulfill their information needs (Craver 1997, xiv). Studies of consumer tolerance for choosing products indicate that "more is less," not "more is more," and that consumers faced with overwhelming supplies of competing goods tend to suffer increased anxiety (Oberman 1991, 189).

There are similarities between the problems of choice that consumers encounter in shopping malls and the problems of increased choice that confront students daily in electronic-information environments. As SLMSs acquire the latest subscription resources and add a Web library to their cyber libraries, access patterns to information change. Suddenly, students can log in to the SLMC's online catalog, switch to a subscription database, click on Google.com, and search the Web or reserve a book from their public library from anywhere and at anytime.

The instructional challenges in this electronic environment are formidable. SLMSs must assist students to choose correctly from more than 1 billion URLs and teach them how to search and retrieve the extraordinary amount of information available in this Web-based medium (Wiggins 2000, 26). We cannot begin to do this soon enough.

Student Information-Seeking Behavior

While our students are "enthusiastic users of electronic resources, often preferring them to their printed counterparts," their eagerness is not matched by their skills at formulating effective searches. According to Sandra G. Hirsh, who completed a study of fifth graders, most of them matched their topic word to what they found online with no regard for content or quality. If the site title matched the keywords in their assignment, they accepted it with no question despite instruction from a SLMS in synonym searching and evaluating their search results (Minkel 2000, 37).

Hirsh's study reinforces Lubans's Internet searching study with ninety-five gifted and talented seventh through tenth graders at a summer program at Duke University in 1998. Lubans reported that the majority of secondary students gave much higher rankings to the Internet for timeliness, accuracy, and authoritativeness than did the 235 members of the freshmen class that he surveyed (Lubans 1998, 1–8). Additional studies involving college students, however, confirm that they too are unable to match even basic subject needs with the appropriate information retrieval databases. When eighty-two undergraduates at the University of Illinois at Champaign-Urbana were given a subject and asked to choose an electronic database from among sixteen, only 22 percent of the students selected appropriate ones. Twenty percent selected databases not even remotely connected to their topic (Oberman 1991, 191–192).

Studies indicate that information users do not fully comprehend the enormous array of available search options and rarely apply the correct ones even when they are cognizant of them. Moreover, students are often frustrated when confronted with too many search options and have difficulty deciding when to employ them. For example, choosing to use a Boolean search may yield more information than choosing to use a keyword search. The result of many information-seeking behavior studies similar to the ones cited in this section is a recognition that there is a defined set of skills that students need to function successfully in a technologically advanced and information-rich environment. The rubric, information literacy, is used to describe the ability of students to: (1) define the need for information; (2) initiate search strategies; (3) locate appropriate resources; (4) assess and comprehend the information; (5) interpret the information; (6) communicate the information; and (7) evaluate the product and process (American Association of School Librarians 2001, 1–8). These abilities are considered life skills, and it has become the responsibility of SLMSs to ensure that students have acquired them before they graduate from high school.

Web-Based Instructional Advantages

While charged with teaching information literacy skills, SLMSs have been hampered by insufficient equipment and access. These problems are finally resolving themselves as school administrators realize the importance of graduating information-literate students. Additional hardware and faster access to the Internet give SLMSs many instructional advantages. By creating or linking to interactive instructional sites, it allows SLMSs to use the Internet itself as a teaching tool. Internet-based tutorials give students the opportunity to read instructions on one part of the screen and execute them in the actual searching device. SLMSs can provide Internet pages that aid in choosing search engines, formulating search strategies, or combining keywords using Boolean logic. Referring to these Web pages during a class makes it easier for SLMSs to teach and students to follow on their computers.

Another advantage of school cyber library instruction concerns the prevention of errors that occurs when students type in a URL address from a handout. Providing permanent instruction links not only lessens the potential for frustrating typing mistakes but also furnishes instructional access on a 24/7 basis. A student who begins work on a project in the evening can refer to a Secrets of Top Web Searchers page again before initiating a search.

Web-based instruction is multidimensional as opposed to its paper-based counterpart, which is one-dimensional. A pathfinder on paper may instruct students to search the online catalog by using designated keywords, but the same pathfinder in electronic format can place a hyperlink to the catalog so that students can go there immediately and type in the recommended keywords.

The potential for interactivity is another advantage of cyber library instruction. SLMSs can use the Web to create test pages, to make electronic links for discussion and feedback of units, and to provide a site for e-mail questions about any difficulty students are experiencing. Cyber library instruction gives SLMSs the chance to promote the differences between the Internet and a SLMC by placing instructional pages that remind students to start with a library because our resources are professionally reviewed, free for use, well organized, have a high degree of permanence, and come with highly trained personal assistance.

Having all of our instruction Web accessible gives SLMSs greater mobility. It is easy to enter a classroom for just ten minutes to refresh students' memories with an overview of a subject-specific subscription resource. Students can click on the page(s) that a SLMS demonstrates and follow along. The necessity for handouts is eliminated. Classes can be maximized too. There is no limit on the number of students who can log on and take a tutorial on the online catalog and then take the online posttest to confirm that they have understood the materials. This assignment can be required as homework and will allow SLMSs more time to individualize instruction and to help students find specific resources related to their own assignments (Thornton 2000, 211).

Web-Accessible Instructional Limitations

As administrators and even SLMSs realize how much easier it is to provide instruction through a cyber library, it may be tempting to think of it as a replacement for the old form of paper-and-pencil–driven lesson plans. Web-based instruction is a supplement to library instruction, not a substitute. It enables SLMSs to level the playing field by having everyone take the same online catalog tutorial and then be prepared to move on to library skills that require critical thinking and more nuanced selections (Dupuis 2001, 21–22).

Technical problems may still be a factor in many schools and even at home. SLMSs who do not have a trustworthy Internet environment will find it difficult to confidently enter a classroom without transparencies or handouts as emergency reinforcements. Many Web-based tutorials employ frames so that users can read instructions on one side of the screen while performing the assignment on the other side. On older-model computers, frames are not tolerated so students owning these models would be at a disadvantage for home use. Downloading assignments that require a sophisticated design is another problem for older-model computers. It can take an exceedingly long time to load the page on the screen (Sears and Wohrley 2000, 65).

There are no quick solutions to these technical problems. Some will be resolved by obsolescence and the recognition that schools need reliable technical support or access to stable off-site servers. In the meantime, SLMSs can carefully design Web-based instructional units that the majority of students can find and load quickly and easily. Most schools, however, are moving ahead with Web-based instruction despite these potential problems because administrators and SLMSs realize that the benefits far outweigh the disadvantages.

Web-Based Instructional Criteria

The task of transferring entire courses of library instruction is not time consuming if they exist in digital format. Most SLMSs have library skills lessons in a word processing document format. Although there can be a few formatting problems with margins and spacing, most word-processed documents easily convert into a Web page through the use of Web-editing software programs including Microsoft FrontPage or Claris Home Page. The problem with a simple conversion is the look and style of the document. Instruction designed for the Web should be more than documents uploaded and linked electronically. Course content needs to be designed for a reader who no longer reads from left to right or from page one to page two. Internet users approach electronically hyperlinked information in a different fashion. Rarely do they read linearly. Instead, they prefer to scan a screen for important keywords that are most important to them. If the information that is relevant takes too long or is too deep in the site to conveniently reach, they simply exit and move on to another site.

The scanning process may take only a few seconds, but Web users are not patient when they are seeking information. Students as well as adults want to find information quickly, and they enter a site with the expectation that the links will be appropriate and will open. They also expect the design to have a purpose. If there is an icon or button on the site, they expect it to open something on the next page.

One of the rules concerning full text and the Web is "chunking." Chunking information means that you analyze a library lesson and remove all unnecessary verbiage, confirm that what appears on the first page is necessary to the following page, and install icons or symbols if they will save words and hasten understanding of the document. Partitioning the information into manageable chunks for a small viewing screen is the objective. In some cases, it may not be worth transferring a series of lesson plans to the Web because making them Web-presentable would be too time consuming. It may be better to use them as a full template and design them anew on a blank screen in one of the Web-authoring programs already mentioned (Porter 1997, 128–131).

With this caveat in mind, consider the following questions before transferring an entire series of lessons onto the Web:

- How much of the course content is appropriate for the Web?

- Does the lesson loan itself to tutorial or handout format?

- Will students work alone or in groups?

- Does the lesson require physical contact with print formats? A scavenger hunt for books in the conventional SLMC is not suited to a Web lesson.

- Does the lesson require a demonstration?

- What parts of the lesson need to be discussed with a SLMS present?

- Can more interactivity be introduced through Web-based instruction?

- Can more visual activities be introduced through Web-based instruction?

- How much of the lesson can be completed by the student without assistance from the SLMS?

- How easy is it to build in a form of online evaluation?

- Does the lesson require a great deal of previous knowledge?

Cyber Library Instructional Services

This section contains ideas and suggestions for instructional services that you may wish to consider for this important part of a cyber library. Some of them may not be relevant to a particular SLMC's core of programs and services. Other sites inspire ideas that you may place on a wish list for when there is additional funding or support personnel. Please keep in mind that many of the instructional suggestions do not have to be created by SLMSs. Almost all of them already exist as a service, and all SLMSs have to do is place an annotated link to them within their own cyber library's subject hierarchy. Several sites are excellent for use as templates should you wish to create a similar set of pages in the school's cyber library.

Orientation/Tour

All SLMSs give tours or orientations to their SLMCs. Some of us accomplish it on the first day when a new class of students arrives for a library skills unit. Periodically, SLMSs also show visitors, boards of governors, trustees, off-site administrators, and colleagues their facilities. The Web is an attractive medium not only to promote the SLMC visually but also to instruct incoming students about its basic programs and services. The Carrier Library of James Madison University (http://library.jmu.edu/library/gold/mod1orient.htm [July 21, 2001]) has an outstanding orientation tour that is visually appealing and instructional. It's basically a Microsoft PowerPoint presentation of fifteen slides or "stops," as the library terms it, that starts with a welcoming picture of the building and is accompanied by a warm message that generally sketches what the Carrier Library provides and contains in its collection. Through the use of friendly pictures and words, this tour conveys an open library where students would not hesitate to ask questions, to relax and read a newspaper, or to just hang out. Based on this site and others, here are some ideas for designing an instructional SLMC tour. Borrow or buy a digital camera for this project to enable you to enhance the color and contrast and make the tour look professional. Use words that welcome students to the SLMC and will make them feel at home. At the end of the tour, they should not only be orientated but also, by the choice of words, have a warm feeling for a wonderful facility.

- **Building**—Invite them into the building and briefly describe the collection, equipment, and friendly SLMSs who are there to serve them.

- **Bulletin Boards/Book Displays**—Is there an area where new materials are exhibited? Does the library sponsor literary trivia contests, author visits, or special book displays in a certain area that students should check?

- **Circulation Desk**—Tell them how easy it is to check out and renew materials and what identification, if any, is required to borrow items. You may also wish to mention the length of circulation for different material formats.

- **Computer Area**—Describe how easy it is to log on to a computer and use it for typing a paper or accessing the SLMC's electronic resources. However, if the computers do not provide access to either e-mail or word processing programs, state it.

- **Copying**—Does the library charge for photocopying? Do students purchase a card for a minimum amount? Is there a place at school to get change?

- **Interlibrary Loan**—What are the procedures for borrowing materials from other nearby SLMCs? Do students have to show the SLMS that they have checked the collection and verified that the item they desire is either checked out or not in stock? How soon do most interlibrary loan materials arrive? How is the student notified?

- **Media Equipment and Resources**—What types of media equipment does the SLMC provide? May a student reserve a video camera or use a tape recorder for a school-sponsored event? Do videos circulate? If so, describe the collection and its circulation requirements.

- **Microforms/fiche**—Show them what fiche and form look like and how they are used to preserve materials in a more compact format. If the SLMC has a reader/printer, tell students about it and mention if there is a charge to print from it. Generally describe the types of materials that the library has on microform.

- **Periodicals**—State how many periodicals the library subscribes to and what the circulation period is for current and back issues. If the SLMC subscribes to an electronic periodicals database, briefly describe it.

- **Quiet Area**—Is there a quiet section of the library where students can study alone without interruption?

- **Reference Area**—Tell them what they will find in this collection area including encyclopedias, almanacs, dictionaries, atlases, and so forth. Inform them that most of these materials cannot be checked out unless they have special permission.

- **Reference Collection**—Encourage them to come and ask for help. At the Carrier Library site, it has written, "Remember, there are no stupid questions." If there is an online reference service, mention it and give the Internet address.

- **Reserve Area**—Tell them what reserve material is and describe the different type of loan periods. When may reserve material be checked out? Does the library charge students if materials are not returned on time?

- **Special Collections**—Does the SLMC have any special collections including yearbooks, college videos, or a local authors' shelf? Are there any circulation restrictions concerning these materials?

Workshops for Faculty or Parents

Years ago, students were the primary instructional audience for SLMSs, but in an information revolution that employs new equipment and searching techniques, faculty and parents have become our teaching responsibility as well. Adults have discovered that the Internet is not something that one can "just click on" and retrieve satisfactory results. Searching an online catalog, electronic databases, and the Web calls for the same information literacy skills that we are trying to inculcate in our student population. Almost all of the searching strategies and techniques that SLMSs teach students need to be taught to faculty and parents. Faculty and parents, however, do not like to acknowledge that their searching-level abilities in an electronic environment may mirror those of their students or children.

While the searching concepts that SLMSs teach are the same for students and adults, the latter group's interests and needs are narrower and more focused. Faculty in particular become noticeably upset if they discover that they are practicing the same tutorial as do their students. Lesson plans with adult users need to be centered around a specific set of needs and interests. Adults and parents will come to workshops when they need information in special areas. Faculty who have little or no electronic searching skills may sign up for a training program when they are offered workshops in some of the following areas.

- **Bells and Whistles Internet for Adults**—Highlight the more obscure search features of search engines such as AltaVista and Google. Foreign-language teachers, for example, may wish to know about and be able to use AltaVista's translation feature. Teach them to use subject directories such as Yahoo and Healthfinder.com for specific topics before they freestyle-search the Internet. Ask faculty or parents to e-mail some topics in which they are interested in obtaining information. Use those topics as demonstration searches for each new search technique.

- **Current Awareness Workshop**—Reserve one faculty meeting per semester to demonstrate and give opportunities for teachers to explore new sites and subscription databases. If there has been a problem with plagiarism, for example, highlight some of the antiplagiarism sites such as Turn It In.com and show them how it works.

- **Departmental Workshops**—Once a year, invite all the members of a department in and show them the latest sites in their respective disciplines. Demonstrate, for example, recent sites containing primary sources to the history department. If there is a new electronic database in their field, create minilessons for it and make time for them to practice using it.

- **New Faculty Workshop**—Present an introductory workshop for new teachers to demonstrate the online catalog, subscription databases, Web library, and appropriate searching techniques. Schedule time for them to ask questions and practice with all of the resources.

- **Parent Power Workshop**—Offer to show parents where all the good homework sites are, what chat rooms are all about, and how filters work. Make time for them to search for topics of personal interest using similar search techniques.

Quick Tips

Many of the concepts and techniques that SLMSs teach are not suitable for a tutorial approach. These papers consist of tips, FAQ pages, or how-to handouts about various aspects of library and Internet research. Students and faculty may have received a copy of them in one of their classes but may have misplaced it or forgotten to take it home when they have an assignment. Placing these pages in a cyber library under a subject heading is a fine way of making them available 24/7. If SLMSs receive an e-mail or telephone request for a tips page, the requestor can be directed to the cyber library and SLMSs can save time by not having to photocopy it and place it in someone's mailbox. Here are some suggestions and ideas for an instructional tips section in a cyber library. Remember to create appropriate hyperlinks for the online catalog or a specific subscription database when you refer to them in a tips page.

- **How Do I Find Materials in the SLMC?**—Students need to know that they can search for books and other materials in the SLMC's online catalog. They also need to know that they can search by author, title, subject, call number, and keywords. If the online catalog supports viewing the items they borrow and reserve, include this information in the orientation too. On this same page, explain each browse function for title, author, and subject. Explain the difference between keyword and subject searching and provide examples.

- **How Do I Find an Article?**—Describe the contents and search capabilities of the SLMC's periodicals subscription databases and the differences between SIRS, for example, which is full text, and another that provides only selective text. Provide an example of a topic that has the keywords highlighted and tell them to do the same with their topic. Tell users to think of synonyms and related words for the topic and to try searching in the database for those words. Explain how a citation database works and that they should consult the SLMC's periodical list to see if the hard copy of a magazine is available. Use a second page, if necessary, to show them how to refine their search by using the words "and," "or," and "not" and searching by year, magazine title, and author.

- **How Do I Narrow My Topic?**—Use a general topic and create appropriate subtopic examples for a ten-page paper, chapter in a book, and book, respectively. Suggest that a topic can be subdivided by date, geographic location, time periods, and so forth and supply examples. Recommend that students try to pose their topic as a question and provide assignment-related sample questions from topics in the physical sciences and humanities.

- **Secrets of Top Internet Searchers**—Recommend that students employ a variety of search engines and subject directories, identify key search terms, select related search terms, use phrase searching whenever possible, check syntax and spelling, search for additional sites similar to ones they found useful, refine their search by the use of Boolean and proximity operators, and try again if they were unsuccessful the first time.

- **What Are the Differences between Primary and Secondary Sources?**—Provide students with examples of primary sources such as letters, diaries, speeches, scrolls, photographs, newspapers, census data, and laws. Include definitions of both types of resources. Pose hypothetical research paper topics involving resources and explain how they fit the definition of primary or secondary within their research topic's context.

Personal Services

Providing students with personal assistance is the most important professional role for SLMSs. Amey and Elliott's study of large numbers of tenth-grade students supported how much they value human interaction. Out of all the resources to which they had access including libraries, television, and other media, students preferred to obtain information from another person (1997, 18). Unfortunately, SLMSs must serve hundreds of students in a setting that is not always conducive to one-on-one help. There are many occasions when SLMSs are unable to provide personal assistance because of teaching commitments. Until the Internet, personal services directed at students ended at the close of the school day. SLMSs still cease answering reference questions, giving term paper counseling, recommending a good book, or teaching students how to find information by late afternoon.

Although the Internet is not an equal substitute for personal interaction and assistance between students and SLMSs, it does allow SLMSs to extend and promote their instructional services in a way that was never possible before.

Reference Assistance

The two main areas where SLMSs are extending personal assistance concern the provision of online reference and homework help. Both have on-site and off-site options. SLMSs in a consortium, however, may wish to explore the latter option in greater depth. If a SLMS is a sole practitioner, it is probably advisable that she/he establishes a link to critically acclaimed reference and homework assistance sites within her/his cyber library. Establishing a school-sponsored virtual reference site would be too time consuming. The following are some sites and examples of personal assistance instructional services that are found at other libraries:

- **Frequently Asked Reference Questions (FARQs)**—SLMSs who have a thorough knowledge of their school's course of study will have no trouble listing questions and answers to reference questions that are posed every year by students attempting to complete various class assignments. If the search process is to be considered part of the learning experience, SLMSs may not wish to provide each question with an answer but instead recommend several relevant books or Internet sites to help guide student research. One of the best examples of FARQs is hosted by the Chicago Public Library (http://www.chipublic.org/008subject/005genref /gisquestion.html). This site contains many answers to routinely posed questions that will be familiar to SLMSs.

- **Reference Service**—Providing students with assistance with finding information and resources to complete class assignments and research papers can be an important instructional aspect of a cyber library. Some SLMSs create a link to the SLMC's e-mail address that contains a form with a link to the FARQs page and boxes for students to enter their name, grade, and e-mail address and an information deadline for a response to their question. The form also has a place to state the question, the type of answer preferred (brief factual answer or ideas for resources to consult), the sources that the student may have already consulted, and the resources that are available to her/him (e.g., Internet connection, public library, and so forth). Other SLMSs create links to well-known reference services that students can access through the school's cyber library. Two of the most highly regarded reference service sites are Kidsconnect Q & A Service (http://www.ala.org/ICONN/kids.conn.html) and the Internet Public Library Ready Reference (http://ipl.org/ref/). Kidsconnect, sponsored by the American Association of School Librarians, is a SLMS volunteer question-answering, help, and referral service for students in grades K–12. In addition to responding to students within two days, the site also provides an FAQs page by K–12 students, a cyber library of Internet resources that is organized by subject, and a set of research guides. The Internet Public Library Ready Reference, staffed by volunteer librarians and library students, answers questions posed by anyone and not just students in grades K–12. While its staff does not have a stated turnaround time for answers, it trys to answer a question right away when someone needs an answer quickly. This site also features FARQs, reference pathfinders, and subject guides. If you are a member of a consortium of SLMSs who wishes to consider establishing a virtual reference desk, visit this site for advice, ideas, and criteria for establishing it (Lagace 1999, 153–174; Foster 2000, 1–2).

- **Homework Help**—Many students have working parents who are not home during the prime-time hours for completing homework. Although there are many Internet sites including Ask Dr. Math (http://forum .swarthmore.edu/dr.math/dr-math.html) and Multnomah County Library Homework Center (http://www.multnomah.lib.or.us/lib/homework/index .html), they lack the live contact that some students need to complete an assignment with an overnight deadline. Live Homework Help (http://Tutor .com) is a fee-based service that connects students to a certified homework help tutor every Sunday through Thursday from 4 P.M. until midnight. The audience is students of all ages. SLMSs may wish to create a link to it from their cyber libraries and include in the annotation information concerning the access charges.

- **Term Paper Counseling**—Although many students seek out SLMSs when they experience difficulty writing term papers, the majority of students may be unaware that it is an instructional service that is offered to everyone. The Internet gives SLMSs an opportunity not only to promote this service by telling students to feel free to either drop in or make an appointment but also to help them with Web pages at junctures where they normally encounter problems. Web pages devoted to topic selection, identifying databases containing primary sources, and developing thesis statements can be of great assistance in lessening the trauma of term papers or major research assignments.

- **Tutoring Services**—Tutors are ever present in many SLMCs where they have taken up residence in nooks and crannies of the SLMC to tutor students in various subjects and for the SATs. In a response to this growing need for tutors, Tutor.com has partnered with the *Princeton Review* to provide online tutoring to schools and individual students. The Boston Public Library in its second year of a pilot project with Tutor.com that connects middle school students via the Internet with trained tutors from Boston-area universities. SLMSs who have had requests for additional tutors may wish to contact them for a trial project with their school or create a link to them to provide individualized tutoring as part of their cyber library instructional services. Connecting to a tutor at this site is an easy process. Students select the subject, view a list of tutors, and begin a session. Students may view tutors' profiles that indicate their qualifications. If the subject is math, for example, they can look at some sample online problems that tutors have solved to see if their explanations are understandable or confusing. The price for each tutor is also posted and ranges from twenty-four dollars to sixty dollars per hour (Oder 2001, 6).

Subject Guides/Pathfinders

SLMSs have been compiling guides to useful SLMC resources on a variety of subjects for years. If they are in digital format, transfer them into the cyber library. If they are numerous, establish subheadings under History, English, Science, and so forth. After the pathfinders have been linked to the cyber library's instruction area, examine each to locate potential hyperlinks. If you have made a reference to searching Scribner's Writers database to find a biographical sketch of Jane Austen, make Scribner's Writers database a hyperlink within the pathfinder so that students can simply click and begin using it. After you have established links to other areas of the cyber library, evaluate it once more to see if there are other links that you can also add to make it even more useful. Most pathfinders in printed formats could definitely benefit from the addition of links to search engines, subject directories, and specific Internet sites. If you do decide to create an online pathfinder, visit the megasite A Pathfinder for Constructing Pathfinders (http://home.wsd.wednet.edu/pathfinders/path.htm#internet). It contains instructions, ideas, graphics, and a host of links to other pathfinder and subject guide sites.

Tutorials

Online tutorials are one of the most valuable components to the instructional services that are offered through a school cyber library because they: (1) provide library instruction on a 24/7 basis; (2) support multiple access; (3) give students a chance to work with the actual research tool as they follow the instructions; (4) provide an opportunity for self-paced learning; and (5) furnish students with immediate feedback concerning their progress. When searching for tutorial design ideas or creating links to tutorials, consider ones that give students the opportunity to read the instructions on one side of the screen while working with the actual research tool. The National Cathedral School Library (http://gold.ncs .cathedral.org/uslibrary_tutorials/internet_home.htm) has several online tutorials about searching the Internet and electronic resources including Wilson Biographies Plus, Ebsco's Host, ProQuest Platinum, and SIRS. The Internet tutorial allows students to read the instructions for image searching, using the search engine AltaVista, while simultaneously performing the search in AltaVista. Once students are successful at image searching, they can continue using the actual research tool linked to the tutorial module for images of personal interest. One of the best library tutorials that also fits this model is TILT (http://tilt.lib.utsystem.edu/). Designed by sixteen subject specialty librarians at the University of Texas, it is the first tutorial to base its instruction on the set of information literacy (IL) standards delineated in the IL position statements of the American Library Association. The tutorial has also garnered several professional awards for innovative instruction. Modules are completed within a sequence that graduates from easy to intellectually challenging. An entertaining research tool called a "Tiltometer" helps students determine which resources would be most helpful in answering specific types of research questions, and the game "It's Time to Play Think Fast" provides outstanding feedback on the student's progress. TILT has an open publication license and SLMSs may easily link to it. Although it is not recommended for elementary or middle school students, high school students can definitely use it successfully.

Designing Tutorials

SLMSs have a number of interesting tutorial choices. You may link to ones that have been critically reviewed, design your own, or rely on a combination of the two. Designing your own tutorial has several advantages. First, you can tailor the information to meet the needs and interests of the students whom you instruct. If you are designing an online catalog tutorial, you can provide examples of titles, authors, and subjects from the SLMC's collection. Second, a self-designed tutorial can also reinforce a library unit on, for example, the American civil rights movement, since all of the tutorial questions, searches, and keywords can be taken from the unit. Third, self-designed tutorials are more reliable than linked ones. SLMSs can count on them being available on the days and times when they are scheduled to teach. Finally, if users encounter problems with a specific aspect of it, the tutorial can be modified at a moment's notice. For SLMSs who decide to design their own tutorials, there are a number of outstanding sites that can provide assistance and inspiration. Learning on the Web (http://teleeducation.nb.ca/lotw/) features a trainer-oriented tutorial to show how to start planning and creating Web-based instructional tutorials (Junion-Metz 2000, 37).

Tutorial Coverage

The biggest tutorial problem that SLMSs face is selecting tutorial-enhancing areas of the curriculum. One place to turn for coverage assistance is the information literacy position statement published by the American Association of School Librarians (http://www.ala.org/aasl/positions/ps_infolit.html). It provides SLMSs with an outline of the steps that are necessary for students to achieve information literacy. Based on these guidelines, SLMSs may wish to search or design tutorials that cover the following areas:

- **Information Needs**—Link to or design tutorials that assist students in correctly identifying what they need to know to complete assignments. Sites that support highlighting keywords, using related search terms, and end in posing questions, hypotheses, thesis statements, or topic sentences are important to include.

- **Search Strategy Formulation**—Find or provide sites that help students identify the types of information they need, ways to organize it, and potential information sources (e.g., the SLMC print collections, electronic databases, the Internet, and so forth). Identify or create sites that establish criteria and provide practice for evaluating the collected information based on authority, accuracy, and timeliness.

- **Location and Access Skills**—Identify or design tutorials that assist students to locate and use online catalogs, electronic databases, cyber libraries, community-based information, and subject experts and to access information within resources through the use of indexes, table of contents, cross-references, keyword searching, and Boolean logic.

- **Information Assessment and Understanding**—Design or link to tutorials that provide opportunities for students to practice scanning material to identify major ideas and relevant topic information, to differentiate between primary and secondary sources, to recognize different points of view including bias and propaganda, to categorize information into useful sections, and to select the most appropriate information for their topics.

- **Information Interpretation**—Locate or furnish tutorials that aid students in taking appropriate notes, understanding the differences between paraphrasing and quoting, organizing the information they have collected, synthesizing it with previously gathered information, and formulating appropriate conclusions based on the materials they have gathered.

- **Information Presentation**—Find or design tutorials that help students select the most appropriate format for presenting information including written reports, videotapes, dramatic productions, Web sites, or speeches. Locate sites that explain and show them the need for source attribution and bibliographic citations.

- **Information Evaluation**—Create or provide tutorials that give students guidance on evaluating their final product. What areas of the product could use improvement? Did their conclusions and final products satisfy the assignment directions? Is there a need for revision?

Materials for Classes

SLMSs who have designed instructional units for teachers in various classes may wish to transfer these units to their cyber library for easy updating of the syllabus, unit timeline, and questions. If a unit has been designed prior to the Internet, SLMSs can update the unit by creating links to Internet sites, search engines, subject directories, and electronic subscription resources. Creating Web pages for instructional units also saves time when students misplace or lose their assignments. SLMSs can simply refer them to the cyber library and they can print it or read it online.

Webquests

Webquests are instructional units that rely mainly on online sources to complete assignments. A typical Webquest can feature tutorials, series of activities, educational games, unit and lesson plans, hot lists, online reference tools, and lists of printed materials. Their only creative limitation is the imagination of the SLMS. This type of instructional unit gives teachers and SLMSs the opportunity to collaborate, to choose from a treasure house of excellent Internet sites, and to design units that look like they have been prepared by a professional publisher by using color, cool graphics, icons, fonts, and hip language. If SLMSs are too busy to create their own, there are megasites containing lists of Webquests in various subject areas that will probably match the school's curriculum needs.

A recent one worth examining was noted in the *School Library Journal*'s "Site of the Month" column. It is called Solar System Webquest (http://www .monet.k12.ca.us/challenge/Teacher_Webpages/OWStemigD/SolarSystemWebquest /solar_system_webquest.htm). Designed for middle school students, this excellent Webquest example site requires students to build a mock science museum. The site instructs third graders to build their own exhibits on planets that are assigned to them. Some of the students prepared posters, assumed the role of a travel agent, constructed models of planets, and even designed an interactive on-line display. Webquests are appropriate for students of any age. There is an excellent site for secondary students that was designed by students for the ThinkQuest competition sponsored by Advanced Network and Services, a non-profit organization that is dedicated to improving education through the use of technology. Called Think Different (http://users.cwnet.com/phillips/wq.thinkdifferent .htm), its purpose is to expose secondary school students to people such as Rosa Parks, Caesar Chavez, Ansel Adams, and Richard Feynman who have thought "out of the box." Students choose one of these "different thinkers" to write about, click on their name to receive biographical information, and are guided in their writing by a useful chart of punctuation, spelling, and grammar rules.

Webquests have the advantage of providing instruction on a 24/7 basis and of supporting quick modifications, additions, and interactivity. They make an outstanding contribution to cyber library instructional services.

Web Rings

Designed in 1994 by Dennis Howe, the creator of EUROPa (expanding unidirectional ring of pages), Web rings are sites that are dedicated to one subject area. They are developed by a group of subject experts who are supervised by a ringmaster. The ringmaster's responsibilities consist of directing future collection site development and maintaining and monitoring the selected links. Web Ring (http://www.webring.com) offers free administrative controls for starting a chain and maintaining links. Its Ring World site contains nine subject categories ranging from the arts and humanities to health, recreation, and sports. Web rings offer a SLMS consortium the opportunity to share collection development in areas where all of the schools cover the same curriculum area. If each SLMS provides Internet resources for a unit on the American civil rights movement, a Web ring would be a very appropriate Internet vehicle for dividing up and sharing various collection responsibilities. One SLMS may agree to compile a list of megasites on the topic, while another might undertake responsibility for finding links to biographical sketches about the most important people involved in the movement. All of the schools then have access to an excellent collection of age-appropriate and SLMS-evaluated resources throughout the year (Stielow 1999, 145–146).

Recommended Internet Sites

The following sites supplement many of the instructional areas that are recommended to include in a cyber library. Some of them provide instruction for original design such as pathfinders and tutorials. Other sites are recommended because of the resources they offer for potential adoption to your cyber library.

Materials for Classes

Yale–New Haven Teachers Institute Curriculum Units
http://www.cis.yale.edu/ynhti/curriculum/units/

Do not think that students in grades 7–12 cannot complete some of these full-text units, because they can. Others may be modified to suit their vocabulary and comprehension level. There are hundreds at this site and they range from the humanities to the physical sciences. Even if you and a faculty member have decided to design your own Webquest or instructional unit, browse through the selection here first, because you will be guaranteed to come up with additional ideas, resources, or insights.

Information Literacy

Information Literacy and the Net
http://www.bham.wednet.edu/literacy.htm

Bellingham Public Schools in Bellingham, Washington, lead the nation in mounting helpful public policies and documents about technology on the Internet. This excellent site is no exception to the high quality of their previous online publications. It features an eight-hour staff development course about how to use student investigations as a means to incorporate information literacy skills. It is extremely thorough in scope and would be an excellent place to start looking if SLMSs are thinking of developing their own IL curriculum.

Purdue University's Online Writing Lab
http://owl.english.purdue.edu

Several requirements of information literacy state that students must be able to communicate and present the information they have learned in appropriate formats. These skills call for the ability to write a cohesive paper, report, and so forth rather than the ability to identify terms and correctly search electronic resources. This writing lab contains all the writing and communication help that students need including assistance for developing thesis statements, building support for them, drawing appropriate conclusions, and checking spelling and grammar.

Reference Services

Bernie Sloan's Bibliography of Sources on Electronic Reference
http://www.lis.uiuc.edu/~b-sloan/digiref.html

If you need more information about how to set up a virtual reference desk or a warning about some of the problems you may encounter, this is place to visit for citations to articles, discussion lists, and newsgroups.

Houston Public Library—Interactive–Ask a Librarian
http://www.hpl.lib.tx.us/hpl/interactive/answers.html

Houston Public Library has an outstanding FAQ section about e-mail reference. It lists the types of questions that librarians are able to answer by e-mail and the sorts of queries that do not loan themselves to an e-mail response. The librarians also provide a useful set of sample reference questions and answers so that their patrons understand the areas where librarians can provide an answer and the areas where they can only recommend resources to help find the answers.

Public Library of Charlotte and Mecklenburg County
(North Carolina)–Ask a Librarian
http://www.plcmc.lib.nc.us/online/asklib/question.asp

This is an excellent site to visit if your school library consortium is thinking of setting up any type of online reference assistance. In addition to providing a traditional e-mail reference question form, the site also directs users to a Research Support service (http://www.plcmc.lib.nc.us/sharedPages /ResearchSupport.htm) that guides students and other users through the information-seeking process. It supplies links not only to a helpful information specialist but also to online resources that consist of relevant Internet sites and online databases.

Subject Guides/Pathfinders

Multnomah County Library's Social Issues Page
http://www.multnomah.lib.or.us/lib/homework/sochc.html

Besides the pathfinder megasite that is referred to in this chapter, you may also want to link to this Oregon Public Library's set of social issues pathfinders. Students in grades 7–12 are always asking for the pro and con sides about issues including gun control, abortion, euthanasia, and affirmative action. This site has divided every debatable topic into "Megasite," "Support," "Oppose," and "Legislation" categories. The sponsoring organization is included in the annotation so that students can be introduced to the idea of bias and propaganda.

Tutorials

Computer Training Tutorials
http://www.ckls.org/~crippel/computerlab/tutorials/index.html

Sponsored by the Central Kansas Library System in Great Bend, Kansas, this site features seven tutorials including "Cleaning Your Mouse," "Keyboard," and "Developing Web Vision." The latter tutorial teaches students how to identify salient information on the Internet. Of all the tutorial sites that have been reviewed in various professional publications, this is the most thorough in terms of tutorial ideas ranging from hard disk cleanup to power protection. Begin with this site if you are planning to develop an extensive tutorial library because you will discover areas for tutorials that you have probably never even thought about.

Do We Really Know Dewey?
http://tqjunior.thinkquest.org/5002/

This site was created by students for the ThinkQuest competition. Designed for all ages, the tutorial is a graduated series of modules for learning the Dewey decimal system. It starts with a brief biographical sketch of Melvil Dewey followed by explanations of: (1) the difference between fiction and nonfiction books; (2) how materials are classified and shelved; (3) how call numbers are selected; (4) how to read library shelves to locate a book; and (5) what call numbers look like on the spine of a book. The site concludes with a challenging set of puzzles and quizzes.

Finding Information on the Internet
http://www.lib.berkeley.edu/TeachingLib/Guides/Internet/Findinfo.html

Considered one of the best tutorials for students in grades 10–12, its contents are robust and the site contains instructor scripts, worksheets, and lessons on specific subjects. Berkeley public librarians have been extremely thorough in designing tutorials for various Web browsers, search engines, subject directories, and even the invisible Web. The latter features specialized searchable databases that are very useful for reference questions and are rarely found by the better-known search engines.

The Good, the Bad, and the Ugly
http://lib.nmsu.edu/staff/susanbeck/evalu.html

Some interactivity exists in this Web evaluation site that links to an actual Web site for actual Web evaluation. It is authored by Susan E. Beck and sponsored by New Mexico State University and is suitable for grades 10–12 and faculty.

Learning on the Web
http://teleeducation.nb.content/lotw2001/c2index.html
If you are interested enough to create your own tutorials, this site will show you how to begin. The authors, Rory McGreal and Michael Elliott of Teleeducation in New Brunswick, Canada, use a tutorial to illustrate various concepts, techniques, and principles of Web searching. Although the site is based on a textbook that is being marketed at the site, Chapters 1 and 2 are so thoroughly explained that they can be used as blueprints for your own tutorials.

National Cathedral School Internet Survival Tutorial
http://gold.ncs.cathedral.org/uslibrary_tutorials/internet_home.htm
Based on the television program *Survivor*, this tutorial series provides students in grades 7–12 with interactive lessons about formulating search plans, using actual subject directories and search engines, and searching the online catalog, Ebsco's Host, Wilson Biographies Plus, and SIRS databases. The program prompts students throughout the tutorial with survivor hints and a "show me" feature that contains the correct search formulation in the actual search engine. A survivor quest or scavenger hunt completes the modules. The authors are Kathleen W. Craver and Sue Gail Spring.

Teach Yourself . . . the Internet
http://www.library.ucla.edu/libraries/college/instruct/instgui.htm
Students probably have to be in grades 10–12 to appreciate this sophisticated site for understanding the flow of information and how to evaluate a Web site. The initial tutorial shows you how information first appears in a newspaper, then a chapter in a book, and finally becomes sufficiently newsworthy to merit publication as a book. The second site Who Dunnit It? provides an interactive exercise that challenges students to correctly identify the source or sponsor of a Web site. It is outstanding. If you decide that it is too advanced for your students, use it for a faculty workshop.

Webquests

Blue Web'n Learning Sites Library
http://www.kn.pacbell.com/wired/bluewebn/
Browsable by contents, subject areas, or grade levels, this Webquest site is outstanding. The content quality and sheer number of sites may even discourage SLMSs from designing their own Webquests. Visit this site before you reinvent the wheel and mine the collection for ideas for your own future Webquests.

The Webquest Page
http://edweb.sdsu.edu/webquest/webquest.html
This excellent megasite is sponsored by the Educational Technology Department at San Diego State University. It features a useful training materials page for SLMSs who wish to learn how to design their own Webquests; a search engine; and a What's New? section. It is also searchable by an annotated subject and grade-level matrix that indicates exactly how many Webquests are available about such topics as art and music for students in grades 4–5. The Webquests are creative and stimulating. For literature-loving librarians, "A Dickens of a Quest" would definitely take first prize in any Webquest contest.

References

American Association of School Librarians. 2001. "Information Literacy on Information Problem Solving." http://www.ala.org/aasl/positions/ps_infolit.html (July 15, 2001).

Amey, Larry, and Stephen Elliott. 1997. "Serving the Cyberteen: Library Service for the 21st Century Adolescent." *VOYA* 20 (April): 14–20.

Craver, Kathleen W. 1994. *School Library Media Centers in the 21st Century*. Westport, CT: Greenwood.

———. 1997. *Teaching Electronic Literacy: A Concepts-Based Approach for School Library Media Specialists*. Westport, CT: Greenwood.

Dupuis, Elizabeth A. 2001. "Automating Instruction." *LJ Netconnect: Supplement to Library and School Library Journal* (Spring): 21–22.

Foster, Janet. 2000. "Reference Questions on Your Web Site." *Internet Spotlight* (July/August): 1–2. http://www.pla.org/webref_jul-aug00.html (January 25, 2002).

Junion-Metz, Gail. 2000. "Teacher Knows Best: Some Web Worthy Tutorials to Help You Create Your Own." *School Library Journal* 46 (May): 37.

Lagace, Nettie. 1999. "Establishing Online Reference Services." In *The Internet Public Library Handbook*, ed. Joseph Janes et al. New York: Neal-Schuman.

Lubans, John. 1998. "Key Findings on Internet Use among Students." http://www.lib.duke.edu /lubans/docs/key/key.html (May 21, 2001).

Minkel, Walter. 2000. "So Far I've Only Found His Head." *School Library Journal* 46 (April): 37.

Oberman, Cerise. 1991. "Avoiding the Cereal Syndrome, or Critical Thinking in the Electronic Environment." *Library Trends* 39 (Winter): 189–202.

Oder, Norman. 2001. "Is Online Tutoring in Your Library's Future?" *LJ Netconnect: Supplement to Library and School Library Journal* (Summer): 6.

Porter, Lynnette R. 1997. *Creating the Virtual Classroom: Distance Learning with the Internet.* New York: Wiley.

Sears, JoAnn, and Andrew Wohrley. 2000. "Guidelines for an Excellent Website." In *Cybrarian's Manual 2,* ed. Pat Ensor. Chicago: American Library Association.

Stielow, Frederick, ed. 1999. *Creating a Virtual Library: A How-to-Do-It Manual for Librarians.* New York: Neal-Schuman.

Thornton, Amy. 2000. "Licensed to Teach." In *Cybrarian's Manual 2*, ed. Pat Ensor. Chicago: American Library Association.

Wiggins, Richard W. 2000. "Coping with the Trillion-Page Web." *LJ Netconnect: Supplement to Library and School Library Journal* (Fall): 26–28.

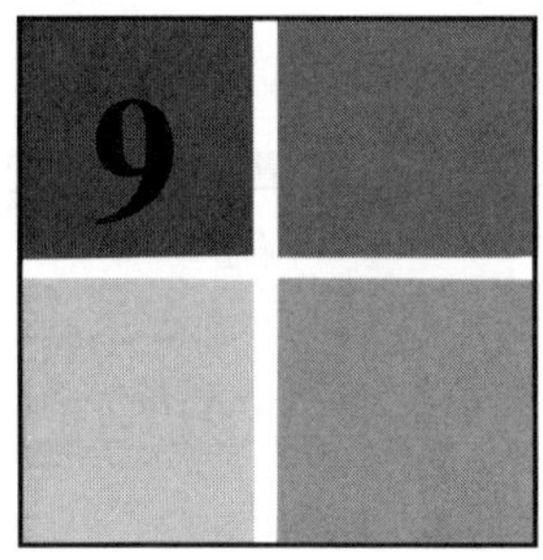

Managing and Evaluating Cyber Libraries

Maintenance Needs

A cyber library collection is more available to the public than are the collection, furniture, newspapers, books displays, and bulletin boards in the conventional SLMC. In the latter type of library, SLMSs regularly straighten the chairs, shelve the day's newspapers, display new periodicals, and update new bulletin boards for a well-defined user group. A cyber library is open to any electronic visitor on any given day or time. Its collection and information must not only be in order but also needs to be current, accurate, and relevant. During certain times of the year, SLMSs evaluate parts of the SLMC's collection to determine if a subject area needs additional acquisitions or if the material has become outdated and should be withdrawn. SLMSs may also modify part of a lesson plan to introduce students to a new online database or reference book. Many of these activities are similar in a cyber library with one exception. Cyber libraries can be straightened up, modified, and updated much more quickly. In a conventional SLMC, there is a tangible product that must be processed in some way whether it is to be acquired for or withdrawn from the collection. A cyber library's collection can be updated or weeded at the click of a mouse. The speed with which acquisitions, modifications, updates, and withdrawals can be performed is deceptive when it comes to maintaining a cyber library, because it is easier to acquire and include more sites, programs, and services than we can competently maintain. A conventional SLMC confines our collection to the allotted number of shelves, our user groups to the number of tables and chairs in the rooms, and our programs, and services to the degree that we have support staff.

When deciding the size of a cyber library, it may be helpful to consider the following developmental stages. Each cyber library stage has certain characteristics that determine the maintenance level. Although you may decide to design a stage-one cyber library, do not think of it as a permanent level. Remember that the only constant involving computers is change. As new hardware and software designs improve access and storage capabilities, it will become even easier to move from different stages and to maintain them.

Stage-One Cyber Libraries

The following characteristics describe stage-one cyber libraries that require minimal maintenance.

- Employ a single school team approach rather than a consortium of SLMSs.

- Comprise less than 30 MB.

- Are hosted off-site by a nonprofit institution.

- Contain little or no internally developed content.

- Feature a subscription Web library from an education portal or provide a link to a well-reviewed one.

- Provide access to no more than three subscription electronic resources.

- Rely on externally developed instructional links for tutorials and other pedagogical techniques.

- Employ externally developed pathfinders and subject guides.

- Maintain a minimal number of links in the cyber reading room.

- Require less than one hour per week to check links and update content.

- Receive minimal school-based technical support.

Stage-Two Cyber Libraries

The following components are present in stage-two cyber libraries that require a medium level of maintenance.

- Employ either a single school team approach or a small consortium of SLMSs.

- Comprise more than 30 MB.

- Are hosted either on-site within the school's Web server or pay for off-site hosting.

- Contain a mixture of internally developed and externally developed Web content.

- Feature a subscribed Web library from an educational portal or an internally developed one of less than 500 annotated links.

- Provide access to more than three subscription electronic databases.

- Rely on a mixture of internally developed and externally developed tutorials and other pedagogical techniques.

- Employ a significant number of internally developed pathfinders and subject guides.

- Maintain a substantial number of internally developed and externally developed links in the cyber reading room.

- Provide a minimal form of communication through e-mail within the cyber library that may support reference questions, reading guidance, or research consultation.

- Require more than three hours per week to check links and update content.

- Receive school-based technical support.

Stage-Three Cyber Libraries

The following elements define stage-three cyber libraries that require maximal maintenance.

- Usually employ a consortial or school district approach to design, construction, and maintenance.

- Comprise more than 30 MB.

- Are hosted either on-site at a dedicated library Web server or pay for off-site hosting.

- Contain a substantial amount of internally developed content.

- Feature a consortium-based Web library numbering more than 1,000 annotated links. The Web library may also contain a search engine and some descriptive cataloging metadata for the sites.

- Provide access to six or more subscription electronic resources.

- Rely mainly on internally developed instructional links for tutorials and other pedagogical techniques.

- Employ internally developed, hyperlinked pathfinders and subject guides.

- Maintain a substantial number of internally developed links in the cyber reading room.

- Provide forms of communication involving e-mail and forms and/or software that support instructional services such as a virtual reference desk, homework help, readers' advisory, or interactive reading programs.

- Require additional support staff to monitor links, update content, and respond to online communication involving reference assistance and other services.

- Receive readily available technical support from a school district–based educational technology department of more than two members.

Striking a Balance

Although these three maintenance stages can overlap, it is important to find a balance among them that allows you to design a cyber library that will expand collection access and services beyond the conventional SLMC but not at the expense of maintaining its collection of books and videos and the real time that is spent providing one-on-one help to students and faculty. Maintaining a cyber library involves technical, educational, financial, and professional issues that should be resolved before construction and design begins.

Technical Internal Maintenance Issues

Improving a cyber library's effectiveness and maintaining its technical accuracy are important tasks. Technical maintenance occurs at two levels: internal and external. Inconsistent internal maintenance can affect the speed of the site and slow the monitoring and updating links process. It is the technical foundation for the entire cyber library and SLMSs or technical support members that should verify that all of the following steps have been taken to ensure that the framework is strong and in place for future growth and enhancements. Most Web-editing software programs are designed to help with internal organization, but it is still vital that you adhere to the following internal site guidelines:

- Establish a consistent plan for naming files and directories.

- Select recognizable terms, words, and abbreviations for file and directory names.

- Employ natural-language hierarchies. For example, if your main directory is to be Reading Lists, do not name it R103. Use the broad term "reading lists" so that sublists such as Halloween, Holiday, and other bibliographies can fall naturally within it and be recognized easily by support staff who may be responsible for inserting updating materials.

- Understand the character limitations of the selected Web-authoring program and operating system. Many programs limit file names to no more than eight characters, a period, plus a three-character extension (e.g., filename.doc).

- Employ lowercase letters since some computer systems can treat a capital letter as a different character.

- Recognize that file name extensions can define specific format types (e.g., html, txt, gif, jpg).

- Confirm that the extensions are appropriate to the file type. Sometimes a software system will automatically add the extensions to the file. Do not delete them. They let you know that the file contains just text (txt) or a picture (jpg).

- Use natural language to describe all files and directories. The cyber library's reading list for Halloween is harder to identify and update the following year with an address such as "/hallowe.edu/f-11.htm" than it would be with an address like "/hallowe.edu/readingl/20-10.htm."

- Apply a system to numbering home pages. If you name home-page file names with "index.htm" or "default.html," site visitors will be ensured of accessing the cyber library's home page rather than a list of internal directories.

- Organize directories and keep them clearly defined. The home page should be in a directory with the domain name (e.g., ncs.cathedral.org /library). All other files belong in subdirectories of this directory. Graphics files, for example, should be stored in a separate directory to facilitate access and updating.

- Verify that you have either duplicated the site in another directory or that you have a backup tape system for it. Avoid at all costs storing the backup copy on the working computer in case it crashes (Stielow 1999, 129–130).

Once this internal maintenance foundation is in place, school cyber libraries at stages one and two of development may wish to consider purchasing a software program that sweeps the site. Mid-Hudson Library System (Poughkeepsie,

NY), for example, used a reasonably priced program called Site Sweeper (http://www.sitetech.com) to discover internal broken links, slow pages, missing file attributes, distorted images, and duplicate title name problems. The software ensures them that the internal structure of their site is well designed and set up for easy internal maintenance (Stielow 1999, 139).

Technical External Maintenance Issues

A well-organized and consistently maintained internal system facilitates external monitoring and link checking. All SLMSs have witnessed students' frustration when they go to retrieve an "available" book only to discover that it is not on the shelf. The same situation is true in a cyber library. Users expect a link to open and be available to them when they click on it. Checking and monitoring internally developed and externally developed links must occur frequently if a cyber library is to continue to serve as a reliable resource for the school community. Link checking must be performed on a scheduled basis for the following reasons:

- The Internet site may have moved and posted a notice. Sometimes Webmasters post a new address when the site is going to be moved and sometimes they program an automatic redirection so that users do not have to type in the new address. At other times, the site has moved and the Webmaster has not left a forwarding address. Then the site must be relocated and the SLMS or a support staff member must replace the old URL with the new URL to ensure continued access.

- The Internet site is dead. Dead links are a nuisance just as lost books are to SLMSs in a conventional SLMC. In some cases, the site has truly vanished for lack of funds, designer interest, or time on the part of the site provider. Many times, however, the site is still flourishing and the creator has neglected to leave a forwarding address. In this scenario, the designated link checker must be a skillful searcher by typing in variations of the old site address to see if some small change has occurred or performing a title search within quotation marks in a large search engine such as Google or HotBot to see if he/she can find its new location.

- A "site forbidden" message appears that indicates the site may be restricting access to users of specific computers or domains. In this case, the link checker may try to correspond with the provider to find out why the site has denied access, try the site again at a later date, or delete the site from the cyber library's collection.

- The site is experiencing technical problems involving congestion, a downed server, a domain name server problem, or an external router problem. The best solution in this case is to record the link as a problem and try to open it again several days later rather than deleting it immediately (Carter 1999, 72–75).

Knowing all the problems that can occur with broken links may help you decide on an approach to link checking. There are a number of automated link-checking programs that will check URLs to see if they are still opening. Net Mechanic.com (http://netmechanic.com) is a link-checking program that is free to small cyber libraries. If a cyber library is at stage three, however, it should purchase a special software product to perform at least the first round of link checking.

Many cyber library specialists do not recommend the use of a link checker because it produces false positives. An automated link-checker will deliver a list of sites that indeed may be dead and should be deleted, but it also will print a list of links that may have moved or be temporarily busy. Some cyber librarians, however, recommend using automated link-checking programs because they can produce a list of potential broken links that are at least smaller than the time it would take to manually check each site to see if is open and working. After an automatic link-checker produces a set of broken links, then SLMSs can employ support staff or trained volunteers to check the list to determine which sites have moved, vanished, or changed addresses. A decision to use an automated link-checker will need to be based on the number of links that need to be maintained. If the cyber library has a thousand or more links, an automated link-checker would still save SLMSs valuable time and effort.

Educational Maintenance Issues

Although it is possible to rely on trained student volunteers for link checking, just as most SLMSs do when they need the shelves read in a conventional SLMC, educational maintenance requires the training of professional SLMSs. Maintaining a cyber library necessitates examining sites because their contents may have changed, weeding sites because they are no longer relevant to the curriculum, acquiring new Internet sites, and responding to user requests for additional sites. It calls for subject expertise across a range of subjects, a thorough knowledge of the curriculum, awareness of Internet review sources, and diplomacy when users suggest an inappropriate site. This is a cyber library maintenance area that can take some time to complete and is the primary reason why

SLMSs may wish to consider linking to other Web libraries because they may not have the time to be responsible for performing the following tasks:

- Check externally developed sites to determine if the content has changed. Many times the focus of the material has not changed but new features have been added that require SLMSs to rewrite the site's annotation. A U.S. census data site that covers 1990, for example, may now include new data from the 2000 census.

- Confirm that sites are still relevant to the collection. If a cyber library contains sites of a topical nature, the SLMS needs to delete them when they are no longer relevant. Teachers sometimes develop narrow units that are based on an area of special interest only to them. If they leave the school, the sites should be deleted since they will not be used by another faculty member.

- Acquiring new sites that reflect the needs and interests of the students and faculty can be time consuming even when SLMSs subscribe to current awareness listservs and periodicals. Finding new sites is, however, necessary to maintain a cyber library's relevance and currency. New sites appear that are improvements over older ones. A simple site of the periodic table may need to be replaced with one that furnishes the periodic table plus the commercial uses and products involved with each chemical element. A site about French artists may be replaced with a similar one that now features a convenient search engine to facilitate the searching process.

- Annotating and cataloging new sites is time consuming even when SLMSs cut and paste the site's description with quotation marks around it as part of their site summary. The decision to increase searching access by site author, keyword, and subject is not to be undertaken without considering the maintenance time. While summarizing a site is considered mandatory, adding descriptive elements is still an option for most SLMSs because of the time factor.

- Respond to user suggestions. This is another maintenance task that can be useful and bothersome at the same time. Students have taken the lead with computers much more than adults have. They talk about new developments, cool sites, and new search engines and share this information with each other more frequently than do their parents and teachers. SLMSs may be surprised to find excellent suggestions for the cyber library from them in various subject and recreational areas. However, students sometimes suggest some pretty whacky sites and their feelings must always be accommodated when their ideas are rejected.

Financial Maintenance Issues

SLMSs who are in the first version of a stage-one cyber library do not face many financial maintenance issues. An educational portal can provide free Web creation template software, linkage to a Web library of school-related Web sources, maintain their own internal link system, and troubleshoot problems with broken links. Sooner or later, however, SLMSs with stage-one cyber libraries will desire to produce some of their own hyperlinked pathfinders or sets of annotated links for class assignments or research projects. Assessing the cost to maintain a cyber library is dependent on which stage library SLMSs desire to construct. Internally developed content, however, is directly proportional to the amount of financial maintenance that is required. Although there is no formula for estimating the funding necessary for a specific amount of internally developed content, SLMSs can try to respond to the following set of questions to help them decide the cost needed to maintain a stage-two or -three cyber library.

- Would the idea of a cyber library consortium make it easier to obtain maintenance funding? Is it easier to persuade school administrators to fund a consortial-based cyber library with hardware, software, and additional support personnel than it is to solicit funds for a single school team approach?

- What are the pros and cons of using an on-site Web server? Is it less expensive to access a Web server off campus? Who will pay for server software updates, provide for backup, and troubleshoot problems? How frequently can an off-site server be updated? Are SLMSs allowed to do it or must the information be sent to the company's Webmaster?

- At what point will a cyber library require either changes in job descriptions for support staff or the hiring of additional personnel to perform monitoring, link checking, and annotating tasks?

- What are the cost benefits of software programs that assist with maintenance tasks such as Site Sweeper or a fee-based link-checking program?

Professional Maintenance Issues

Cyber libraries are not static as books stacked on shelves are. The electronic medium in which a cyber library resides is always undergoing change. New software is created, design styles change, and the means to offer communication services become easier. All of these changes require SLMSs and/or staff members to professionally maintain themselves by learning about the latest bells and whistles, discovering new instructional methods, and sharing their experiences with other cyber librarians. Here are some professional development activities that school cyber librarians may wish to engage in to maintain their cyber libraries.

- Subscribe to appropriate current awareness sites. Bigchalk.com, for example, provides several "Top Sites of the Week" that are designated as suitable for either elementary and secondary school students.

- Join or participate in local online or real cyber librarian discussion groups and discuss current problems and concerns.

- Read electronic and/or print publications that address cyber library issues.

- Attend conferences regarding cyber library design, construction, maintenance, and so forth.

- Enroll in a course about Web management and/or take an instructional course involving a Web-authoring program.

- Encourage support staff to take any Web-related courses that will assist them in managing and maintaining a cyber library.

- Visit vendor exhibits to learn about the latest cyber library technologies.

- Become an active in a cyber library consortium or try to form one to expand the school's current cyber library.

Cyber Library Evaluation

Technology has created an environment of unremitting change. Almost everyday new developments occur in computer hardware, software, and more importantly in the ability to store, organize, and communicate information. The search engine Google, for example, increased from 30 million pages to 1.3 billion in just two and one-half years (Dobrzynski 2001, 1). Access to information is no longer edifice and time bound. As a result, our students and faculty have come to expect that library materials in every format type be available on a 24/7 basis. They also expect us to remain current with all of the technological changes taking place and actively respond to them by providing improved electronic materials, databases, programs, and services. In this type of protean medium, evaluating a cyber library becomes an ongoing process from the day of its electronic debut.

Cyber Library Design Evaluation

There are two aspects to appraising a cyber library: design and usability. While the current design may be "state of the art," within a year it can probably be classified as second or third generation as new design standards emerge and are adopted by other libraries. Design needs to be looked at from a generation perspective. Most of us, for example, could probably classify a school library site that features clip art apples and little red schoolhouses as a first-generation cyber library. While the content may be rich with full-text materials, a cyber reading room, and tutorials, the design conveys a site that is considered out of date. Dated icons and overused clip art are the equivalent to the display of Beatles posters in a conventional SLMC. Students would feel as if they are entering a museum rather than a vital, active library containing new materials and exciting programs and services.

This analogy is weak in one perspective. In a conventional SLMC, students are required to enter with their classmates for instruction and research purposes. They are a captive audience. In a cyber library, they are not. They are visitors with many other electronic information options. The design of a cyber library is critical because it needs to capture and hold their interest. Just as SLMSs attempt to attract students with book displays and brightly colored posters, so must we captivate the users of our cyber libraries. Our only problem, however, is time. The pace of change in an electronic medium is much faster than it is in a conventional SLMC. To match this computerized tempo, we must constantly evaluate the look and feel of a cyber library. Here are some suggestions for evaluating the attractiveness of a cyber library.

- Whenever you see a list of "the ten most visited Web sites," evaluate them for all of their features. See if you can discern what is cool and current and why users revisit them.

- Check out car dealer sites. They usually contain the latest bells and whistles including interactivity, sound, and video. While you may not be able to afford any of the latest technologies, you will have an idea of what's hot in the area of design, navigation tools, and so forth.

- Return to library sites that you used as models to see if they have changed their organization or entrance structure. Notice if it now takes fewer clicks to get to frequently used information.

- Examine library sites to see if library terminology has changed. Are librarians using "information desk" rather than "reference desk"?

- Look at a site from an esthetic standpoint. What features do you consider "eye candy"? Can you incorporate them into your own cyber library?

Cyber Library Automated
Usability Tools

The most important evaluation of a cyber library is to determine its usability. SLMSs need to know, for example, if the cyber library's resources are user-friendly. Many of the methods that SLMSs rely on to determine usability in a conventional library are available in a cyber library. In a conventional library, SLMSs monitor circulation, title counts, the age of an item, and verification that the item is listed in a standard bibliography to determine its usability. In a cyber library, the following electronic tools are available to achieve similar objectives.

1. **Counters**—The function of this type of software is to allow SLMSs to collect information concerning how many times the cyber library is being accessed and which areas are receiving the most use. Most Web servers have this type of software installed so that the reports are generated automatically. Cyber librarians can use the data to determine, for example, if the cyber reading room is a more popular destination than the online catalog. It can also be employed to show if the cyber library is being used more often than other parts of the school's Web site, which can be extremely important as a justification measure for additional funding requests.

2. **Transaction Logs**—Many vendors of electronic resources either collect usage data and mail it to you periodically or provide options within their software for you to collect it. Examples of data include the number of information requests per database, the number of sessions, number of menu choices, quantity of items to examine, and the number of citations displayed. This information can be used not only to assess renewal of an electronic resource but also to determine if students are using it as a postinstructional tool.

3. **Network Usage Logs**—The information generated from a network log is useful to determine the load on the network or router, user access points, and peak times of use. SLMSs who are Web managers can use these statistics to justify budget increases for hardware and possibly support personnel.

4. **Cookies**—Most SLMSs think of cookies as tracking devices that vendors place on their sites to monitor our usage of their site, but cyber librarians can also install them to measure school cyber library traffic and use by individual users. Although cyber librarians may not be interested in discovering the usage of school-site computers, you may wish to know the addresses of remote users and which sites they are visiting most frequently in your cyber library. SLMSs who are in

need of budgetary justification may wish to employ a cookie service. One example, Net-Trak Services (http://www.net-trak.stats.net/) supports tracking of the following information: (1) each single hit to a page; (2) average number of hits per day; (3) total number of hits for the past two days; (4) past 100 hosts/IP addresses that visited the cyber library; and (5) individual browser counts and operating systems that visited the site. Vendors of cookie services also allow the user to program the number of pages that they wish to attach cookies. Cyber librarians could implant a cookie on the cyber reading room to see if students were accessing, for example, the summer reading lists (Stielow 1999, 136–138; Gregory 2000, 58–63).

Cyber Library Personalized Usability Tools

The previous usability tools are easy for SLMS to employ because they are generated automatically. They can definitely assist in quantitatively measuring use of a cyber library. They do not, however, measure the quality of its resources and the ease or difficulty that students or faculty may experience when accessing different parts of the site. Measuring this type of use requires surveys and assessments that can be performed with a focus group of students, a printed or online survey, or scripted with a pop-up box on the screen. The chosen method is dependent on time and justification factors. If SLMSs need this type of documentation for future funding, it may be worth the time to form focus groups ranging from inexperienced to experienced users to determine how their cyber library is used. If you wish to gather data to improve the look, contents, and navigation of the site, it may be timesaving to place an online survey on the cyber library site and make adjustments based on the respondents' recommendations. All of the following collection methods allow SLMSs to collect valuable qualitative user information.

1. **Focus Groups**—This is the most open-ended method to evaluate cyber library usability. While the questions can be standardized, the responses leave room for commentary and sometimes surprising revelations. Focus groups can be delineated by grade level, thus enabling SLMSs to determine how difficult the site is for seventh graders to use, for example, than it is for twelfth graders. Employed judiciously, this method may allow SLMSs to quickly ascertain usability problems and make the necessary modifications to the cyber library.

2. **Surveys (Online and Printed)**—Less open-ended than focus groups, this method allows SLMSs to pose questions in a variety of areas. It can also be a time-saver if SLMSs can motivate students and

faculty to respond to the survey through e-mail or an online form via the cyber library.

3. **Pop-Up Surveys**—Vendors are using this quick-and-dirty method to evaluate usability of a product. Sometime during actual use of a resource, a pop-up box appears on the screen that requests users to evaluate its usability. While many students and faculty may not take the time to respond to a survey about cyber library resources, they may be more likely to answer one or two questions that pop up within a specific resource. SLMSs should consider using this method to obtain a fast read on a new site or cyber library service.

Usability Questions

The paramount goal of a usability study is to find out what students and faculty experience when they visit the cyber library. If automated usage data indicate that students are spending the majority of their time accessing the online catalog, it could mean that they may find it the most useful of all the information resources or that they are finding it difficult to search and find material. The answers to these questions can be used to redesign various aspects of a cyber library site, to renew various fee-based resources, or to justify additional expenditures. Once you have constructed a cyber library, many of the questions about its usability will arise naturally. The following general queries can be easily modified into specific ones.

- How simple is it for a beginner to access all of the cyber library components?

- How simple is it for an experienced user to do the same? Are there shortcuts that could be installed for more experienced users?

- Is the cyber library easily navigated? Must users orient themselves each time they return to it?

- What types of mistakes do students make when they use the site? How easy is it for them to recover from a mistake without exiting from the cyber library?

- Do users find the instructional pathfinders, tutorials, and so forth helpful?

- How has the system worked for remote users? Has it been crashing, for example, on busy school nights with assignment deadlines? How fast does it load from home?

- How frequently do students experience sites that do not open?

- Are the subject hierarchies logical and easy to follow?

- Are there parts of the cyber library that should be moved to the first page and/or contents that should be moved to the third page?

- What sites are missing? Are there content areas that need more sites and information? (Hudson 2001, 12–15; Gregory 2000, 60–61)

Cyber Library
Evaluation Caveats

As soon as you search other sites to evaluate their design elements, navigational structure, and interactivity, you will know where your cyber library rests in comparison to other sites. Although it is important to be responsive to the fast pace of change, do not incorporate new ideas so quickly that you dramatically alter the look of your cyber library. Remember that you have spent time developing a site that may reflect the school's colors, logo, and general atmosphere. This type of overall design should remain as a foundation. Making many changes too frequently can disorient students and faculty. You must still provide them with an electronic anchor even though you may have changed the library term "circulation" to the more recognizable "checking out." Try to make changes gradually and in small increments rather than altering the entire site.

While the use of network logs and transaction logs does not violate users' privacy, the application of cookies can be a troublesome area for SLMSs. It is strongly advised that cyber librarians disclose any practice of collecting personally identifiable information about students or faculty and reveal the use they will make of the information.

Technical problems must also be considered if you decide to install software such as link checkers, cookies, and counters. Some of them may affect loading time and slow response time considerably. Be sure to check and test any additional evaluation software before you purchase and load it onto your cyber library.

Recommended Internet Sites

These sites include additional information about maintenance and evaluation issues. Some sites concerning training students as technology assistants are also included for SLMSs who may lack sufficient support staff to assist with some of these tasks.

Maintenance-Related Sites

Beginner's Central
http://www.northernwebs.com/bc

If you are going to have students serve as technology trainers and help maintain the cyber library by checking links, this comprehensive site can provide some useful ideas on what students should know. Use Chapter 1 that begins with an introduction to the Internet and includes lessons about simple and advanced searching techniques. Chapter 2 discusses off-line operations and file downloading, and Chapter 3 shows students how to configure e-mail and news readers. The site also has information on myths of the Internet and concludes with a set of problems to test student trainees' knowledge in each area.

ezAttach
http://www.ezAttach.com

i-drive
http://www.idrive.com

Myspace
http://www.freediskspace.com

SLMSs who do not have another location to store a backup of cyber library files can do so for free at any one of these three sites. All of them allow students and faculty to archive data at no charge. Plan to use this as a safe alternative to creating a backup file on the Web server. If the server were to crash, the backup would be lost too. Storing it off-site is a safer maintenance alternative.

Finding Stuff on the Web
http://www.ckls.org/~crippel/computerlab/tutorials/web
/searching/page1.html

This site contains a set of beginner tutorials that range from how to use a mouse to learning to type on an interactive keyboard. Many of the tutorials are relevant to specific software programs such as Microsoft Word and Excel, but there are many that will help you train students for hardware and software troubleshooting.

Evaluation Sites

Giving People What They Want: How to Involve Users in Site Design
http://www-106.ibm.com/developerworks/library/design-by-feedback
/expectations.html
> Provides an excellent series of questions that cyber librarians should answer regarding construction of their site. The questions can easily be adapted for a school cyber library online evaluation form.

Rosenfeld, Lou. 1997. "30-Minute Web Site Tune-Up." WebReview.com
(January 24)
http://www.webreview.com/1997/01_24/strategists/01_24_97_2.shtml
(January 25, 2002)
> Authored by librarian-trained Lou Rosenfeld, this article provides excellent criteria for formulating questions about what makes a Web site usable. It goes into detail about the need for a logical navigation system and understandable terminology. Each of the areas discussed contains a quick fix so that cyber librarians can quickly correct their mistakes.

Usability.gov
http://usability.gov/index.html
> Sponsored by the National Cancer Institute, this site contains an excellent overview of the topic. Pay particular attention to section "Lessons Learned" before designing a usability survey. It features a section on research-based Web design that is one of the most comprehensive on the Internet. Each guideline provides a scholarly citation to a study that supports the site's recommendations for a usable cyber library.

References

Carter, David S. 1999. "Building Online Collections." In *The Internet Public Library Handbook*, ed. Joseph Janes et al. New York: Neal-Schuman.

Dobrzynski, Judith H. 2001. "So, Technology Pros, What Comes after the Fall?" *New York Times* (July 29): 1, 11–12.

Gregory, Vicki L. 2000. *Selecting and Managing Electronic Resources*. New York: Neal-Schuman.

Hudson, Laura. 2001. "From Theory to Virtual Reality." *LJ Netconnect: Supplement to Library and School Library Journal* (Summer): 12–15.

Rosenfeld, Lou. 1997. "30-Minute Web Site Tune-Up." WebReview.com/ (January 24). http://www.webreview.com/1997/01_24/strategists/01_24_97_2. htmls (January 25, 2002).

Stielow, Frederick, ed. 1999. *Creating a Virtual Library: A How-to-Do-It Manual for Librarians*. New York: Neal-Schuman.

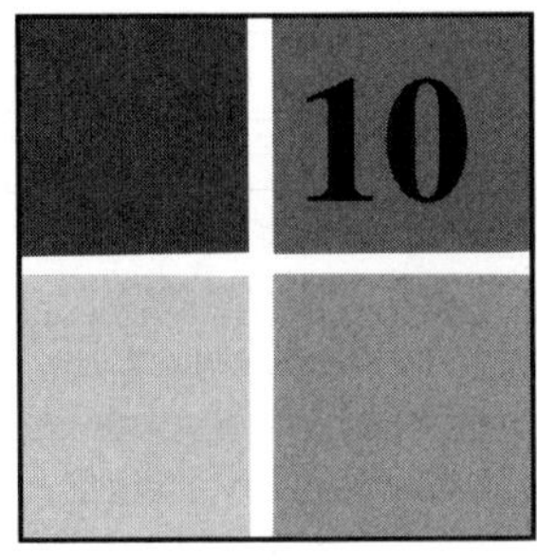

Promoting Cyber Libraries

The Need for Promotion

Cyber libraries need to be promoted for several reasons. First, because they do not have a physical presence. When a new conventional SLMC opens or a new addition is built, an open house is usually held. Students, faculty, staff, administrators, and parents are invited to attend. It is a justifiably exciting and worthwhile community event for it represents a commitment on the part of the majority of taxpayers that SLMCs are a vital and integral part of the educational process. Enclosed within the invitation to a new SLMC opening is a set of directions so that all of the invitees know where it is located. The new library is usually festooned with balloons and filled with flowers and plants. New books are on display and there are special activities that may feature a local author, storyteller, booktalks, and equipment demonstrations. Special bookmarks are distributed and the finale may be a birthday cake with the library's logo and one candle signifying its upcoming first year of operation.

In preparation for this event, the media have been contacted and are filming the opening for the local evening news. Flyers were distributed around town to publicize the upcoming open house. Announcements have been made on the radio about it. Everything has been done to ensure a large turnout and total enjoyment by everyone who comes. People leave with a memorable experience not only about the new SLMC but also of the school and perhaps the community in which they have decided to raise their children.

While a cyber library is just as thrilling to open, explore, and use as a conventional SLMC, promoting it at a higher level is an absolute necessity because it cannot be seen, smelled, or touched. People who did not attend the hypothetical open house of the conventional SLMC will pass a new building and be able to read the sign that identifies it as a SLMC. A cyber library, however, remains totally invisible unless you provide students, faculty, parents, staff, alumni, and administrators with online experiences that are memorable and the directions to visit it again and again.

The second reason for promoting a cyber library concerns some demographic, educational, and technological trends that are going to have a major impact on the future development of schools and SLMCs. Less than 25 percent of our community's households have children in them (Johnson 2000, 12). We are an aging population. If schools are going to be able to pass bond issues and operating referendums, they have to promote their services—not just to parents but to the community as well.

Competition among schools has also become a major factor. Years ago, independent schools were the only segment of the educational market that competed for students, but this is no longer the case. Charter schools, for example, are creating a competitive market among public schools. In less than a decade, more than 2,000 of them have been established. The appearance of magnet schools has also created a competition for the brighter students or students who wish to specialize in the physical sciences or the arts among schools within the same district.

The emergence of a "wired generation" has also changed approaches to teaching and learning. Students have higher and different expectations of what computers can and should do. They see them as an absolute necessity for acquiring information, entertaining themselves, and producing assignments and term papers (Ryan 1999, 123–124). This trend has created both an opportunity and a challenge for educators. Distance learning, once the province of higher education, is finally becoming a reality in secondary schools. The competition for virtual high schools has already started. Last spring, the North Central Association of Colleges and Schools accredited two university high schools that have offered correspondence courses to high school students for decades and authorized them to bestow high school diplomas. Both Indiana University High School and the University of Missouri at Columbia High School are accredited virtual schools. Students who have not succeeded in a traditional school or who are being home-schooled or just do not wish to attend a traditional school will soon be able to choose an online or virtual school as an option (National Association of Independent Schools 2001, 12).

The field of education is going to become more competitive and complex than it was a few years ago. Schools that feature new resources for online education and Web-based instruction will be at a decided advantage. This advantage can only be maintained, however, if they spend the time and effort to promote their services.

Promotional Barriers

Perhaps the higher barriers to promoting cyber libraries are the very people who so ably design them: SLMSs. Research shows that librarians perceive themselves generally as "undervalued, not recognized and not appreciated; they tend to convey a self-defeating image, and it is hard to find examples of positive writing from librarians other than those in the corporate world" (Houghton and Todd 2000, 284). Survey research conducted by the American Library Association reported that "although librarians thought fairly highly of themselves, they didn't believe that others did" (284). It is a waste of valuable time to try to ascribe perceptions to ourselves or our users. We must recognize, however, that SLMSs have an image problem.

Every profession has an image problem. Viewers of the film *Jurassic Park*, for example, heard the audience cheering when the actor portraying the lawyer was devoured by a huge Tyrannosaurus rex while cowering in an outhouse. Our professional image, unlike a lawyer's reputation for deception and obfuscation, is of shyness. This characteristic is so readily associated with our profession that Librarybook, Inc. entitled a new subscription newsletter "The Shy Librarian: Marketing and Public Relations for Librarians."

Shyness, introversion, and reluctance can be debilitating factors and costly ones in a competitive educational environment. Perhaps after mastering the learning curve of new software programs, educating ourselves about artistic design, searching for wonderful Internet sites, creating instructional tutorials, and packaging it into a brand-new cyber library, we think that it is crass to promote it. We may think of self-promotion as unseemly and not in keeping with our membership in a "helping profession."

New marketing techniques, however, show that effective publicity does not entail self-promotion. Professional promoters tell their clients to speak less of themselves and instead focus on the benefits provided to their users. Students and faculty do not care how special you think you are. They care about how much SLMSs can do for them and how much you care about them. School librarianship is a service profession, and our current, educational service is a cyber library that is invisible to our users unless we promote it.

Developing a Promotion Plan

If you had the luxury of affording a marketing firm, the first thing that its firm members would prepare for you is a plan to market your cyber library. They would ask you the following questions:

- What is the overall mission and specific goals of a cyber library?

- What are the specific objectives concerning the growth and direction of the cyber library? Do you wish, for example, to start adding modules such as internally developed tutorials soon?

- Do you have a demographic profile of the primary audience including its needs, interests, likes, and dislikes?

- In what position do you wish to be in comparison to other cyber libraries? Do you want to be professionally recognized for making a contribution to the field? Do you desire to simply maintain a presence on the Web without public acknowledgment? Do you wish to be on the cutting edge with a stage-three cyber library that features the latest bells and whistles?

- What combination of media and advertising do you want? Do you have some funds that you could use to promote your cyber library? What balance do you wish to strike between more expensive print promotion and online promotion?

Promotion Issues

Approach promoting a cyber library from a long-term rather than short-term perspective. In the twenty-first century, it is an ongoing process. Think of all the time, effort, and energy that you invested in creating a cyber library that has greatly expanded your collection and made many of your services available on a 24/7 basis. Now plan to spend the time to show, tell, teach, and talk about it to all the people who need to use it.

One of the recent trends in market research is a switch from the idea of market share to a focus on one-to-one marketing. Market share meant producing a quality product that everyone wished to buy. The more people who bought a company's product, for example, the greater the firm's share of the market. One-to-one marketing focuses on the client instead of the product. The goal is to sell many products to them over the course of a lifetime. Libraries, especially corporate and academic, are responding to this type of marketing when they provide online reference help, term paper counseling, readers' advisory, and research consultation services. They are responding to a need that has been fueled by e-mail, interactive Web sites, and customization features of products being sold online such as computers and many types of sports equipment.

The goal of one-to-one marketing is to achieve customer share instead of market share. For SLMSs, this means trying to get students, faculty, administrators, and parents to use some parts of the cyber library, then come back again for other services and be so pleased with it that they become free promoters of their cyber library (National Association of Independent Schools 2001, 13).

Drucker, in *Management Challenges for the 21st Century* (1999), recommends that we pose questions not about the cyber library but about our users or potential customers. We should be asking questions about what they want and need and what results they consider to be satisfactory (28–29). Analyzing the characteristics, needs, and interests of the primary and secondary user groups was described in Chapter 1. The data collected in this area helped SLMSs develop their mission statements, goals, and Web library contents. Refer to the capacity to segment the different user groups. Segmenting groups allows us to target or customize our services to them. If we serve high school seniors, why not offer a short cyber course called "College Connections" that shows them how to use college libraries, choose from a larger set of online databases, and identify new types of resources such as census data files, microfilm, and so forth? To make it fun, SLMSs can show them how to obtain housing information, see pictures and diagrams of actual dormitory rooms, find out how roommates are assigned, surf for college cafeteria menus, and where to go online to buy the least-expensive tickets to return home at Thanksgiving.

Segmenting a cyber library's audience also helps you determine how you wish to be viewed by your primary users. If your cyber library's mission is to offer a collection of filtered Internet sites that are only relevant to the curriculum, you will need to design instruction, pathfinders, and other aids that promote those services to students, faculty, staff, alumni, administrators, and parents (St. Lifer 2001, 44–46).

Promotion Team Members

Although segmenting the market of a cyber library allows you to customize your services, it does not mean that you should not enlist a variety of interested groups to support your message. Think of the following groups as members of your promotional team. They do not have to meet or get to know each other. You need, however, to remain in contact with all of them to keep them up-to-date and to solicit their advice and ideas for promoting the cyber library.

1. **Administrators**—After you have shown local administrators the cyber library, ask them for help in promoting it. If you know that a principal needs research on homework overload, for example, show him/her how he/she can obtain relevant articles and Internet sites from the cyber library's subscription electronic resources and the Web library. If local administrators are dutifully impressed with the product, offer to make a joint presentation of the cyber library to the board of education or board of governors. Administrators will enjoy seeing something as exciting and educational as a cyber library. Think of how many of their evenings are devoted to dreary issues including

security, budget, and finding teachers. Plan to take whatever time they will allot you and show them where they can find information relevant to something they may address at future meetings. At an opportune moment, ask members if they know anyone with marketing and public relations experience who would be willing to give you some free advice.

2. **Students**—They are not only your primary user group but also the sounding board for the message you want to promote about the cyber library. They are candid barometers of what sounds and looks cool and what will surely be an electronic flop. Form a teen advisory board composed of tech-savvy students and ones who love to read. Show them the parts of the cyber library that they will find most helpful for assignments, reading ideas, and computers. Ask them to be ambassadors for your cyber library. Would they be willing to help design a logo, posters, or talk the site up at future times for class announcements or meetings?

3. **Faculty**—They can be ardent supporters when you show them what is available for them and their classes in a cyber library. You may even hear a sigh of relief when they see all the resources organized and available at the click of a mouse. After you have presented the cyber library at a faculty meeting, identify the opinion makers at the school and request their assistance in promoting the site. Ask them if they know anyone in the marketing business who might be willing to help you promote the cyber library's resources more widely.

4. **Alumni**—They may or may not be active in your school setting. If they are, plan to offer a workshop on homecoming weekend that introduces them to relevant sites and tutorials within the cyber library. Alumni are very interested in searching for friends through the Internet and in traveling and medical information. Use the Web library or search engines to show them sites and give them time to practice searching on their own. Remind them to bookmark your cyber library when they return home and ask their advice for promoting it in various media formats.

5. **Parents**—They are one of the most powerful groups to help you promote a cyber library. Demonstrate the advantages of a cyber library for them at an open house or parents' breakfast. Many parents are wondering and worried about chat rooms. Show them what they are and give them some Internet safety tips. Have all of your instruction available from the cyber library so that they can refer to it at a later date. Solicit their opinions on ways to promote it. Ask if they or

anyone they know has experience developing a promotion strategy. Do they know anyone who has experience writing copy for print ads, radio spots, television spots, or Web sites? Do they know anyone with experience producing advertisements in print, radio, television, or electronically? Remind them to make a bookmark for the cyber library on their home computers.

6. **Friends of the Library**—Many schools have a designated group of supporters that provide funding for special library programs and services. They may be instrumental in promoting the cyber library because of their own professional marketing expertise or their contacts within the community. At a future meeting, highlight areas of the cyber library that would motivate them to help you with marketing and promoting it. When demonstrating various cyber library sections, emphasize the benefits to not only the students but also the community.

Promotional Tools

In addition to showing the cyber library to members of your promotional team, avail yourself of the following promotional tools to publicize the cyber library and its services and programs. Remember that you have to promote an invisible library, so employ all of the resources to make it visible.

1. **Print Resources**—Print descriptions of the cyber library and its URL in every publication you can think of where students, faculty, alumni, administrators, and parents may encounter it. If the print resource targets parents, make sure that your description of the cyber library contains some information for them. If students are getting ready to take the SAT, write a description of the relevant Web library sites and run it in the school newspaper. Here are some suggestions for promoting the cyber library in print including:

    ◆ Student newspaper

    ◆ Student magazine

    ◆ Alumni magazine

    ◆ Local newspapers (free and subscription)

    ◆ Brochure and/or flyer

    ◆ Bookmarks (containing the SLMC logo and cyber library URL)

- ◆ Parent newsletter

- ◆ Public library newsletters

2. **Broadcast Promotion Resources**—If the cyber library is a stage three and designed to serve a large school district, seek funding to place advertisements on local radio and television stations. Broadcast advertising varies in cost by the number of advertisements and their placement in the viewing schedule. They are more expensive, for example, if you wish them to be aired during prime time or on certain days. The cost will also vary depending on the station's popularity and the demographics of the audience it attracts. Consider the following places for broadcast announcements of a cyber library.

   - ◆ Local radio and educational television stations

   - ◆ High school radio stations

   - ◆ School-aired daily announcements

   - ◆ Local school-supported events

   - ◆ Community events that feature an announcer (fairs, festivals, and so forth)

3. **Interviews, Press Releases, and Features**—Another way of promoting a cyber library takes the form of news. If your cyber library is highly regarded by administrators and other "powers that be," you may be able to promote it through interviews that are published or featured in local school district newsletters or a board of education–sponsored television or radio program. If you host an Open Cyber Library party, you may wish to arrange for the following:

   - ◆ The presence of the school's public relations administrator

   - ◆ Attendance by reporters from the local newspaper and television programs

4. **Online Resources**—Many of the online resources that you can use to promote the cyber library are free. You just need to be creative in thinking of cyber spots that students, faculty, alumni, parents, and administrators visit frequently and arrange for a brief announcement and the link to appear. One click and they are visiting your site. Consider placing a description and link of the cyber library by using these online resources.

- Attach a scrolling banner across the cyber library home page notifying everyone that the library is open for business.

- E-blast—use an e-mail message that can be addressed to all faculty, parents, and students.

- Ask the public library to link to your site from theirs.

- Announce the cyber library to a wider population by sending the URL to Web search engines; What's New sites; newsgroups and magazines that list Web sites; newsletters and mailing lists; and books that list Web sites, Web directory pages, and school library site pages.

- Make the cyber library the default page on all library terminals.

- Confirm that the library is listed on the menu selection on the school's home page.

- Ask the school Webmaster to place an advertisement for the cyber library on the site's home page and maintain it for two to three weeks.

5. **Personal Resources**—Personally promoting a cyber library can run the gamut from teaching with cyber library resources, including tutorials and pathfinders, to delivering five-minute presentations to various constituent groups. Take the time to schedule some of these activities as part of your promotional cyber library strategy.

   - Presentations to administrators including board of education and/or board of governors

   - Faculty workshops, both instructional and recreational

   - Back to School Night

   - Professional days and faculty meetings

   - Parent breakfasts

   - Homeroom visits

   - Student announcements

6. **Professional Publications**—Another method of promoting the cyber library is through the use of professional publications. Fellow cyber librarians need to know of our successes as well as our failures so that we can learn from each other in a medium that has no official standards. We also need to hear of any research that has been conducted

about the use of a cyber library, the effectiveness of online tutorials, and so forth. Here are some publications that would be interested in cyber library issues.

- *Classroom Connect* (http://www.classroom.com) highlights outstanding Web sites for its readers and provides the address so that interested cyber folks can contact you.

- *Knowledge Quest*, a monthly publication of the American Association of School Librarians, solicits manuscripts about cyber libraries.

- *School Library Journal*'s "Web Site of the Month" column. Every month a different school's or public library's site is reviewed for either its overall framework and design or a special program or service.

7. **Word of Mouth**—All of us can recall books that were published by obscure presses and then simply by word of mouth rocketed onto the best-seller lists. Rebecca Well's *The Divine Secrets of the Ya-Ya Sisterhood* was such a title. In a country as large as ours, it is hard to believe how one-to-one conversation about a book could produce a demand for millions of copies and appearances by a surprised and gratified author. Word of mouth is an excellent form of promotion. All SLMSs have to do is show their cyber library to students and faculty and listen for their comments and criticisms. Respond to both and you will have created an environment that is positively contagious for promoting your cyber library.

Twilight or Daylight

Articles are starting to appear in our professional publications that speak of a twilight time for libraries. Some writers are saying the librarians have fulfilled their historic mission and now it is time for them to wither away and die. This prophecy can only be realized if we, as SLMSs, fail to provide the professional programs and services our students and faculty need and deserve. A cyber library is a wonderful extension of a conventional SLMC. It gives us a greater opportunity to practice our profession through teaching, instructional design, reference services, readers' advisory, Webographies, and much more.

Never before have SLMSs been so essential to their parent institutions. Their media programs and services are educationally imperative if schools are to provide students with the skills, training, and knowledge they must have to prosper in America.

My vision for school library media centers is not without hope. Despite the changes occurring with the economy, technology, and society, I believe that we have been given an unprecedented opportunity to shape our future. Creating cyber libraries puts us in a position that is central to the goals and objectives of educational institutions. We must become the physical and cyber centers for information access, storage, dissemination, and instruction. Our educational mission is to design library programs and services that assist faculty to teach and help students to learn. As SLMSs, we must become the agents of change, not reactors to it.

Recommended Internet Sites

The following sites contain places where SLMSs can register their new cyber libraries and/or place them in contention for awards and recognition if they are so interested. Please remember that awards abound on the Internet. Many of them are considered bogus and can sometimes bestow the dubious distinction of "The Bottom 95%" or "Loving It Award." If your cyber library does receive a legitimate award such as the *School Library Journal*'s "Web Site of the Month," it is considered good netiquette to link to it discreetly through a small icon or link it to an awards page on your site.

Announcement Sites

Epages' FAQ: How to Announce Your Web Site
http://ep.com/faq/webannounce.html

If you are wondering where and how to announce the launching of your cyber library, this site provides the links to all the popular places and pointers for Web directory pages, Web search engines, newsgroups, mailing lists, and much more.

What's New with NCSA Mosaic
http://www.ncsa.uiuc.edu/SDG/Software/Mosaic/Docs/whats-new.html

When you are ready to announce your cyber library, send the URL through an online form at http://www.ncsa.uiuc.edu/SDG/Software/Mosaic/Docs/whats-new.html. This Web-announcing site features content-rich sites that other schools would be interested in linking to. It takes about ten to fourteen days for your cyber library to appear.

Yahoo
http://www.yahoo.com/

Yahoo furnishes a list of the most recent resources within the past week. The form for announcing your cyber library can be accessed at http://www.yahoo.com/bin/add/. SLMSs can choose the appropriate category from a drop-down menu, add the title, URL address, and a description.

Promotional Ideas Sites

Blue Web'n Learning Sites Library
http://www.kn.pacbell.com/wired/bluewebn/

Considered one of the best educational site reviewers, Blue Web'n is a legitimate awarder of recognition to top-quality Internet sites. Review some of its list of award-winning sites to see how your cyber library compares. If you wish to submit your cyber library to Blue Web'n, click on Suggest a Link and include your cyber library's URL, title, description, main subject area, and e-mail address.

Free Links
http://www.freelinks.com/awards.html

Although this site is geared to the business community, the tips on Web design, promotion, and marketing can also be applied to a school cyber library. It also contains a link popularity search box for you to check various search engines to determine who links to your cyber library. All you have to do is enter the cyber library's URL to generate a link popularity report.

Webmaster T's World of Design
http://www.tsworldofdesign.com/promotion/cool.htm

Although these "Cool Sites and Award Sites" target companies for awards, there are a number of links to awards that would probably be granted to a stage-three cyber library. If you are interested in promoting your cyber library online, this site, developed by librarian-trained Robert Woodhead, contains a step process that includes guidance ranging from submitting your cyber library to search engines and indexes to writing catchy and accurate descriptions of it.

References

Drucker, Peter. 1999. *Management Challenges for the 21st Century*. New York: Harvard Business School Press.

Houghton, Jan M., and Ross J. Todd. 2000. "Overcoming Image: Strategies for Librarians in the New Millenium." In *Cybrarian's Manual 2*, ed. Pat Ensor. Chicago: American Library Association.

Johnson, Doug. 2000. "Building Digital Libraries for Analog People." *Knowledge Quest* 27 (May/June): 10–15.

National Association of Independent Schools. 2001. *Marketing Independent Schools in the 21st Century*. Washington, DC: National Association of Independent Schools.

Porter, Lynette R. 1997. *Creating the Virtual Classroom: Distance Learning with the Internet*. New York: Wiley.

Ryan, Sara. 1999. "Serving Young People—What You Can Do." In *The Internet Public Library Handbook*, ed. Joseph Janes et al. New York: Neal-Schuman.

St. Lifer, Evan. 2001. "Tapping into the Zen of Marketing." *Library Journal* 126 (May 1): 44–46.

Bibliography

"ALA Task Force Report on Privacy and Confidentiality in the Electronic Environment." 2000. http://staffweb.library.vanderbilt.edu/ala_tf/Report.htm (July 2, 2001).

Albanese, Andrew Richard. 2001. "The E-Book Enterprise netLibrary's Digital Mission." *Library Journal* 126 (February 15): 126–128.

Albee, Barbara, and Brenda Dingley. 2001. "U.S. Periodicals Prices—2001." *American Libraries* 32 (May): 72–78.

"Alexa Research Report Shows Inefficiencies of Web Users." 2001. *LJ Netconnect: Supplement to Library and School Library Journal* (Spring): 5.

American Association of School Librarians. 2001. "Information Literacy on Information Problem Solving." http://www.ala.org/aasl/positions/ps_infolit.html (July 15, 2001).

American Memory Project. http://lcweb.gov (July 20, 2001).

Amey, Larry, and Stephen Elliott. 1997. "Serving the Cyberteen: Library Service for the 21st Century Adolescent." *VOYA* 20 (April): 14–20.

Ariel, Glen, and David Millman. 1998. "Access Management of Web-Based Services." *D-Lib Magazine* (September). http://www.dlib.org/dlib/September98/millman/09millman.html (January 25, 2002).

Arms, William Y. 2000. *Digital Libraries*. Cambridge: MIT Press.

Benson, Allen C., and Linda M. Fodemski. 1999. *Connecting Kids and the Internet*. 2nd ed. New York: Neal-Schuman.

Benzing, Matthew. 2000. "Browser Plug-Ins: Customization for Multimedia." In *The Cybrarians Manual 2*, ed. Pat Ensor. Chicago: American Library Association.

Block, Marylaine. 1998. "Creating an Internet Collection Development Policy: Principles of Selection." *Knowledge Quest* 27 (September/October): 46–47.

Bobicki, Jeff. 2001. "All of the News, None of the Hassle." *LJ Netconnect: Supplement to Library and School Library Journal* (Winter): 8

Braun, Linda W. 1998. "Building a Better Web Site." *School Library Journal* 44 (July): 24–27.

————. 2001. "Letting Teens Take the Lead." *LJ Netconnect: Supplement to Library and School Library Journal* (Winter): 26–29.

Breeding, Marshall. 2000. "Security and Authentication Issues." In *Cybrarian's Manual 2*, ed. Pat Ensor. Chicago: American Library Association.

"Building a School Web Site." 2001. *Classroom Connect* 7 (April): 15.

Burnett, Tim. 2001. "Set up a Free Web Site This Summer." *Classroom Connect* 7 (Summer): 7–8.

Carter, David S. 1999. "Building Online Collections." In *The Internet Public Library Handbook*, ed. Joseph Janes et al. New York: Neal-Schuman.

Copyright. http://netizen.uoregon.edu/document/copyright.html (July 3, 2001).

Cox, Paul. 1997. "Cyberdegrees." *Wall Street Journal* (November 11): R26.

Coyle, Karen. 2001. "Protecting Privacy." *LJ Netconnect: Supplement to Library and School Library Journal* (Winter): 14–17.

Craver, Kathleen W. 1994. *School Library Media Centers in the 21st Century*. Westport, CT: Greenwood.

————. 1997. *Teaching Electronic Literacy: A Concepts-Based Approach for School Library Media Specialists*. Westport, CT: Greenwood.

Crawford, Walt. 1998. "PaperPersists: Why Physical Collections Still Matter." http://www.Onlineinc.com/onlinemag/JanOL98/ (January 23, 2001).

Cummins, Julie. 2001. "Dead Trees and Wooden Nickels." *School Library Journal* 47 (March): 11.

Cyberspace Laws. http://www.cyberspacelaws.com (July 3, 2001).

Dobrzynski, Judith H. 2001. "So, Technology Pros, What Comes after the Fall?" *New York Times* (July 29): 1, 11–12.

Drucker, Peter. 1999. *Management Challenges for the 21st Century*. New York: Harvard Business School Press.

Dupuis, Elizabeth A. 2001. "Automating Instruction." *LJ Netconnect: Supplement to Library and School Library Journal* (Spring): 21–22.

Ebrary.com. http://ebrary.com (July 20, 2001).

e-Global Library. http://JonesKnowledge.com (July 20, 2001).

Ensor, Pat, ed. 2000. *The Cybrarian's Manual 2*. Chicago: American Library Association.

"Falling through the Net: Toward Digital Inclusion: A Report on Americans' Access to Technology Tools 2000." 2000. http://www.esa.doc.gov/fttn00.htm (October 10, 2000).

Foster, Janet. 2000. "Reference Questions on Your Web Site." *Internet Spotlight* (July/August): 1–2. http://www.pla.org/webref_jul-aug00.html (January 25, 2002).

"Frequently Asked Questions about Portals" 2000. *LIS News* (July 7). http://lisnews.com/article.php3?sid=20000707104903.

Garlock, Kristen L., and Sherry Pointek. 1996. *Building the Service-Based Library Web Site: A Step-by-Step Guide to Design and Options.* Chicago: American Library Association.

Gibbons, Susan. 2000. "Some Emerging eBook Business Models: netLibrary, Questia and Ebrary." Rochester Regional Library Council (December 2000). http://www.lib.rochester.edu/main/ebooks/newsletter1-2/vol2-business_models.htm (January 25, 2002).

Goerwitz, David. 1998. "Pass-through Proxying as a Solution to the Off-Site Web Access Problem." *D-Lib Magazine* (June). http://www.dlib.org/dlib/June98/stg/06goerwitz.html (January 25, 2002).

Gorman, Michael. 2001. "Technostress and Library Values." *Library Journal* 126 (April 15): 48–50.

Gregory, Vicki L. 2000. *Selecting and Managing Electronic Resources.* New York: Neal-Schuman.

"Growing Pains: The Challenge of Overcrowded Schools Is Here to Stay." 2001. http://www.ed.gov/pubs/bbecho00/bbecho00.doc (March 23, 2001).

Guidelines and Considerations for Developing a Public Library Internet Use Policy. http://www.ala.org/alaorg/oif/internet.html (July 3, 2001).

Hodge, Brian. 2001. "Windows on the World." *Smart Computing* 12 (September): 88–90.

Houghton, Jan M., and Ross J. Todd. 2000. "Overcoming Image: Strategies for Librarians in the New Millenium." In *Cybrarian's Manual 2*, ed. Pat Ensor. Chicago: American Library Association.

"How Can I Use Standards in My Classroom?" 2001. *Classroom Connect* 7 (March): 6.

Hudson, Laura. 2001. "From Theory to Virtual Reality." *LJ Netconnect: Supplement to Library and School Library Journal* (Summer): 12–15.

Hughes, Jane E. 2001. "Access, Access, Access! The New OPAC Mantra." *American Libraries* 32 (May): 62–64.

"Internet Access in U.S. Public Schools and Classrooms: 1994–2000." 2000. http://nces.ed.gov/pubsearch/pubsinfo.asp?pubid=2001071 (May 15, 2001).

Internet Public Library. http://www.ipl.org/ (June 2, 2001).

Janes, Joseph, et al. 1999. *The Internet Public Library Handbook.* New York: Neal-Schuman.

Johnson, Doug. 2000. "Building Digital Libraries for Analog People." *Knowledge Quest* 27 (May/June): 10–15.

Johnson, Roberta. 2001. "Global Conversation: Readers' Advisory on the Web." *Booklist* 97 (January 1 and 15): 912–913.

Junion-Metz, Gail. 2001. "The Librarian's Internet Food for Thought: How Kids and Adults Learn." *School Library Journal* 47 (April): 33.

———. 2000. "Teacher Knows Best: Some Web Worthy Tutorials to Help You Create Your Own." *School Library Journal* 46 (May): 37.

KidsClick! http://sunsite.berkeley.edu/KidsClick! (June 23, 2001).

Klein, Leo Robert. 2000. "The Web Design and Sin." *LJ Netconnect: Supplement to Library and School Library Journal* (Summer): 37–39.

———. 2001. "The Web Is Not Your Library." *LJ Netconnect: Supplement to Library and School Library Journal* (Winter): 36–37.

Kovacs, Donald, and Michael Kovacs. 1997. *The Cybrarain's Guide to Developing Successful Internet Programs and Services.* New York: Neal-Schuman.

Lagace, Nettie. 1999. "Establishing Online Reference Services." In *The Internet Public Library Handbook*, ed. Joseph Janes et al. New York: Neal-Schuman.

Librarians' Index to the Internet. http://lii.org (July 8, 2001).

Louv, Richard. 1990. *Childhood's Future.* Boston: Houghton Mifflin.

Lubans, John, Jr. 1998. "Key Findings on Internet Use among Students." http://www.lib.duke.edu/lubans/docs/key/key.html (May 21, 2001).

Lynch, Patrick, and Sarah Horton. 1999. *Web Style Guide: Basic Design Principles for Creating Web Sites.* New Haven, CT: Yale University Press.

Majka, David. 2001. "The Conqueror Bookworm." *American Libraries* 32 (June/July): 61–63.

McCaffrey, Meg. 2001. "One-Stop Reading." *School Library Journal* 47 (July): 22.

Meyer, Randy. 2000. "It Takes a Cybervillage." *LJ Netconnect: Supplement to Library and School Library Journal* (Fall): 20–25.

Minkel, Walter. 2001. "A Chapter a Day." *School Library Journal* 47 (May): 31–32.

———. 2001. "Dot-Coms Offer Libraries for a Fee." *School Library Journal* 47 (January): 35.

———. 2000. "E-Book Anxieties." *School Library Journal* 46 (February): 29.

———. 2001. "Great Expectations: Will Yourhomework.com Make Librarians' Dreams Come True?" *School Library Journal* 47 (April): 39.

———. 2000. "Life's a Beach." *LJ Netconnect: Supplement to Library and School Library Journal* (Fall): 42–43.

———. 2001. "Not So Elementary: How Young Is Too Young Online?" *School Library Journal* 47 (January): 41.

———. 2001. "A Picture Is Worth . . ." *LJ Netconnect: Supplement to Library and School Library Journal* (Winter): 38–39.

———. 2001. "Policy Discussion: Add Web Sites to Your Materials Selection Policy." *School Library Journal* 47 (March): 41.

———. 2000. "So Far I've Only Found His Head." *School Library Journal* 46 (April): 37.

———. 2000. "Web Site of the Month." *School Library Journal* 46 (July): 30.

Minkel, Walter, and Roxanne Hsu Feldman. 1999. *Delivering Web Reference Services to Young People*. Chicago: American Library Association.

National Association of Independent Schools. 2001. *Marketing Independent Schools in the 21st Century*. Washington, DC: National Association of Independent Schools.

Oberman, Cerise. 1991. "Avoiding the Cereal Syndrome, or Critical Thinking in the Electronic Environment." *Library Trends* 39 (Winter): 189–202.

Oder, Norman. 2001. "Is Online Tutoring in Your Library's Future?" *LJ Netconnect: Supplement to Library and School Library Journal* (Summer): 6.

O'Leary, Mick. 2000. "Grading the Library Portals." http://www.onlineinc.com/onlinemag/OL2000/oleary11.html (July 18, 2001).

Parker, Kimberley. 2000. "Collecting Electronic Resources: What You Don't Know You Can Learn." In *Cybrarian's Manual 2*, ed. Pat Ensor. Chicago: American Library Association.

Pastore, Michael. 2001. "Internet Use Continues to Pervade U.S. Life." http://cyberatlas.internet.com/big_picture/demographics/article/0,,5901_775401,00.html (August 27, 2001).

Pine, B. Joseph II, and James H. Gilmore. 1999. *The Experience Economy: Work Is Theatre and Every Business a Stage*. Boston: Harvard Business School Press.

Porter, Lynette R. 1997. *Creating the Virtual Classroom: Distance Learning with the Internet*. New York: Wiley.

Project Gutenberg. http://www.promo.net/pg/ (July 21, 2001).

"Rating Educational Portals." 2001. *Beacon Learn North Carolina* (Spring). http://www.learnnc.org/newlncs/beacon.nsf/doc/9CAC871555C46AD485256A4C0064909B.

Reynolds, Janice. 2000. "Distributive Learning Evolves to Meet Needs of Lifelong Learners." *e-Education Advisor* 1 (Fall): 1–15.

Rifkin, Jeremy. 2000. *The Age of Access*. New York: Putnam.

Robinson, Brian. 1999. "Leading Computer Companies Combine of Offer Education 'Portal' Services" CNN.com (August 18). http://www.cnn.com/TECH/computing/9908/education.portal.idg/index.html (July 17, 2001).

Roger, Eleanor Jo, et al. 2001. "The Public Library and the Internet: Is Peaceful Co-Existence Possible?" *American Libraries* 32 (May): 58–61.

Rosenfeld, Lou. 1997. "30-Minute Web Site Tune-Up." WebReview.com (January 24). http://www.webreview.com/1997/01_24/strategists/01_24_97_2.shtml (January 25, 2002).

Ryan, Sara. 1999. "Serving Young People—What You Can Do." In *The Internet Public Library Handbook*, ed. Joseph Janes et. al. New York: Neal-Schuman.

Schumacher, Mary Louise. 1999. "The Struggle to Find Librarians." *Washington Post* (August 26): DC5.

Sears, JoAnn, and Andrew Wohrley. 2000. "Guidelines for an Excellent Website." In *Cybrarian's Manual 2*, ed. Pat Ensor. Chicago: American Library Association.

Simcox, Schelle. 1999. "Creating a Successful Web Site." In *The Internet Public Library Handbook*, ed. Joseph Janes et al. New York: Neal-Schuman.

Smith, Harry K. "Educational Portals." http://plato.ess.tntech.edu/foed334=02/Resources/ed_portals.htm (August 27, 2001).

Smith, Susan, et al. 2001. "Make It a Team Approach." *LJ Netconnect: Supplement to Library and School Library Journal* (Winter): 18–20.

Stielow, Frederick, ed. 1999. *Creating a Virtual Library: A How-to-Do-It Manual*. New York: Neal-Schuman.

St. Lifer, Evan. 2001. "Tapping into the Zen of Marketing." *Library Journal* 126 (May 1): 44–46.

Thomas, Karen. 2000. "One School's Quantum Leap in Florida: A Class of 2004 Will Do Its Learning Online." *USA Today* (April 6): 1A–5A.

Thorton, Amy. 2000. "Licensed to Teach." In *Cybrarian's Manual 2*, ed. Pat Ensor. Chicago: American Library Association.

Traw, Jeri L., comp. 2000. *Library Web Site Policies*. Chicago: American Library Association.

Weissman, Sara. 2001. "Know Your Audience." *LJ Netconnect: Supplement to Library and School Library Journal* (Spring): 42.

"Why Content? The Unassailable Argument for Why You Need Website Content." 2001. ScreamingMedia Inc. http://www01.screamingmedia.com/en/content_services/why_content/data.php (August 27, 2001).

Wiggins, Richard W. 2000. "Coping with the Trillion-Page Web." *LJ Netconnect: Supplement to Library and School Library Journal* (Fall): 26–28.

Links
Citation List

A & E Television
http://www.aande.com

About.com's List of Animal Cams
http://biology.about.com/science
/biology/cs/animalcams/index.htm

Adams Books Company
http://www2.adamsbook.com/adams
/homepage.tmpl$Showpage

Aerodynamics of Bicycles
http://www.princeton.edu/~asmits
/Bicycle_web/bicycle_aero.html

Airlines of the Web
http://flyaow.com/

Alibris-Out-of-Print Books
http://www.alibris.com/

AltaVista
http://www.altavista.com

Amazon.com
http://www.amazon.com

Amendments to the Constitution
http://cornell.edu/constitution/
constitution.table.html#amendments

**American Association
of School Librarians**
http://www.ala.org/aasl/positions
/ps_infolit.html

American Library Association
http://www.ala.org/aasl/positions
/ps_libraryrecords.html

American Memory Project
http://rs6.loc.gov/amhome.html

Amtrak Home Page
http://www.amtrak.com

Amusement Park Physics
http://www.learner.org/exhibits
/parkphysics/

AOL@School.com
http://www.aol@school.com

Apple Learning Interchange
http://www.ali.apple.com

Art History Sources on the Web
http://witcombe.sbc.edu/ARTHLinks
.html

Ask Dr. Math
http://forum.swarthmore.edu
/dr.math/dr-math.html

Ask Jeeves for Kids
http://www.ajkids.com/

**Association for Library Services
to Children 700+ Great Sites**
http://www.ala.org/parentspage
/greatsites/amazing.html

Atlas of the Human Body
http://www.innerbody.com/htm
/body.html

**Australian Libraries Gateway—
Guidelines for the Preparation
of a Collection Development Policy**
http://www.nla.gov.au/libraries
/resource/acliscdp.html

Avoiding Plagiarism
http://www.careton.ca.wts
/plagiarism.html

B. J. Pinchbeck's Homework Help
http://www.bjpinchbeck.com

Baker & Taylor
http://www.btol.com/index.cfm

Barnes & Noble
http://barnesandnoble.com/

Beginner's Central
http://www.northernwebs.com/bc

**Bellingham School District 501
Copyright Compliance Instruction**
http://www.bham.wednet.edu
/copyrght.htm

Berkeley Public Library for Kids
http://www.ci.berkeley.ca.us/bpl
/kids/index.html

**Bernie Sloan's Bibliography of
Sources on Electronic Reference**
http://www.lis.uiuc.edu/~b-sloan
/digiref.html

Best of the Hubble Space Telescope
http://www.seds.rog/hst.html

Best of the Web
http://www.botw.org/

Bigchalk.com
http://bigchalk.com

Bigwords.com
http://www.bigwords.com

Blackboard.com
http://blackboard.com

Blue Web'n Learning Sites Library
http://www.kn.pacbell.com/wired
/bluewebn/

Bookfinder.com
http://www.bookfinder.com/

Books@Random Library
http://www.randomhouse.com
/library/rgg.html

Bradford Robotic Telescope
http://baldrick.eia.brad.ac.uk/rti
/index.html

Building the Web.com
http://www.buildingtheweb.com

**Calgary Public Library's
"Electronic Reading Game"**
http://www.public-librar.calgary
.ab.ca/wra2000/wra2000.htm

Carnegie-Mellon University
http://www.informedia.cs.cmu.edu/

Chapter a Day
http://www.chapteraday.com

Chasing El Niño
http://www.pbs.org/wgbh/nova
/elnino/

Chicago Public Library
http://www.chipublic.org/008subject
/005genref/gisquestion.html

Children's Garden
http://commtechlab.msu.edu/sites
/garden/index.html

**Choose the Best Engine for Your
Purpose**
http://www.nueva.pvt.k12.ca.us
/~debbie/library/research
/adviceengine.html

Choosing a Summer Camp
http://www.bosbbb.org/prac18.htm

Circuit Builder Tutorial
http://www.jhu.edu/~virtlab/logic
/log_cir.htm

Classroom Clipart
http://classroomclipart.com/cgi-bin
/kids/imageFolio.cgi

Classroom Connect
http://www.classroom.com

College and University Rankings
http://www.library.uiuc.edu
/edx/rankings.htm

College Board Online
http://www.collegeboard.com/

Common Errors in English Grammar
http://www.wsu.edu/~brians/errors
/index.html

Computer Training Tutorials
http://www.ckls.org/~crippel
/computerlab/tutorials/index.html

**Consumer Gateway for 40 Federal
Agencies**
http://www.consumer.gov/

Consumer Information Online
http://www.pueblo.gsa.gov/

Consumer World
http://www.consumerworld.org/

Copyright
http://www.netizen.uoregon.edu
/documents/copyright.html

**Copyright Act of 1976
(amended 1994)**
http://www.4.law.cornell.edu
/uscode/17/

Copyright and Fair Use
http://fairuse.stanford.edu/

Copyright Website
http://www.benedict.com/

**Core Documents of American
Democracy**
http://www.access.gpo.gov/su_docs
/locators/coredocs/index.html

Cosmology and the Big Bang
http://csep1.phy.ornl.gov/guidry
/violence/cosmology.html

C-Span
http://www.c-span.org/

Cyberspace Laws
http://www.cyberspacelaws.com

Davesite's Interactive HTML Tutorial
http://www.davesite.com/Webstation/html/

Dead Sea Scrolls
http://www.ibiblio.org/expo/deadsea.scrolls.exhibit/intro.html

Definitions of Words and Phrases Commonly Found in Licensing Agreements
http://www.library.yale.edu/~llicense/definiti.shtml

Digital Libraries
http://www.bookwire.com/LJDigital/diglibs.articles

District Copyright Web Publishing Rules
http://www.bham.wednet.edu/copyrule.htm

Do We Really Know Dewey?
http://tqjunior.thinkquest.org/5002/

Eagle Eyes NCS Web Library
http://.207.188.221.237/

Earth Cam
http://www.earthcam.com

Earth Viewer
http://www.fourmilab.ch/earthview/vplanet.html

Earthshots: Satellite Images of Environmental Change
http://edcwww.cr.usgs.gov/earthshorts/slow/tableofcontents

Ebrary.com
http://www.ebrary.com

EdGate.com
http://edgate.com

EdNow.com
http://www.ednow.com

Educational Web Adventures
http://www.eduweb.com/adventure.html

efollett.com
http://www.efollett.com/

e-Global Library
http://JonesKnowledge.com

Electric Schoolhouse
http://www.eschoolhouse.com

Encyclopedia Mythica
http://www.pantheon.org/mythica.html

Epages' FAQ: How to Announce Your Web Site
http://ep.com/faq/webannounce.html

Epals
http://www.epals.com/

Excite
http://www.excite.com

Experimental Climate Prediction Center
http://meteora.ucsd.edu/%7Epierce/elnino/en97/en97.html),

Exploratorium
http://www.exploratorium.edu/

ezAttach
http://www.ezAttach.com

Famous American Trials
http://www.law.umkc.edu/faculty/projects/ftrials/ftrials.htm

Fast Facts and Reference Sources
http://gwu.edu/~gprice/handbook
.htm

Federal Web Locator Sites
http://www.inctr.edu/fwl/

Fiction Mailing Lists
http://www.fictional.org/ralists.html

Field Museum (Chicago)
http://www.fieldmuseum.org/

Finding Information on the Internet
http://www.lib.berkeley.edu/TeachingLib
/Guides/Internet/Findinfo.html

Finding Stuff on the Web
http://www.ckls.org/~crippel
/computerlab/tutorials/web
/searching/page1.html

Florida Library Youth Program
http://dlis.dos.state.fl.us/flyp200

Flying Inkpot's World Newspaper Links
http://www.inkpot.com/news/

FLYP
http://dlis.dos.state.fl.us/bld
/FLYP2000

Free Links
http://www.freelinks.com/awards
.html

Gale's Literary Criticism Index
http://www.galenet.com/servlet
/LitIndex

Galileo Project
http://es.rice.edu/ES/humsoc
/Galileo/

Gallery of Interactive Geometry
http://www.geom.umn.edu/apps
/gallery.html

**Giving People What They Want:
How to Involve Users in Site
Design**
http://www-106.ibm.com
/developerworks/library
/design-by-feedback/expectations
.html

The Good, the Bad, and the Ugly
http://lib.nmsu.edu/staff/susanbeck
/evalu.html

Google
http://www.google.com

Grateful Med Search Engine
http://igm.nlm.nih.gov/

Gravity Tutorials
http://www.curtin.edu.au/curtin
/dept/phys-sci/gravity/contents.htm

Great Lakes Atlas
http://www.epa.gov/grtlakes/atlas
/intro.html

Great Sites Selection Criteria
http://www.Ala.org/parentspage
/greatsites/criteria.html

**Guide to Summer Camps:
Summer 2002**
http://www.washingtonparent.com
/guides/guide-camps.htm

**Guidelines and Considerations for
Developing a Public Library
Internet Use Policy**
http://www.ala.org/alaorg/oif
/internet.html

Guidelines for School Web Pages
http://macserver.stjohns.k12.fl.us
/guidelines.html

HarperCollins Reader Resources
http://www.harpercollins.com
/readers/reader.resources.htm

High Wire Press
http://highwire.stanford.edu/

HighWired.com
http://www.highwired.com

**Historical United States Census
Data 1790-1970**
http://fisher.lib.virginia.edu/census/

History Channel
http://www.historychannel.com
/index.html

**Houston Public Library—
Interactive–Ask a Librarian**
http://www.hpl.lib.tx.us/hpl
/interactive/answers.html

Iconbrowser
http://www.ibiblio.org/gio
/iconbrowser/icons/icons1-6.html

ICONnect
http://www.ala.org/ICONN/kidsconn
.html

i-drive
http://www.idrive.com

**Indiana University's Digital
Library**
http://www.dlib.indiana.edu/

Information Literacy and the Net
http://www.bham.wednet.edu
/literacy.htm

Information Please Online
http://www.infoplease.com/

Ingram Book Company
http://www.ingrambook.com/

**Interactive Frog Dissection: An
Online Tutorial**
http://cury.eduschool.virginia.edu
/go/frog

**International Coalition of Library
Consortia**
http://www.library.yale.edu/consortia
/statement.html

**International Standards Copyright
Office for Changes in the Law**
http://lcweb.loc.gov/copyright/

**Internet and Public Libraries . . .
Issues and Opportunities**
http://www.iage.com/rusa.shtm

Internet Library for Librarians
http://www.itcompany.com
/inforetriever

Internet Movie Database
http://us.imdb.com/

Internet Public Library
http://ipl.org/

**Internet Public Library:
Controversial Science**
http://ipl.org/ref/RR/static
/sci0800.00.html

**Internet Public Library: Issues
and Conflicts**
http://ipl.sils.umich.edu/

**Internet Public Library Ready
Reference**
http://ipl.org/ref/

Internet Public Library Services for Librarians
http://www.ipl.org/svcs

Internet Sites for Research
http://www.multnomah.lib.or.us/lib/homework/

IPL Especially for Librarians: Organizing the Web
http://www.ipl.org/svcs/organizing.html

IUP Role-Play Exercise for School (Public) Library Staff
http://www.iage.com/roleplay.shtm

Jerusalem Mosaic
http://jeru.huji.ac.il/jerusalem.html

Kathy Schrock's Guide for Educators
http://www.capecod.net/schrockguide/

Keypals Club
http://www.mightymedia.com/keypals/

KIDS Report
http://scout.cs.wisc.edu/scout/KIDS/index.html

KidsClick!
http://www.sunsite.berkeley.edu/KidsClick!

Kidsconnect Q & A Service
http://www.ala.org/ICONN/kids.com.html

Learning on the Web
http://teleeducation.nb.content/lotw2001/c2index.html

A Legal and Educational Analysis of K–12 Internet Acceptable Use Policies
http://ces.uoregon.edu/responsibilities/analysis.htm

Librarians' Index to the Internet
http://lii.org/

LibraryHQ
http://libraryhq.com

LibraryLand
http://sunsite.berkeley.edu/LibraryLand

LibrarySpot
http://www.libraryspot.com

Licensing Digital Information
http://www.library.yale.edu/~llicense/intro.shtml

Licensing Resources
http://www.library.yale.edu/~llicense/liclinks.html

Lightspan, Inc.
http://lightspan.com

Linear Accelerator Center on Particle Physics
http://www2.slac.stanford.edu/vvc/home.html

LIS News
http://lisnews.com

Live Homework Help
http://Tutor.com

Louvre
http://www.paris.org/Musees/Louvre/

Mamamedia
http://mamamedia.com

Math Forum
http://forum.swarthmore.edu/

Metropolitan Museum of Art
http://www.metmuseum.org/

Mindsurf Networks
http://www.mindsurfnetworks.com

Mineral Gallery
http://mineralgalleries.com/

Morton Grove's Webrary
http://www.webrary.org?RS/Rsmenu
.html

**Multnomah County Library
Homework Center**
http://www.multnomah.lib.or.us/lib
/kids/homework/index.html

**Multnomah County Library's
Social Issues Page**
http://www.multnomah.lib.or.us/lib
/homework/sochc.html

**Museum of Science's Virtual
Exhibits (Boston)**
http://www.mos.org/home.html

Myspace
http://www.freediskspace.com

Nancy Keane's Booktalks
http://nancykeane.com/booktalks

**National Cathedral School Library
Internet Database**
http://207.188.221.237/

**National Cathedral School Library
Internet Survival Tutorial**
http://gold.ncs.cathedral.org
/uslibrary_tutorials/internet_home
.htm

**National Cathedral School's
Internet Collection Development
Policy**
http://ncs.cathedral.org/uslibrary
/Library/Lib_Policies
/Internet_Collection_Policy.htm

**National Drought Center and
Drought Science**
http://enso.unl.edu/ndmc/

National Gallery of Art
http://www.na.gov/

National Public Radio
http://www.npr.org/

Net Mechanic.com
http://netmechanic.com

netLibrary.com
http://www.netLibrary.com

Netscape Netcenter
http://www.netscape.com/Websites

Net-Trak Services
http://net-trak.stats.net/

New York Public Library
http://digital.nypl.org

News Online
http://www.newspapers.com/

**19th Century British and
American Authors**
http://lang.nagoya-u.ac.jp/~matsuoka
/19th-authors.html

Noodletools.com
http://noodletools.com

Ocean Sciences Education Teacher Resource
http://www.vims.edu/bridge

Oklahoma 2000 Summer Reading Program
http://www.connectok.com
/summerfunsite

On-Line Books Page
http://www.cs.cmu.edu/People/spok
/aboutolbp.html

Orientation to Carrier Library
http://library.jmu.edu/library/gold
/mod1orient.htm

Overbooked
http://freenet.vcu.edu/educaton
/literature/bklink.html

Ovid
http://www.ovid.com

Ozone Hole Tour
http://www.atm.ch.cam.ac.uk/tour/

Page Tutor
http://www.pagetutor.com/pagetutor
/makapage/

A Pathfinder for Constructing Pathfinders
http://home.wsd/wednet.edu
/pathfinders/path.htm#internet

PBS Online
http://www.pbs.org/

Perseus Project
http://www.perseus.tufts.edu/

Personality: What Makes Us What We Are?
http://www.learner.org/exhibits
/personality

Peter Milbury's Network of School Librarian Web Pages
http://www.school-libraries.net/

Plate Tectonics Exhibit with Animations
http://www.ucmp.berkeley.edu
/geology/tectonics.html

Privacy
http://netizen.uoregon.edu
/documents/privacy.html

Privacy Resources Electronic Information Privacy Center
http://www.eipc.org

Project Gutenberg
http://www.ibiblio.org/pub/docs
/books/gutenberg/index.html

Public Library of Charlotte and Mecklenburg County (North Carolina)
http://www.plmc.lib.nc.us/

Purdue University's Online Writing Lab
http://owl.english.purdue.edu

Questia.com
http://questia.com

Rail Europe: Eurail Passe and More
http://www.raileurope.com/us
/index.htm

Rainforest Action Network Center
http://www.ran.org/

Reading Group Choices
http://www.readinggroupchoices
.com/

Red Rival
http://www.redrival.com

Research Support
http://www.plcmc.lib.nc.us
/sharedPages/ResearchSupport.html

San Francisco's Fine Arts Museum
http://www.thinker.org/

SchoolCity
http://schoolcity.com

Science Fair Project Resource Guide
http://www.ipl.org/youth
/projectguide/

Scout Report
http://www.scout.cs.wisc.edu/scout
/report/subscribe.html

Sensation and Perception Tutorials
http://psych.hanover.edu/Krantz
.tutor.htm

700+ Great Sites: . . .
http://www.ala.org/parentspage
/greatsites/amazing.html

Shakespeare's Globe Theatre
http://www.rdg.ac.uk/globe/home
.htm

Site Sweeper
http://www.sitetech.com

Smithsonian
www.si.edu/info
/museums_research.htm

Smithsonian Gem and Mineral Collection
http://www.150.si.edu/150trav
/discover/evolve.htm

Solar System Simulator
http://space.jpl.nasa.gov/

Solar System Webquest
http://www.monet.k12.ca.us
/challenge/Teacher_Webpages
/OWStemigD/SolarSystemWebquest
/solar_system_webquest.htm

The Soundry
http://library.thinkquest.org/19537/

Stanford University
http://diglib.stanford.edu/

Subject Guides
http://web.uflib.ufl.edu/subguide.html

Supreme Court Cases
http://supctlaw.cornell.edu/supct/

Symphony Interactive Guide
http://library.thinkquest.org
/22673/index.html

Teach Yourself . . . the Internet
http://www.library.ucla.edu/libraries
/college/instruct/instgui.htm

Think Different
http://users.cwnet.com/phillips
/wq.Thinkdifferent.htm

Thomas Legislative Information
http://thomas.loc.gov

TILT
http://tilt.libutsystem.edu/

Tony's List of Live Cam Worldwide
http://chili.rt66.com/ozone/cam.htm

Top Ten Reasons School Library Media Specialists Should Connect to the Internet
http://ericir.syr.edu/ICONN /ihome.html

Toronto Public Library (Canada)
http://www.tpl.toronto.on.ca /KidsSpace/SRC

Tracking Hurricanes
http://www.miamisci.org/hurricane /instructions.html

Tutor.com
http://Tutor.com

University of California at Berkeley
http://elib.cs.berkeley.edu/

University of California at Santa Barbara
http://www.alexandria.ucsb.edu/

University of Illinois
http://dli.grainger.uiuc.edu/idli/idli /htm

University of Michigan
http://www.si.umich.edu/UMDL/

University of Virginia's William Blake Archive
http://www.iath.virginia.edu/blake/

Usability.gov
http://usability.gov/index.html

VarsityBooks
http://www.varsitybooks.com

Vatican Museum Exhibit
http://metalab.unc.edu/expo /vaticanexhibit/Vatican.exhibit.html

Virtual Chemistry Textbook
http://library.thinkquest.org/3659/

Virtual School Bus
http://www.field-guides.com/

Virtual Tourist
http://www.virtualtourist.com/?s=1&

Visible Human Project
http://www.nlm.nih.gov/research /visible/visible_human.html

Visit Your National Parks
http://www.nps.gov/parks.htm

Visual Interpretation of the Table of Elements
http://www.chemsoc.org/uiselements /pages/pertable_fla.htm

Visual Physics
http://library.thinkquest.org /10170/main.htm

Weather Channel
http://www.weather.com/

Web Elements
http://www.shef.ac.uk/~chem /web-elements/

Web Pages That Suck.com
http://www.webpagesthatsuck.com/

Web Ring
http://www.webring.com

WebCamVideo.com
http://webcamvideo.com/domi/satel /en.htm

WebChess
http://www.june29.com/Chess/

Webmaster T's World of Design
http://www.tsworldofdesign.com
/promotion/cool.htm

Webquest Page
http://edweb.sdsu.edu/webquest
/webquest.html

Web's Reference Search Engine
http://www.xrefer.com

Web66: AK12 World Wide Web Project
http://web66.coled.umn.edu/

Whatis.com
http://whatis.techtarget.com/

What's New with NCSA Mosaic
http://www.ncsa.uiuc.edu/SDG
/Software/Mosaic/Docs
/whats-new.html

White House Virtual Tour
http://www.whitehouse.gov/

WhyFiles
http://whyfiles.org

World Mythology Database
http://windows.vcar.edu/cgi-bin
/tour_def/mythology/mythology.html

World Travel Guide Online
http://www.wtgonline.com/navigate
/world.asp

WWW Virtual Library
http://www.vlib.org/Overview.html

WWW Virtual Library: Meteorology
http://dao.gsfc.nasa.gov
/DAO_people/towens/VLM

WWW Virtual Library: Museums
http://vlmp.museophile.com/

Yahoo.com
http://www.yahoo.com/

Yahoo Religion Links
http://www.yahoo.com/society_and
_culture/religion_and_spirituality/

Yahoo World and U.S. Weather
http://www.weather.yahoo.com

Yahooligans
http://www.yahooligans.com/

Yahoo's Newspaper List
http://dir.yahoo.com/news/

Yahoo's What's New Listing
http://www.yahoo.com/new/

Yale Style Guide
http://info.med.yale.edu/caim
/manual/contents.html

Yale–New Haven Teachers Institute Curriculum Units
http://www.cis.yale.edu/ynhti
/curriculum/units/

Index

About the Author

Kathleen W. Craver, Ph.D., is Head Librarian at the National Cathedral School in Washington, D.C. Dr. Craver is the author of *School Library Media Centers in the 21st Century* (Greenwood, 1994), *Teaching Electronic Literacy* (Greenwood, 1997), and *Using Internet Primary Sources to Teach Critical Thinking Skills in History* (Greenwood, 1999), which won the 2000 American Association of History and Computing Book Prize.